CHRISTOCENTRISM IN CHRISTIAN SOCIAL ETHICS

A Depth Study of Eight Modern Protestants

E. Clinton Gardner

UNIVERSITY
PRESS OF
AMERICA

Copyright © 1983 by

University Press of America,™ Inc.

P.O. Box 19101, Washington, DC 20036

ISBN (Perfect): 0-8191-2955-0
ISBN (Cloth): 0-8191-2954-2

All rights reserved
Printed in the United States of America

241
G226c

This book is gratefully dedicated
to my students and colleagues
in Christian Ethics

ACKNOWLEDGEMENTS

The ensuing essay is the fruit of many years of reflection upon the nature, the meaning, and the sources of Christian ethics. It was largely through the influence of Professor H. Richard Niebuhr that I was led to a vocational interest in this field. Professor Niebuhr's interpretation of Christian ethics as a human response to the divine action provided a liberating alternative to the legalism and moralism of my Southern Protestant heritage; most importantly, it did so, however, through a transformation rather than a rejection of the latter. Thus it was from him that I gained an appreciation of the theocentric dimensions of Christian faith and ethics. The present essay represents an attempt to clarify the meaning of Christian faith in relation to the special task of social ethics.

While it is impossible to identify all of those who have contributed to the development of this volume, I wish to acknowledge my special indebtedness to the authors who are included in this study. I also owe a special debt of gratitude to my colleagues and students in the study of Christian ethics; it is to them that this volume is gratefully dedicated. For many years the Society of Christian Ethics--together with its predecessors--has provided a stimulating forum for the discussion of both theoretical and practical issues in the field. My special thanks for the goodly fellowship and support which my colleagues in this Society have provided across the years.

I also wish to express my deep appreciation to President James T. Laney of Emory University and Dean Jim L. Waits of the Candler School of Theology for their support and encouragement in many ways, including leave from teaching responsibilities in order to pursue the writing of this volume.

I am happy to record a special word of thanks to Ms. Nancy Wilkinson for the preparation of the manuscript for publication.

Finally, I take particular pleasure in expressing my enduring gratitude to Ruth for her companionship and support throughout our marriage and to our children--Edward, Marilyn, and Arnold--who have enabled us to know the joys and blessings of parenthood.

Emory University E. Clinton Gardner
September, 1982

CONTENTS

Acknowledgements   v

1. THEOLOGICAL FOUNDATIONS OF SOCIAL ETHICS   1

   Recent Trends in Protestant Ethics   1
   Prerequisites for a Social Ethic   6
   Christocentrism in Ethics   10
   Procedure of the Present Study   17

2. THE QUESTION OF A STARTING POINT   21

   Ethics Based on Christology:
      Barth, Bonhoeffer, and Lehmann   22
   Ethics Based on Christology and Creation:
      Brunner, Reinhold Niebuhr, and Ramsey   28
   The Primacy of Moral Experience:
      H. Richard Niebuhr and Gustafson   40

3. THE NATURE OF THE GOOD   49

   Obedience to the Command of God:
      Barth, Bonhoeffer and, Brunner   50
   Conformity to a Moral Principle (_Agape_):
      Reinhold Niebuhr and Ramsey   60

4. THE NATURE OF THE GOOD (Continued)   73

   A Pattern of Response to God's Action
       (1) Lehmann: Maturity   74
       (2) H. Richard Niebuhr: The Fitting   76
       (3) Gustafson: The Well-being of
           Creation   82

5. THE NATURE OF THE MORAL AGENT   89

   The Self as Obedient:
     Barth, Brunner, Bonhoeffer, and Ramsey 90
   The Self as Purposive:
     Lehmann, Reinhold Niebuhr, and Gustafson 104
   The Self as Responsible:
     H. Richard Niebuhr 119

6. THE STRUCTURE OF COMMUNITY: CONTINUITY AND CHANGE   125

   Structures of Redemption:
     Barth and Lehmann 126
   The Dualism between Creation and Redemption:
     Brunner, Bonhoeffer, and Reinhold Niebuhr 134
   The Transformation of Community:
     H. Richard Niebuhr, Ramsey, and Gustafson 151

7. TOWARD A CHRISTIAN SOCIAL ETHIC   175

   The Role of Empirical Reason in Social Ethics 176
   Theological Symbols and the Structure of Morality 186
       (1) Moral Criteria 187
       (2) Human Agency 192
       (3) The Covenant Form of Community 198
   The Movement from Theory to Practice 203
       (1) The Divine Commonwealth 205
       (2) Response to the Divine Action 209
       (3) Regulative Principles of Human Community 213
       (4) Responsibility in the Formation of Social Policy 216

Notes   219

Index   251

CHRISTOCENTRISM IN CHRISTIAN SOCIAL ETHICS

x

THEOLOGICAL FOUNDATIONS OF SOCIAL ETHICS

Recent Trends In Protestant Ethics

The purpose of the present study is to examine the theological foundations for social ethics which are found in contemporary Protestant interpretations of Christian ethics. More specifically, its aim is to analyze the major issues in the typically Protestant debate between those who attempt to build Christian ethics upon exclusively Christological foundations and those who seek to undergird the former with a broader theological base.

Clearly, this debate has roots which go back to the Reformation and, indeed, beyond the Reformation to the New Testament itself; the present study is restricted, however, to an analysis of the controversy as it appears in contemporary Protestant thought. While many of the issues in the present-day debate are the same as those which appeared in the Reformation and in early Christianity, the latter have assumed new forms in our day, and they are raised in a new theological and cultural context. Questions concerning the possibility of human knowledge of the divine will, the nature of the good, the possibilities and limits of human existence, and the relationship between Christian faith and culture have been persistent themes throughout Christian history.[1] Today, however, these questions are being raised in different forms which reflect modern humanity's new understanding of itself and its place in the cosmos--a new understanding of human freedom and the ability to control the historical future; a new consciousness of human interdependence and our common destiny upon this planet; and a radical questioning of all traditional forms of authority, both religious and secular. The old issues are now being raised in the context of the vast expansion of human knowledge through the natural and the social sciences, the increasing secularization of modern life, and the rapid growth of pluralism in faith and morality; all of these developments have profoundly shaped the religious and moral sensibilities of contemporary persons.

Thus, the question of ethics concerning the meaning and grounding of morality is raised anew in our day at every level--personal, interpersonal, and social. But it is the problem of ethical reconstruction at the level of social ethics which has become most critical in so far as Christian ethics is concerned since the first quarter of the present century. Not only have the traditional religious sources of moral authority been undermined by the growing secularization of modern society, but the very possibility of a Christian social ethic in a pluralistic setting has been called into radical question by the prevailing forms of neo-orthodox and existentialist theology which have dominated large segments of Protestantism, particularly in Europe, since World War I. Neo-orthodox theology has generally interpreted Christian ethics as a branch of dogmatics, and it has tended to limit human knowledge of the divine will exclusively to God's self-disclosure in Jesus Christ. The moral authority of such an ethic is dependent upon the moral agent's acceptance of such a concept of revelation. The attempt to base Christian ethics exclusively upon Christology has been challenged on the theological ground that it does not give adequate attention to general revelation through creation. This issue is important both for understanding the on-going cultural life of the Christian community and also for the participation by believers in the common life of the inclusively human community which is both religiously and ethically pluralistic. Existentialist theology, on the other hand, has tended to interpret faith in individualistic terms and to reduce ethics to momentary acts of obedience, or <u>agape</u>. As a result, existentialist interpretations of Christian ethics have focused primarily upon the justification of the believer followed by new acts of radical obedience and love. They have emphasized the individualistic and occasionalist aspects of moral decisions and neglected the social and historical (temporal) dimensions of human existence. In a word, those interpretations of Protestant ethics which have been informed primarily by Neo-Reformation and existentialist forms of theology have limited themselves largely to analyses of moral criteria which are pertinent to relationships that are essentially personal, interpersonal, and confessional in character; and the more inclusive, more complex and morally ambiguous field of social ethics has remained largely unexamined in these circles.

Thus far special attention has been called to the impact of neo-orthodox and existentialist patterns of thought upon Protestant ethics in the second and third quarters of the present century. The reasons for this emphasis have been two-fold. First, these forces exercised a dominant and pervasive influence in the shaping of Protestant theological ethics during this period. Secondly, these forces helped make the very possibility of a Christian social ethic particularly problematic in a pluralistic setting. It needs to be pointed out, however, that those ethicists who were most influenced by these motifs differed widely in the manner in which they adapted and utilized the latter. Thus a major concern of the present study will be to compare the ethical methodologies of such men as Barth, Brunner, and Reinhold Niebuhr in this regard. In addition, we will be concerned with the ways in which other Protestant moralists have attempted to reconstruct the theological foundations of Christian ethics in the contemporary period. Helmut Thielicke, for example, has sought to overcome the dualism of traditional Lutheran pietism which flourished in Germany prior to World War II. This tradition affirmed the autonomy of the secular world in the name of the doctrine of "the two kingdoms." Thielicke, among others, challenged such a dualistic interpretation of Luther and attempted to construct a social ethic based on a reinterpretation of the idea of "the two kingdoms."[2] While making the doctrine of justification decisive, he placed far greater significance than did Luther upon the eschatological implications of the gospel for the believer's life in culture. Thielicke stands basically in the Lutheran tradition and re-interprets the concept of "the two kingdoms" in terms of the dialectical tension between two "intersecting aeons." Other Protestants who have attempted to provide a more dynamic interpretation of Christian ethics, including both its personal and its social dimensions, include Dietrich Bonhoeffer in Germany and Paul Lehmann in the United States. Lehmann, in particular, draws upon biblical images which are fundamentally political in character-- messianism and liberation, for example--to describe the divine action and the divine will for human conduct.

In this country the Social Gospel, with roots going back into the nineteenth century, gained increasing influence in theological and ecclesiastical circles through the early decades of the present century. This movement represented an attempt to relate the demands of the gospel to the problems of social injustice in the industrialized urban centers of the North.[3] In many respects John C. Bennett and, in a more qualified sense, Reinhold Niebuhr, stand in this tradition. Both of these men, however, felt the impact of Neo-Reformation theology, and both moved toward a greater realism in their anthropology and social ethics than was characteristic of the Social Gospel generally. In the main, Bennett continues to represent the Liberal tradition in Protestant ethics whereas Reinhold Niebuhr, reflecting a greater impact of neo-orthodox and existentialist thought, developed a more dialectical method of relating Christian faith to culture.

In the ensuing study particular attention will be given to the ethics of H. Richard Niebuhr. Deeply influenced by Ernst Troeltsch as well as by the newer movements in continental theology, Niebuhr undertook to construct a broader theological base for Christian ethics than was present in the latter. Ethical analysis, he believed, properly begins with the effort to understand moral experience in its broadly human as well as its distinctively Christian terms. Moreover, he found important resources for Christian ethics both in the social sciences and in moral philosophy; and he drew upon these to supplement the resources of Scripture and theology. On the basis of such an analysis of moral experience he developed a theocentric interpretation of Christian ethics as human response to a three-fold pattern of divine action. In this respect his concept of "radical monotheism" constituted a critique of the tendencies toward Christocentrism in faith and ethics which he discerned in contemporary European theology, particularly in that of Barth.

Two of H. Richard Niebuhr's students--Paul Ramsey and James M. Gustafson--have, like their mentor, endeavored to broaden the theological base of Christological ethics, and they have attempted to deal more intentionally than Niebuhr with the role of ethics in providing moral direction. The interpretations of Christian ethics which Ramsey and Gustafson have developed differ in a number of fundamental ways, however; hence, they provide two important and widely influential contemporary approaches to theological ethics. Ramsey is essentially a deontologist who seeks to supplement "primary Christian ethics" based upon agape by drawing increasingly upon the natural law tradition in theological ethics; in contrast, Gustafson's ethics is focused primarily upon virtue and the character of the moral agent.[4] Again, Ramsey's method of decision-making is essentially deductive; Gustafson's is basically inductive and teleological. Both attempt to provide a theological basis for social ethics in a pluralistic setting, but they do so on different theological grounds.

No attempt is made in the present essay to examine the entire field of contemporary Protestant ethics.[5] Nor does it lie within the scope of this study to provide a comprehensive analysis of the ethical thought of any of the particular persons under consideration. Rather, our intention is to inquire how selected contemporary Protestants have dealt with certain key issues in social ethics and what theological models they have employed in this process. How does each understand the task of Christian ethics, and upon what underlying theological convictions is such an understanding based? Insofar as Christian ethics includes social ethics, what theological resources are available for the development of the latter? Why, on the other hand, do some theologians and moralists define the task of Christian ethics in such a way as to preclude concern with the broader issues of constructive social ethics?[6] Clearly, many of the most fundamental issues which will be raised in the present study are basically theological. Yet, it must be emphasized that this is not an essay in systematic theology, although it does pose important questions for the latter from the standpoint of the adequacy of particular theological positions to illuminate and inform human existence and decision-making in relationship to the institutions and structures of society.

Prerequisites For A Social Ethic

For purposes of the present study, the term "social ethics" will be used to refer to the ethical dimensions of issues which arise in relationship to "the organization of human communities and the shaping of social policies."[7] According to Gibson Winter, "the subject matter of social ethics is moral rightness and goodness in the shaping of society." Winter proceeds to identify the following three elements as essential components for a social ethic: an understanding of the social conditions in which action is contemplated, evaluative norms, and religious vision.[8] The term "social conditions" refers to the state of society; it represents the subject matter of the social sciences.[9] "Evaluative norms" signifies the moral order which provides the basis for moral decisions. Finally, "religious vision" refers to "the ultimate or comprehensive order"--that is, to a vision of humanity in relationship to that ultimate reality in which the moral order is grounded.

Although various approaches to social ethics differ regarding the importance which is ascribed to each of the foregoing elements, every social ethic must take all three into account. Thus, one interpreter may stress the conditions which are considered necessary for the continued existence of society. A second may emphasize the primacy of specific demands for goodness and duty rooted in a moral order which is given. Upon the basis of this view, conformity to the requirements of such an order is more important than the survival of society. Similarly, a third ethicist might give primary weight to man's relationship to ultimate reality understood as the object of final loyalty. Understood in personal or in ontological terms, such a loyalty to the principle of Being would in effect relativize all attempts to reduce the moral order to abstract laws and principles. In the end, however, the task of social ethics requires that consideration be given to each of these components of decision-making and policy formation. Using these concepts, Winter defines social ethics as "the expression of ultimate commitments in the shaping of man's future, embodying a view of man and his fulfilment in concrete recommendations for public policy."[10]

Winter's analysis of the fundamental elements in social ethics suggests a method of testing the adequacy of various forms of theological ethics in providing the foundations for a Christian ethic which includes social ethics without being limited to the latter. His basic study in this field is essentially a phenomenological inquiry into "the nature and structure of man as a social being."[11] Winter recognizes the major contribution which George Herbert Mead made to an understanding of the self in social terms. He believes, however, that Mead's background in behavioristic thought led the latter to an unwarranted emphasis upon the conditioning impact of social forms and a corresponding neglect of the intentional, creative dimensions of the relationship between selves and society.[12] For Winter, the basis for a more adequate understanding of the relationship between human creativity and social conditioning in everyday experience is found in Alfred

Schutz's phenomenological studies of the nature of the social world. Following Schutz, Winter posits the "We-relation" as the fundamental form of the experience of sociality and humanness. The possibility of the actualization of the self as being-in-the-world "depends upon the inter-subjective experience of self and other in the 'We-relation'." Thus understood, "[s]ociality is not a product of external forces or so-called interaction; rather, interaction, communication, and the emergence of complex social structures are <u>derived</u> typifications of the essential sociality of man."[13]

Viewed in phenomenological terms, human sociality is experienced as the manifestation both of intentional selves (the "We-relation") and as intersubjective, empirical forms through which such selves are related to each other.[14] The intentionality of selves as moral agents and the participation of selves in institutional forms in which sociality and humanness are expressed are thus seen to be united in moral experience. It is at this point also that the relationship between the social sciences and social ethics can best be clarified. The task of the former is to describe empirically the social forms in which our humanity is expressed; the task of social ethics, on the other hand, is to evaluate these forms in terms of the possibilities which they hold for human fulfilment. The contributions which the social sciences make to ethics are indispensable, but these disciplines do not provide an adequate account either of human freedom and transcendence or of the evaluative norms of human action including both its societal and its personal modes.[15]

Our purpose in drawing upon Winter's analysis has been to identify certain basic elements which constitute the phenomenological structure of the self in its relationship to the social world. Winter is also helpful in providing a basis in experience for joining together the external, institutional forms in which human sociality (community) is expressed, on the one hand, and the free, creative, intentional aspects of selfhood and moral agency, on the other. Unless some space for intentional action is presupposed, there is little point in speaking of human relationships to society in ethical terms. Winter's analysis provides one way of pointing to the presence of this dimension of humanness in the experience of the social world.[16] The task of social ethics is to show how moral agency is related to each of these aspects of human experience. Like other forms of ethics, social ethics also has the two-fold purpose of providing moral illumination and moral direction. Hence, the adequacy of any particular social ethic may be tested by its comprehensiveness and internal consistency in providing such clarification and guidance regarding issues of public policy.

For purposes of the present study it will be useful to describe the elements which Winter has identified as essential components of any social ethic in somewhat different terms. Winter's study is essentially a foundational work for social ethics; its aim is to identify the <u>kinds</u> of building blocks which are essential in the construction of a social ethic. Our purpose, on the other hand, is to analyze the thought of selected theological ethicists in terms of the issues which have been disclosed through a phenomenological examination of the social world.[17] These issues now need to be reformulated in terms of theological ethics. First, any social ethic must provide some account of the nature of the good and some normative criteria of moral judgments. This includes the specification of such criteria and the justification of the latter in terms of some ultimate source or ground of the good. Secondly, every social ethic presupposes some conception of human freedom and responsibility in history, the meaning of human fulfilment, and the nature and locus of evil in human history. In the third place, every social ethic must provide a basis both for the construction of social institutions and for the criticism of all such structures. This includes an interpretation of the role and function of institutions in relationship to human fulfilment, moral agency, and social change.

These three components which are essential parts of any social ethic are interrelated and interdependent. The manner in which one is perceived affects the perception of each of the others. Hence, no one component can be adequately understood in isolation from either of the other constituents. Thus, the identification and, particularly, the weighting of moral criteria on the part of one ethicist will be greatly influenced by the latter's concept of human nature and also by his understanding of society. Similarly, one's perception of the nature and function of social institutions is shaped in profoundly important ways by one's understanding of the ultimate ground of the good. Hence, it should be clear that we are not here attempting to devise a check-list for determining whether or not a particular social ethic is good or bad by reason of its including, or its failure to include, one or more of the elements which we have specified. Rather, we have been seeking to identify certain features of any social ethic as distinguished from other forms of moral reflection which are limited to personal or even to interpersonal aspects of experience. It may be useful to note, however, that the most difficult area of Christian social ethics is the problem of social structures.[18] Traditionally, this issue has been dealt with in terms of the "two cities" (Augustine), the "two kingdoms" (Luther), the "orders" of creation (or of preservation), and the Kingdom of God (the Social Gospel). Unless attention is given to this problem, Christian ethics is limited to personal and interpersonal relationships, and social ethics in turn becomes an autonomous secular discipline.

Christocentrism In Ethics

Stated in theological terms, the present essay represents a critique of Christocentrism in Protestant social ethics. Thus understood, it is concerned with one fundamental question concerning Christological ethics, namely, the relationship of the latter to the task of social ethics. Moreover, the term "Christocentrism," which is widely used in contemporary

Christian ethics, focuses attention as sharply as possible upon the central issue of the exclusivism of Christology in relationship to a Christian understanding of the basic categories of Christian ethics.

The term "Christocentrism" has widely different meanings in theological ethics. Stated in one form, the purpose of this essay is to identify and clarify the major issues which are involved in the debate between those who use Christological categories to provide the fundamental framework of interpretation for Christian ethics and those who maintain that such categories are by themselves insufficient for this task. H. Richard Niebuhr, for example, viewed Christ-centered faith as perhaps the greatest single threat to "radical monotheism" within the churches today, if not indeed throughout Christian history.[19] Although he was strongly influenced by Barth, especially in the period prior to the publication of The Kingdom of God in America (1937), Niebuhr became increasingly critical of the latter's tendency toward a "completely Christocentric and solely Christo-morphic form of thinking and acting."[20] In general, Niebuhr spoke of Christocentrism in faith and ethics in three different albeit interrelated ways, namely, in reference to the center of value, in reference to revelation, and in reference to symbolic forms of ethical analysis.[21]

In an essay on Niebuhr's ethics entitled "The Transformation of Ethics," which appeared in Faith and Ethics, Paul Ramsey cited Niebuhr's description of evangelical ethics as "God-centered" and accepted Niebuhr's characterization of his own ethical position in terms of "radical monotheism."[22] Yet, Ramsey went on to describe Niebuhr's ethics as "the ethics of Christocentric monotheism" and to interpret the latter's category of "Christ Transforming Culture" in terms of "Christocentric faith."[23] It is evident that in Ramsey's usage the term "Christocentric" has at least two possible meanings--one referring to the locus of revelation and one referring to the final object of trust; moreover, he does not make clear how his usage is related to Niebuhr's.

Ramsey also employs the concept of "Christocentrism" in his analysis of the ethics of Karl Barth and Reinhold Niebuhr. In these instances he uses the term to designate a concept of revelation according to which God has revealed himself either exclusively or quintessentially through Jesus Christ. He speaks with approval, for example, of Barth's "Christocentric" doctrine of man although he does not concur with Barth in the latter's complete rejection of all general anthropology and ethics.[24] In like manner, Ramsey refers to Reinhold Niebuhr as "a Christocentric theologian" and describes his moral theology as being similarly "Christocentric."[25] It is clear, however, that natural reason has a far more significant role in Reinhold Niebuhr's thought than it does in the case of Barth. The issue of revelation is an important one, but it is not the only issue at stake in Christocentric theology and ethics; moreover, the term "center" may have different meanings when applied even to the single concept of revelation in different theologians. Sometimes it is used to describe a position--Barth's, for example--which limits revelation to Jesus Christ; at other times it is used to describe a position--Reinhold Niebuhr's, for example--which makes revelation in Jesus Christ decisive but not exclusive.

In *Christ and the Moral Life*, James M. Gustafson also focuses attention upon the role of Christ in revelation in his analysis of the ethics of Barth and Bonhoeffer. "Both are theocentric in their ethics," he writes, "but God reveals himself exclusively in Jesus Christ and thus, for both, the theocentric interpretation of the moral life becomes Christocentric."[26] Gustafson is quite correct in pointing out that in the case of Bonhoeffer and Barth Christocentrism includes the view that "God reveals himself exclusively in Jesus Christ"; but he fails to give sufficient attention to other meanings of Christocentrism which we have noted in contemporary Christian ethics, particularly, the question of Christ as the ultimate source and ground of value.[27]

The significance of Christocentrism in Christian

ethics is similarly illustrated by the recurrence of this theme in <u>Christian Social Ethics in a Changing World</u>, one of a series of four preparatory studies for the World Conference on Church and Society, held in Geneva in the summer of 1966. In one of the contributions to that volume under the title, "Luther's 'Two Kingdoms' Ethic Reconsidered," William H. Lazareth suggested that social ethics needs both "Christocentric depth" and "Trinitarian breadth."[28] Both of these elements are present, he believes, in Luther's doctrine of the "two kingdoms." N. H. Søe also contributed an essay called "Natural Law and Social Ethics" to the same volume; in it he developed "a Christological view of natural law," based upon an essentially Barthian understanding of revelation.[29] It is interesting to note, however, that Søe found Barth's own attempt to deal with this issue in <u>Church Dogmatics</u>, IV/3, inconsistent with the latter's Christocentric view of revelation. Summarizing the emergent trends which he saw in recent ecumenical Protestant ethics, John C. Bennett noted certain broad areas of agreement, but he also identified a number of areas of debate within, as well as among, the various theological traditions. A major factor contributing to this diversity, Bennett suggested, is found in the difference in methodology between those whose approach to theology and ethics is Christocentric and those whose approach might be called "Neo-liberal."[30] Significantly these differences cut across the various theological and ethical traditions.

In a certain sense, the debate over Christocentrism in ethics may be considered a debate concerning the possibility, the method, and the structure of Christian social ethics. Participation in this debate thus provides a convenient basis for the selection of representative ethicists to be included in this study. Moreover, the basic elements of a social ethic which we have identified provide a corresponding phenomenological structure for analyzing and evaluating the contributions of such ethicists to the task of social ethics. Hence, in the ensuing study we will be concerned with the treatment of the following issues in the on-going debate concerning the role of Christology in theological ethics: the nature and ground of the good, including human knowledge of that good; the doctrine of human nature; and the role of social institutions. Since ethicists vary in the attention which they devote to different ones of these issues, the selection of persons for consideration--and the depth of treatment accorded each person's position-- will vary from topic to topic.

Before proceeding to an analysis of the three major areas of debate in social ethics it may be helpful to indicate certain areas of agreement among the writers whom we will be considering in the subsequent chapters. We are interested both in discovering areas of agreement in contemporary Christian ethics concerning the possibility, the task, and the methodology of social ethics and also in identifying basic issues which are in dispute concerning these matters. Recognition of certain points upon which there is consensus will aid us in identifying the issues upon which there is debate. In the first place, there is basic agreement that Christological images and symbols are indispensable in any Christian understanding of faith and ethics. Indeed, as H. Richard Niebuhr affirms, the Christ symbol is both a "fundamental" and an "indispensable" metaphor for Christians to use in understanding themselves, their fellow men, and God.[31] Without the aid of this symbol, the concept of the Christian life would be meaningless, and it would be impossible to differentiate between the latter and any other form or style of life. The question at issue between theocentric and Christocentric ethicists, therefore, is not whether the Christ-symbol is indispensable but whether by itself it is sufficient and if not, whether it is the dominant symbolic form for theology and ethics. These two questions are radically different. If they are confused, it becomes impossible to understand Niebuhr's polemic against the tendency which he saw in much contemporary theology to substitute Christology for theology. The differences among Paul Ramsey, John Bennett, Reinhold Niebuhr, Barth, Bonhoeffer, and Lehmann are, from this perspective, differences among ethicists for whom the highest norm is finally disclosed in Christ. These writers differ only--but importantly--in their conceptions of the nature of this norm (<u>agape</u>, obedience, responsibility), their perceptions of the manner in which this norm is actualized in human conduct (the role of law and principles of conduct), their conceptions of human nature, and their understandings of the relationship of Christology to the doctrine of the Trinity.

Secondly, there is general agreement among all of the ethicists under consideration that moral values are essentially relational rather than objective in an abstract sense or relativistic in a subjective-psychological sense. All of the writers who have just been mentioned reject legalistic and idealistic definitions of moral norms and values. The differences among the former in this regard have to do primarily with two questions, viz., the ultimate grounding of value (in God or in Christ) and the issue of continuity-discontinuity in ethics.

In the third place, the debate over Christocentrism in contemporary Protestant ethics is not a debate concerning the primacy of reason over faith, or of works over grace. There is common agreement that Christian ethics rests upon Christian faith and that salvation is a gift of grace rather than something which is earned. The differences that exist pertain to the way in which the availability of grace is conceptualized--in terms that emphasize the unity of the divine nature and action in creation and redemption (H. Richard Niebuhr, Paul Ramsey, John Bennett), in terms which emphasize the exclusiveness of God's redemptive action in Christ (Barth, Bonhoeffer), or in terms which emphasize the role of the Holy Spirit in accounting for the common moral insights which non-Christians share with Christians (Paul Lehmann).

Finally, there is general agreement that Christians have a responsibility in and for culture. In this sense Christian ethics includes social ethics. The question at issue in the present debate is not whether Christian ethics is the ghetto ethic of a withdrawn community; it is, rather, the question of how Christian faith is related to life in the secular community. It is basically a question of the adequacy of predominantly Christological symbols in ethics for understanding and structuring human life in culture. Among the tests of such adequacy are the capacity of these symbols to provide a framework for understanding the common humanity of all persons and the institutional aspects of human life in culture, consistency between the recognized responsibility of Christians for society and the theological foundations upon which this responsibility is based, and ultimately the faithfulness of a particular interpretation of the divine nature and will to God's self-disclosure as understood in Judeo-Christian history. The final test of faithfulness to God's self-disclosure within the community of faith can be answered only confessionally. The answer which each person gives to this question is an answer which is given in the decision of faith. Hence, it perhaps needs to be emphasized that it is not the purpose of this study to argue that one particular interpretation of Christian ethics is right and another is wrong, that one is faithful and another is unfaithful, in this ultimate sense. Our purpose is, rather, much more modest and much more analytical-descriptive. In the first place, we will attempt to identify typical Christological and theological symbols which different contemporary writers use in dealing with the basic components of social ethics, and we will examine the manner in which these symbols are used by these authors. In the second place, we will seek to evaluate these symbols in terms of their ability to illuminate particular issues in social ethics.

The truth of faith is not determined by its social utility, but the profundity and power of biblical faith have been attested both in the history of Israel and in the history of Christianity by its ability to provide a perspective in terms of which the meaning and coherence of all human history could be understood. Hence, it becomes pertinent to ask whether contemporary Christian ethics is able to provide such a center of meaning for contemporary humankind. Christocentric ethics seeks to do this through the use of basically Christological symbols and forms; theocentric ethics seeks to do this through the use of less exclusive symbols.[32] Both kinds of symbols are found in Scripture, and both have been used throughout Christian history. Moreover, the meaning which a particular symbol bears changes from one cultural setting to another. Thus, the kingdom of God has had a vastly different meaning for Christians who stood in a conservative, pietistic tradition from what it had in the Social Gospel.[33] Hence, it is important to see how different symbols are used in different interpretations of Christian ethics, and it is necessary continually to test such usages against the original as well as the generally accepted meanings of these concepts in Christian history.[34] The power of such symbols is measured finally, however, by their capacity to give meaning and coherence to human life as it is experienced in the present day. The ensuing study is intended as a contribution to this larger, on-going task of theological-ethical reflection.

Procedure Of The Present Study

In summary, then, our procedure in the present essay will be to undertake an analysis of the debate over Christocentrism in contemporary Protestant ethics from the standpoint of certain issues which are raised in social ethics. These issues were identified on the basis of a phenomenological analysis of human experience of the social world. This analysis pointed to a fundamental structure of human sociality which includes both empirical and normative components and dimensions. As indicated above, the empirical description of the social world (societal relationships) is the task of the social sciences. The special task of social ethics, on the other hand, is to examine the implications of such an empirical understanding of society for human freedom and moral choice. While the specific concern of social ethics is humankind's relationship to society, the former is a part of the more inclusive discipline of ethics. This means that, like the latter, social ethics must give some account of the nature and ground of the good, some interpretation of human nature, and some form of moral guidance for concrete decisions. In view of its special focus upon society, it must give particular attention to the social dimensions of human existence and the societal forms in which our common humanity is expressed.

The relationship between the empirical and normative components of social ethics is interactive rather than static; hence, it can best be understood in dialogical terms. Social ethics is dependent upon an empirical description of societal relationships for its analytic and prescriptive tasks; moreover, the tools which ethicists use in the collection of such data are the same as those used in the social sciences. This does not mean, however, that the presuppositions of social scientists--or of social ethicists in so far as they are social scientists--are unimportant or that their methodologies are value-free. It means, rather, that social ethics is dependent upon the same methods and procedures as the social sciences for empirical data concerning social processes and relationships. Ethicists must, however, question the selection as well as the adequacy of particular interpretations of such data. They may, for example, question the significance of the latter for understanding human nature--the worth of human beings, the sources of moral evil, and the possibilities and limits of human history; and they may challenge the alleged implications of these data for decisions affecting public policy. Thus, in social ethics the gathering of empirical data and evaluative interpretation of such data are related dialogically in the process of policy formation.

From the standpoint of methodology, the fundamental issue which social ethics poses for theological ethics is, therefore, the question of the latter's openness to the social sciences for their indispensable assistance in the identification and definition in concrete form of the issues which are the proper subject matter of social ethics. Such definition includes an analysis of the probable consequences of alternative forms of action in so far as such consequences can be projected upon the basis of empirical data. Thus, the debate in Christian ethics concerning the possibility and nature of social ethics is at bottom a debate concerning the relationship between general and special revelation, or between reason and revelation. This question underlies our entire study, and it must be dealt with in each of the succeeding chapters. Stated another way, the theme running through each of the major topics under consideration is that of the continuity, or discontinuity, between a Christian and a secular understanding of the nature and ground of the good, human nature, social institutions, and the prescriptive task of ethics. Due to the critical nature of this issue for the ensuing study as a whole, a special chapter will be devoted to it as a methodological problem in contemporary theological ethics (Chapter 2). Chapters 3 and 4 take up the question of the nature and ground of the good. In Chapter 5 we turn to a consideration of human nature, including moral agency. Chapter 6 consists of an examination of the nature and function of social institutions from the perspective of theological ethics. A concluding section (Chapter 7) represents an attempt to assess the resources in those forms of theological ethics which have been examined for the development of a social ethic. Such an assessment will be made primarily in terms of the capacity of these resources to provide a theological-ethical framework for understanding human life in society and in terms of their ability to provide moral direction in the field of social policy. As noted above, both of these criteria are implicit in ethics as a discipline whose aim is to provide both moral analysis and moral guidance.

2

THE QUESTION OF A STARTING POINT

The question of the proper starting point for Christian ethics has different significance for different theologians. Insofar as the debate over Christocentrism is a debate concerning such a starting point, it is primarily a debate about the nature and locus of revelation. The answer which is given to this question affects the way a particular ethicist treats each of the other elements of moral experience. More important than the choice of a particular starting point, however, is the question of how the latter is perceived. Is it chosen, for example, because it constitutes the <u>critical</u>, or decisive, source of the Christian's understanding of the divine will? Or, does the selection of a particular starting point imply that there is <u>only</u> one source (locus) of moral insight and illumination? Further, how are the distinctively Christian and broadly human understandings of moral agency and norms related?

Basically, the ethicists included in this study answer the question of the proper starting point for theological ethics in one of the following three ways. Members of the first group maintain that Christian ethics is based exclusively upon Christology; hence, for them, the only proper starting point for moral reflection is God's self-disclosure in Christ. For a second group, knowledge of the good rests partly upon special revelation in Christ and partly upon reason grounded in creation. For them, Christian ethics has two different albeit related sources of moral understanding. Members of the third group begin with moral experience. In a word, the fundamental issue in this methodological debate about the proper starting point of moral reflection is the question of the basis and scope of Christian ethics. A decision concerning the starting point is a decision which affects both the nature of the issues which are raised and the sources of moral illumination which are available for addressing these issues. Such a decision is particularly critical in the field of social ethics and in a society that is religiously and morally pluralistic.

Ethics Based On Christology:
Barth, Bonhoeffer, And Lehmann

Karl Barth, Dietrich Bonhoeffer, and Paul Lehmann are representative of those contemporary theologians who have insisted most strongly that Christian ethics is based exclusively upon God's revelation of himself in Jesus Christ. For them the question of the starting point for ethics is critical since it identifies the only source of knowledge of humanity's true good. Moreover, Christian ethics does not consist of a body of objective moral truth--moral laws or principles or ideals; rather, it is concerned primarily with the question of the relationship of the moral agent to Christ in faith. In this view faith tends to be defined dogmatically in terms of assent to particular Christological beliefs rather than as trust in and loyalty to a "center of value" that is apprehended more fully in religious and moral experience than it is in creeds.[1] Not only does Christian ethics rest exclusively upon faith in Christ for knowledge of the good, but that knowledge to which it points cannot be defined abstractly in terms of moral laws or principles or ideals. Rather, it must be perceived concretely in each new moment of decision. All three writers distinguish sharply between Christian ethics and general ethics.

For Barth the only proper starting point for Christian ethics is the electing grace of God.[2] The fundamental question of ethics is the question of human existence; and the answer to this question is found only in the grace of God which is addressed to humanity through the Word of God. Since knowledge of this Word is known only through Christ, the ethical question can be raised aright only when it is raised Christologically. While Barth bases Christian ethics finally upon the doctrine of God, he is careful to insist that the answer to the ethical question of the good is not dogmatics per se, not even the doctrine of God, but rather the electing and commanding grace of God which is both sovereign and free.

In the light of man's confrontation with the Word of grace, the question of the meaning of human existence is answered in terms of the covenant-relation which God has established with humanity in Jesus Christ. This covenant relation expresses two fundamental elements in man's relationship to God which define the perspective in which it becomes meaningful to talk about Christian ethics, viz., the doctrine of God's electing grace and the doctrine of the divine command.[3] The first of these elements is primary, for it points to God's free and sovereign act of grace in electing man to be his covenant partner. In this context it is important to note that, while the meaning of this election has been revealed in Christ, God's decision to be for man and to establish a covenant relationship with him preceded the creation of humanity; hence, for Barth, the divine election is the fundamental and over-arching context in which the meaning of human existence must be understood. But the significance of the covenant is not exhausted in grace, for the God who elects man to be his covenant partner in that very act claims man for his purposes and places him under the divine command. "There is no grace," Barth writes, "without the lordship and claim of grace."[4] God's purpose in electing man is to rule over man, to take man into his service as a covenant partner and commission him to share in the divine work. "Ruling grace is commanding grace."[5] As the Lord of the Covenant, God summons man to obedience. Hence, the one Word of God which establishes the covenant is both Gospel and Law.

The Word of grace is addressed anew to man in each new moment of decision. Hence, the answer to the ethical question can be defined only in a formal way as the command of God. To attempt to specify in advance what the content of this command will be would be to attempt to limit the freedom and the sovereignty of God. What must finally be said, therefore, is that the norm of all human conduct is "the sovereign decision of God" who always summons man to concrete forms of responsibility.[6] Barth writes:

> Man's action is good in so far as he is the obedient hearer of the Word and command of God....Good human action is action set free by the command of God, by His claim and decision and judgment.[7]

Like Barth, Bonhoeffer and Lehmann also attempt to base Christian ethics exclusively upon a Christological foundation. For Bonhoeffer, the starting point of Christian ethics is "the reality of God as He reveals Himself in Jesus Christ."[8] God is the ultimate reality, and neither the world nor man nor the ethical can be understood apart from the self-disclosure of God in Jesus Christ.

For Bonhoeffer, Christian ethics--in contrast to all other ethics--is fundamentally concerned with "the will of God," and the latter can be known only as it is revealed concretely in Jesus Christ.[9] All other conceptions of the good and duty are finally abstract and false because they are based upon false presuppositions about the true nature of man and the world. The question of the good can be answered, therefore, only as it is answered Christologically through revelation. The question of the good is fundamentally "the question of participation in the divine reality which is revealed in Christ."[10] Bonhoeffer calls this participation "conformation." Christian ethics is an ethic of formation in the likeness of Christ--that is, a conformation which is wrought in man by Christ. Moreover, the Church is the concrete place where this conformation takes place. Bonhoeffer writes:

> Ethics as formation is possible only upon the

foundation of the form of Jesus Christ which is present in His Church. The Church is the place where Jesus Christ's taking form is proclaimed and accomplished. It is this proclamation and this event that Christian ethics is designed to serve.[11]

In a word, Jesus Christ is "the origin, essence, and goal of all that is real."[12]

For Bonhoeffer, God's will is disclosed to man in the form of "commandment." Bonhoeffer's understanding of the commandment of God is similar to Barth's interpretation of the "command of God." In both instances the Word of God is addressed to man in concrete terms; it is a word of permission and also a word of obligation, a word which both frees and binds its hearer. It leaves no room either for interpretation or for application, but only for obedience or disobedience. Succinctly stated, God's commandment is, according to Bonhoeffer, "the only warrant for ethical discourse."[13]

Like Barth and Bonhoeffer, Lehmann also emphasizes the uniqueness, or distinctiveness, of Christian ethics. Any serious discussion of the latter must begin, he believes, with consideration of a "prior question" about the nature and the possibility of a Christian ethic.[14] As a theological discipline, Christian ethics differs sharply from moral philosophy both in its object and in its method. Hence, the former cannot begin with efforts to discover the good based on human reason. Neither, however, can it be identified with biblical ethics, or with New Testament ethics, although there is a close relationship between the former and the latter. Like Barth, Lehmann subsumes Christian ethics under theology or dogmatics; hence, the methodological question of the proper starting point is critical. Not only does the answer which is given to this question differentiate Christian ethics from philosophical ethics as well as from thinking about ethics in other religious traditions; it also "fundamentally differentiates one interpretation of Christian ethics from another."[15] This decision determines both the nature and the procedure of the discipline as a whole--its substantive content, the context in which reflection takes place, and the structure of Christian behavior.

Lehmann defines Christian ethics as "the disciplined reflection upon the question and its answer: What am I, as a believer in Jesus Christ and as a member of his church, to do?"[16] This definition focuses attention decisively upon the reality and the nature of the Christian Church as the only proper "point of departure" for Christian thinking about ethics. The <u>koinonia</u> is the place where the divine will is discerned--where the divine action is recognized and understood and where the will of God is apprehended in concrete terms. Christian ethics is not concerned with abstract notions of the good, but with the concrete will (action) of God. In short, it is "oriented toward revelation and not toward morality."[17]

Thus far in our discussion of Barth, Bonhoeffer, and Lehmann, attention has been focused upon their insistence that God's revelation in Jesus Christ constitutes the only source of man's knowledge of the good understood in terms of the will of God. Not only does the divine revelation in Christ provide the only proper starting point for Christian reflection about ethics; it provides the only basis for the latter. Hence, there is little room for empirical inquiry into the nature either of selves as moral agents or of social institutions. For Barth as well as for Bonhoeffer, the commandment of God "does not spring from the created world. It comes down from above."[18]

This interpretation does not mean, however, that these ethicists reject all responsibility on the part of Christians to participate in culture. Indeed, precisely the opposite is the case. The Lordship of Christ means, on the one hand, that man is freed from legalistic and pietistic forms of morality by the One who is Lord of culture; and it means, on the other hand, that man is summoned to new, concrete forms of obedience.[19] Culture is included within the realm of redemption. The totality of human life is now understood fundamentally from the perspective of redemption rather than creation. Thus, the state, the economy, and the family are "orders" of redemption rather than orders of creation or the fall; their true meaning and purpose can be apprehended only in the light of the reality of Christ's present Lordship over them. As the Lord of all things, Jesus Christ is not only the Redeemer but also the Creator of all so that redemption and creation are seen to be united in him.

Those ethicists for whom Jesus Christ is the only source of knowledge of the divine will emphasize the distinctiveness and the particularity of Christian ethics. They stress the fundamental importance of the faith-relationship understood in terms of God's self-revelation in Christ as the only basis for knowledge of "the good." Moreover, Barth, Bonhoeffer, and Lehmann all tend to be strongly contextualist in their understandings of the manner in which God reveals his will, whether through his commands or through his action. Faith in Christ defines the fundamental perspective for the Christian as he participates in culture. In so far as observable action is concerned, however, Christian ethics has little specifiable content that distinguishes it from other forms of conduct. On the one hand, Christ frees his followers to participate in the empirical, historical life of culture; and, at the same time, he summons them to concrete acts of obedience to himself amid the institutionalized forms of culture. Yet, such an interpretation of the nature and basis of Christian ethics poses serious problems for the construction of a Christian social ethic, and it does so for two main reasons. First, the existentialist understanding of revelation upon which this interpretation rests results in a failure to give adequate attention to an empirical analysis of the cultural forms and processes in which our humanity is expressed. Secondly, the exclusivism of revelation upon which this view rests obscures both the necessity and the possibility of the discovery of a broadly human ground of common moral understanding which is prerequisite for community in a society that is religiously pluralistic.[20]

Ethics Based On Christology And Creation:
Brunner, Reinhold Niebuhr, And Ramsey

While the writers whom we have considered thus far have attempted to construct Christian ethics upon an exclusively Christological foundation, Emil Brunner, Reinhold Niebuhr, and Paul Ramsey base their ethics upon a double foundation of Christology and creation. For each of these moralists, both the possibility and the distinctiveness of Christian ethics rest upon God's self-disclosure in Jesus Christ; in addition, however, God's will is also revealed through his work in creation. Hence, Christian ethics must include the effort to understand both forms of God's relationship to the world and their implications for human conduct. As we shall see, Brunner and Reinhold Niebuhr tend to view the relationships between redemption and creation in dualistic terms whereas Ramsey interprets the latter in transformationist terms. For John C. Bennett, who is also representative of this group, this relationship is best understood in terms of an "overlap" between Christian ethics and general ethics.

How, then, do these theologians view the question of the starting point of Christian ethics? In their view, how decisive is this issue? Are they Christocentric in the same sense as Barth, Bonhoeffer, and Lehmann? What difference does it make that they base their ethics upon a double foundation? In view of the significant differences among them as well as the importance of their contributions, it seems necessary to consider the answers of each ethicist to these questions in some detail.

The great significance of Emil Brunner's landmark study of Protestant ethics, The Divine Imperative (1932), lay in the fact that in that work he forcefully posed the question of the nature and the basis of Protestant theological ethics.[21] The publication of this work preceded that of Barth's major systematic treatments of this problem in the later volumes of Church Dogmatics (II/2, 1942; III/4, 1951; and IV/2, 1955) by at least a decade. While Barth's answer to this question is more systematic and more exclusively Christological than Brunner's, both men are in basic agreement that the fundamental question of Christian ethics concerns its basis, that is, the presuppositions which determine the form in which the ethical question is raised and the method by which the question of the Good or the Ought is answered. In Paul Lehmann's terms, both raise the "prior question" of the starting-point of Christian ethical reflection. Both agree that there is no way of moving from general--or natural--ethics to theological ethics because the two are based on radically different presuppositions. Natural ethics rests upon reason; theological ethics rests upon revelation. For both Barth and Brunner, moreover, man's knowledge of God is limited exclusively to the divine self-revelation in Jesus Christ as the Word of God.

Beyond this agreement, however, there is a fundamental difference between Barth and Brunner concerning the manner in which God's will is made known to man. Brunner himself alluded to this difference in the Preface to the German edition of <u>The Divine Imperative</u>, where he spoke of two tasks confronting a Protestant theological ethic in the early 1930's. The first and most important of these was "a fresh consideration of the bases and fundamental conceptions of an evangelical doctrine of right conduct."[22] In this context he acknowledged his indebtedness to Barth and Friedrich Gogarten. In addition he saw a second task, namely, the need to think through "the concrete problems of particular spheres of life." In Brunner's view there is a dialectical relationship between these two endeavors, and he saw his own work as an effort to recover this relationship on a Christological basis.

As compared with Barth, Brunner distinguishes more sharply between the Command of God as Creator and the Command of the Redeemer. Brunner stands, in this respect, in the Lutheran tradition whereas Barth belongs to the Reformed tradition. Brunner attempts to construct his ethics upon the Reformation doctrine of "justification by grace alone" whereas Barth develops his ethics in relationship to the basic theological doctrines of God, Creation, Reconciliation, and Redemption. For Brunner, all authentic Protestant ethics are "interim ethics"--i.e., ethics which lie between the Fall and the Resurrection. Through Jesus Christ the will of God as Creator and the will of God as Redeemer are seen to be ultimately one. As Creator, God wills to preserve the structure and form of that which he has created, and he commands us to "accept the world, adjust ourselves to it, (and) obey its concrete demands."[23] These are not two separate commandments, but one; for in Jesus Christ love is revealed to be the basis of Creation as well as Redemption.

Despite the ultimate harmonization of the demands of the Creator and the Redeemer in Christ, the dualism between these two forms of the divine command persists in Brunner's ethics. In subsequent sections of our study we will see how this dualism works itself out, particularly in relationship to his social ethics. Here our concern has been to see how the basis for this dualism is grounded theologically in Brunner's concept of revelation. The God who has revealed himself in Christ as Redeemer is the same God who has revealed himself--through his historical revelation--to be the Creator. Through creation God discloses the form and structure of human existence--i.e., the forms of community. Man cannot be obedient to the Creator if he does not "pay heed to the laws of life and to the life which is peculiar to man in accordance with his creation."[24] Knowledge of human nature and the human condition are necessary if one is to serve the neighbor in keeping with the divine will. Since they contribute to this knowledge, empirical studies such as biology and anthropology have a "definite place within a Christian ethic."[25]

If Brunner's social ethics rests upon a dualistic understanding of the relationship between creation and redemption, Reinhold Niebuhr's ethic rests upon a more dialectical conception of the latter. Christian ethics is dependent upon Christian faith both for its understanding of the final norm of human existence and for the motivation to seek the realization of that norm in history. As previously noted, Niebuhr stands within the Social Gospel tradition in a number of important respects. Like the latter he believed that the gospel has far-reaching implications for society as well as for the moral conduct of individuals; and like the Social Gospel, also, he tended to reduce the ethic of Jesus to the single principle of love.[26] Yet Niebuhr was highly critical of liberal Christianity, including the Social Gospel, for its tendency to interpret Christian ethics in moralistic and rationalistic terms. In the teachings of Jesus, love is an ideal which is understood in universalistic and perfectionistic terms. As such it is an "impossible possibility" for human history; nevertheless, it is the final law of all human life and constitutes the ultimate norm by which the latter is judged. For Niebuhr, the moralistic interpretation of Christian love in liberal Christianity was associated fundamentally with an idealistic and rationalistic conception of human nature; hence, the former was finally irrelevant to the struggle against evil in human history.

In *An Interpretation of Christian Ethics* Niebuhr sought to recover the radical quality of Christian ethics through an examination of the ethic of Jesus and the religious foundations upon which the latter was based. Both the radical character and the power of Jesus' ethic are derived from his faith in a transcendent power which constitutes the ground for belief in the meaning and coherence of human life despite the presence and power of evil in the world. It is this prophetic-religious faith which provides the "dimension of depth" in moral experience, thus creating "the tension between what is and what ought to be."[27] It is this religious dimension of depth rooted in transcendence, in short, which provides the basis not only for the love perfectionism but also for the realism of Christian ethics. Insistence upon Creation as a work of God saves prophetic religion from cynicism concerning the possibilities and achievements of partial meaning within history; it also provides the ground for confidence in the final fulfilment of human life at the end of history.[28] As in the Social Gospel, the ideal of love has far-reaching implications for the struggle for social justice, but for Niebuhr the former cannot be applied directly or immediately to the latter.[29] In the struggle for social justice Christian ethics is dependent both upon faith and upon reason; however, the reality of love as the final norm for society as well as for the individual is disclosed Christologically.

Whereas in this earlier work Niebuhr found the meaning of love depicted in the teachings of Jesus, in his later writings he held that the norm of <u>agape</u> was most fully revealed in the Cross of Christ. In his Gifford Lectures on <u>The Nature and Destiny of Man</u> the crucified Christ is the "wisdom of God and the power of God."[30] Indeed, the Atonement now becomes "the significant content of the Incarnation." The perfection of Christ is "the perfection of sacrificial love." This perfection is most fully revealed in the Cross, for this is "the point in history where the sinful rivalries of ego with ego" are most clearly transcended and overcome.[31] While Niebuhr is in agreement with other Christological ethicists in locating the source of man's knowledge of the norm for human life in revelation, he differs from Barth and Lehmann in relating this revealed knowledge of <u>agape</u> as the law of life dialectically to man's essential nature as this is apprehended by reason. Niebuhr states the issue precisely which he writes:

> Protestant theology is right in setting grace in contradiction to nature in the sense that the vicious circle of false truth, apprehended from the standpoint of the self, must be broken and the self cannot break it.... But Protestant theology, more particularly radical Protestant theology (Barth), is wrong in denying the 'point of contact' (<u>Anknuepfungspunkt</u>), which always exists in man by virtue of the residual element of <u>justitia originalis</u> in his being.[32]

According to Niebuhr, faith is the presupposition of proper self-knowledge, for the self can understand itself only when it views itself from a vantage point beyond the self, i.e., from a perspective in terms of which both the sinfulness and the essential nature of the self can be fully understood. Because of his transcendence over nature and reason, man is able, on the basis of natural reason, to recognize the need for such a perspective, but natural reason cannot, by itself, provide the latter. Hence, true self-knowledge must be grounded in revelation. "To understand himself truly," Niebuhr writes, "means to begin with a faith that he [man] is understood from beyond himself, that he is known and loved of God and must find himself in terms of obedience to the divine will."[33] Moreover, it is the claim of Christian faith that such a vantage point for true wisdom about human nature is given in the Atonement. Indeed, the Cross of Christ is the only source of knowledge from which an adequate understanding of human freedom and transcendence can be derived. In the Atonement the freedom of God is manifest in the paradoxical relationship between the divine mercy and the structure of the created world.[34]

For Niebuhr, the Atonement presupposes the biblical doctrine of Creation, for the latter is "the only ground upon which the full height of the human spirit can be measured...the essential meaningfulness of its history in the finite world asserted, and a limit set for its freedom, and self-transcendence."[35] Man has some knowledge of God as Creator and as Judge on the basis of general revelation mediated by common human experience. A longing for forgiveness and reconciliation is also part of man's common experience, but apart from faith there is no assurance either that God is merciful or that his mercy finally transcends his judgments. Knowledge of God's love and of the relationship of his love to his justice can be known only by special revelation. Christian faith declares that this precisely is the meaning of the Atonement; such faith affirms, moreover, that the Cross of Christ is the "final" revelation of God's nature because it represents the freedom of God over his own law. The Cross of Christ is "the revelation of God's freedom in the highest reaches of its transcendence";[36] for here God takes the consequences of man's sinfulness into himself, thereby revealing the depths of the divine mercy and at the same time disclosing to man the meaning of his humanity and the law of his freedom.

True knowledge of the meaning of human life and history is rooted in Christology, but the knowledge that is thus grounded in faith is dialectically related to man's knowledge of himself based upon reason. On the one hand, revelation stands in contradiction to all of man's efforts to interpret the meaning of human life from the standpoint of himself as its center; but, on the other hand, once it is accepted, this disclosure of history's final meaning becomes the basis of true wisdom concerning the nature and meaning of human existence. The knowledge of revelation is not alien to man, nor is it superimposed upon man's rational knowledge of himself. Rather, the word of revelation concerning the meaning of human life and history "completes" the incomplete knowledge of natural reason, "clarifies" the obscurities and contradictions that are found in history, and "corrects" the falsifications of human knowledge.[37]

Not only does the Cross of Christ disclose the ultimacy of mercy in the divine nature, but it also reveals to man that _agape_ is the norm--or law--of his own essential nature. Through the Cross of Christ _agape_ is revealed to be the most perfect expression of the divine goodness, and it is also revealed to be the norm of man's authentic selfhood. That is to say, through the Cross man recognizes that the _agape_ of Christ--the sovereign expression of the divine goodness and freedom--corresponds precisely to his own created nature. _Agape_ is thus revealed to be the norm of human conduct; but the norm itself is grounded in the essential nature of man, and, hence, it can be validated by common experience. "The ethic of the Cross," Niebuhr writes, "therefore clarifies, but does not create, a norm which is given by the very constitution of selfhood."[38]

Like Brunner and Reinhold Niebuhr, Ramsey also makes Christological revelation the starting point for

Christian ethics. Epistemologically speaking, all three of these writers base their ethics primarily and fundamentally upon Christology (love), but all three also believe that Christian morality has a secondary basis in reason grounded in creation (natural justice). As we shall see, however, Ramsey's conception of the relationship between revelation and reason in Christian ethics differs in important ways from those of Brunner and Niebuhr. Whereas Brunner tends to interpret this relationship in dualistic terms and Niebuhr in dialectical categories, Ramsey's position is intentionally transformationist. Particularly in his later writings, Ramsey is concerned to give a more positive role to natural justice than is characteristic of Neo-Protestant ethics generally, including both Brunner and Niebuhr, but he is also concerned to defend the primacy of revealed agape as the fundamental norm of rational justice.[39]

For each of these moralists the basic problem for Christian social ethics is that of a proper understanding of the relationship of love to natural justice. While Ramsey finds a powerful expression of the transformationist motif in Brunner's The Divine Imperative, he argues that the former was unfortunately replaced by a dualistic understanding of this relationship in Justice and the Social Order. The strong ethical dualism of the latter work is rooted in an underlying theological dualism between God's relationship to the world as Redeemer and his relationship to it as Creator and Preserver. Thus, Brunner's fundamental error lay in his abstraction of the notion of justice from the totality of God's action--i.e., from "the whole idea of God."[40] Despite the transformationist thrust which he finds in The Divine Imperative, however, it is evident that Ramsey wants to move beyond the "duality" or "polarity" between the Command and the orders even in that earlier work. Brunner himself provided the basis for such a movement in his emphasis upon the transformation of the social order although even here he made "the obedient preservation of the present existing order" man's "first duty" and the task of participating in its transformation a secondary duty. Thus, while the more transformationist ethic of The Divine Imperative is greatly to be preferred to the dualism of Justice and the Social Order, it would be better still "to refrain from calling either one or the other of these tasks (justice or love) man's 'first' or 'second' duty under his covenant with God and with man...."[41]

While Ramsey interprets Reinhold Niebuhr as "a radical revisionist among natural law theorists," he nevertheless finds a qualified form of dualism in the latter's conception of the relationship between love and natural justice. In Niebuhr the dualism is more dynamic and hence more dialectical than it is in Brunner, but here, too, it is rooted in an abstraction of God's redemptive action from his creative/ordering work in human history. In ethical terms it is expressed in Niebuhr's perfectionist interpretation of *agape* as an "impossible possibility" for human history and in the resultant dichotomy between life "within history" and "beyond history."[42] For Ramsey, the true criterion of Christian love is not self-sacrifice but commitment to the good of the neighbor, and it is for this purpose that *agape* makes use of natural justice as it seeks to become embodied in the midst of the conflicts and tensions of history. "What can be more 'right' and 'conformable to *agape*'," he asks, "than a wise concern for the life and interests of others?"[43] In this way the transformation of justice by love takes place "in fact" and not "in principle" only.

The fundamental structure of Ramsey's interpretation of Christian ethics is set forth in his first major work, Basic Christian Ethics, which appeared in 1950. He described that volume as "an essay in the Christocentric ethics of the Reformation."[44] According to Ramsey, *agape* is the "'primitive idea' of Christian ethics"; it is the fundamental notion in terms of which all other ethical and theological ideas receive "derivative definition" in Christian faith. The term "basic Christian ethics" refers to "the fundamental moral perspective of the Christian," and that perspective is defined in terms of "obedient love." Moreover, the only source for knowledge of what such love means is Scripture understood Christologically--i.e., with Christ as the center. Christian ethics includes social ethics, but the latter is not basic. Nevertheless the former must take up the task of the latter, and in its search for a social policy Christian ethics must draw upon the resources of other forms of ethics. In particular, Ramsey argued, contemporary Christian ethics must form an alliance with philosophical idealism. Such an alliance, however, should be neither a partnership of equals nor a permanent "concordat." On the contrary, <u>agape</u> always "occupies the ground floor"; it always remains "dominant and free" in relationship to insights and principles drawn from other sources.[45] Thus H. Richard Niebuhr aptly characterized Ramsey's position in <u>Basic Christian Ethics</u> as "Christ transforming Natural Law."[46] Ramsey does not essentially depart from this fundamental position in his later work although he does undertake to develop the role of natural law in Christian social ethics much more fully and more systematically in his more recent discussions of this theme. Natural justice becomes more important in the methodology of Christian social ethics, but it remains secondary in the order of authority. It does not become "basic Christian ethics" in this sense. Rather, the proper relationship of Christian ethics based on revelation to moral insights based on reason is that of "Christ transforming, renewing, reshaping, and redirecting" the latter.[47]

It has been noted that Ramsey's ethics is intentionally Christocentric. It is clear, however, that for him the basic meaning of this concept refers to the source of human knowledge of moral truth rather than to the believer's final object of faith and trust. Thus, his ethics is Christocentric because it is based upon the revelation of the divine will in Christ as the decisive measure of human action and because it makes the love of Christ the controlling--the primary or basic--principle of moral conduct. It is in this sense that Ramsey writes: "The Christian, indeed, is consistently more Christocentric, considerably less merely theocentric, in his religious and ethical outlook than was Jesus himself."[48]

Like Reinhold Niebuhr, Ramsey interprets Christian ethics primarily in terms of agape understood as a moral principle. The meaning of Christian love is decisively measured by "the controlling love of Christ"; moreover, such love is "the principle par excellence of Christian ethics."[49] The appeal to agape interpreted in the light of the New Testament enables Ramsey--like Niebuhr--to recover the radical and distinctive quality of Christian love. Further, by rooting agape in the fundamental biblical idea of the covenant, Ramsey keeps love integrally related to social justice.

Nevertheless, Ramsey's tendency to make agape-- even "obedient agape"--the fundamental principle of Christian ethics involves him in a number of difficulties when he attempts to deal with the totality of Christian ethics. These difficulties are related, in part at least, to the Christocentric structure of his ethics. For example, there is a certain ambiguity in Ramsey's designation of agape as "basic," or "primary," Christian ethics. Sometimes this term is used to describe the distinctive quality of Christian morality.[50] At other times, however, Ramsey seems to include the entirety of Christian ethics in the single principle of agape and to equate the latter with the more fully structured concept of "covenant." When this occurs, the relationship between agape and covenant becomes problematic, especially when the latter is used as a paradigm of moral discourse in a pluralistic society.[51] In a similar manner Ramsey calls the just war doctrine a "product of agape in Western thought."[52] Yet on occasion he qualifies this judgment as when he writes: "the norm of Christian love, and not natural justice only, was still the main source both of what the Christian could and should do and of what he could and should never do in military action."[53] Here, too, the relationship between agape and natural justice remains ambiguous at the point of whether or not the former is actually dependent upon the latter for a fuller understanding of the meaning of social justice.

To the extent that Ramsey is seeking to analyze

the <u>distinctive</u> quality of Christian ethics, his analysis is necessarily based upon Christology. To the extent that he raises the broader question as to what is "basic"--or "primary"--in Christian ethics as a whole, however, he poses a deeper ethical and theological issue, viz., that of the relationship between the particular and the universal in Christian morality. If, in addition to its particularity, the latter also includes universal elements which are grounded in Creation, the question must be asked whether it is appropriate to speak of the former as "primary" and to call the latter secondary. Christian ethics is not an ethics of redemption for Ramsey just as it is not for Brunner. Ramsey believes, however, that Brunner separates the Command of the Creator too sharply from the Command of the Redeemer; hence, Ramsey seeks to set forth a more unified conception of Christian ethics in transformationist terms. However, he does not entirely escape the criticism which he levelled against Brunner when he declared that a truly transformationist ethic must be based upon "the <u>whole</u> idea of God."

While Ramsey draws upon the insights of natural law to supplement <u>agape</u> in the task of social ethics, he does not have a doctrine of natural law--or natural justice--as a basis for his ethics.[54] His intention has been to give natural law (justice) a more positive role in Christian ethics than it has for Brunner and Reinhold Niebuhr, and he has attempted to do so on the basis of a Christocentric understanding of <u>agape</u>. While his Christology remains undeveloped in so far as a systematic theological statement of his position is concerned, he is strongly attracted to the <u>kenotic</u> model of Paul rather than the Logos view that Christ was "half-God, half-man" and speaks, instead, of Christ as one whom "God put...forward."[55] With Barth, he speaks of creation as the external basis of covenant and also of God's covenant as the internal meaning of creation.[56] Clearly Ramsey does not mean to imply, however, that he accepts Barth's doctrine of creation. Yet, he has resisted the development of his own theory of natural justice and his own doctrine of creation in order to maintain the transformationist position against a hierarchical synthesist interpretation of the relationship of Christ to natural justice.[57] Not only does his Christocentrism lead him to focus on the theme, "Christ <u>transforming</u> natural justice"; the former apparently precludes the development of a doctrine of creation. Such a concept seems necessary in theological ethics, however, in order to relate the moral life to "the <u>whole</u> idea of God."

The Primacy Of Moral Experience: H. Richard Niebuhr And Gustafson

When we turn to H. Richard Niebuhr and James M. Gustafson, the question of the starting point of ethical inquiry becomes much more complex than it is for the first two groups. For Barth, Bonhoeffer, and Lehmann Christian ethics rests squarely and exclusively upon a Christological foundation, that is, upon dogmatics. Although Christian ethics, at least for Barth and Lehmann, does not reject philosophical ethics, there is nevertheless a radical incompatibility between the two based upon "the irreconcilability of their respective views of human self-determination."[58] Theological ethics must take philosophical ethics seriously in so far as the questions which the latter raises are the "stuff"--or concerns--of its own reflection and provide a conceptual base for ethical discussion. But the radical difference between the two is shown by the fact that philosophical ethics does--and must--reject theological ethics since the latter is based upon radically different presuppositions.[59] For philosophical ethics, the Good is fundamentally a good to be known and achieved by man; for theological ethics, the nature and the possibility of the Good are given in the divine claim which comes to man through the revealed Word.

In comparison with the first group, Brunner, Reinhold Niebuhr, and Ramsey have a more positive place for natural morality in the total structure of Christian ethics. In comparison with H. Richard Niebuhr and Gustafson, however, they tend to interpret

God's redemptive will more exclusively in terms of
<u>agape</u> and to separate his redemptive will (<u>agape</u>) more
sharply from his creative/ordering will (justice). For
both H. Richard Niebuhr and Gustafson, moral experience
constitutes the primary datum for ethical reflection.
As such it provides a phenomenological basis for a more
unified understanding of the relationships between
faith and reason and between Christian ethics and moral
philosophy than is found in the first two groups.

In examining the question of the starting point
for ethics in H. Richard Niebuhr, it is necessary to
distinguish clearly between the moralist's point of
view (perspective) and the object of ethical inquiry
(human moral experience).[60] Every observer, Niebuhr
notes, has some point of view. Niebuhr uses the term
"Christian" to identify the standpoint in terms of
which he seeks to interpret human existence. In this
sense, his belief "that man exists and moves and has
his being in God; that his fundamental relation is to
God" constitutes Niebuhr's "starting point" rather than
the conclusion of his study of moral philosophy.[61]
Niebuhr also describes this point of view as "theistic," but the term "Christian" seems more precise
since it identifies the historical particularity of his
own understanding of God by one who is a member of the
Christian community.

In addition to the moralist's point of view
(perspective), the question of the starting point
raises a second important issue for Niebuhr's ethics,
viz., the object of moral inquiry. In <u>The Responsible
Self</u>, the object of investigation is "human moral life
in general" rather than simply the Christian life as is
the case, Niebuhr notes, in Christian ethics. This
distinction is of fundamental importance in understanding the basic difference between his conception of
Christian ethics and those interpretations which are
based exclusively upon Christology. "It is at this
point," he writes, "that I part company" with those
theologians who make the Christian life "discontinuous
with other modes of human existence."[62] Niebuhr does
not deny that Christian ethics has a distinctive qual-

ity that makes it distinguishable from other forms of morality; indeed, he moves toward such a Christian ethic in the later sections of The Responsible Self, but he does so on the basis of a generalized pattern or structure of responsibility which he finds typified in broadly human moral experience. Such a structure is necessary, he believes, as a model in terms of which both the continuity and the discontinuity between Christian ethics and other forms of morality can be comprehended and understood.

Thus, the distinctiveness of Niebuhr's approach to theological ethics as compared with other approaches which we have considered lies in his insistence upon the primacy of moral experience in defining the basic structure of the moral life. Although he considered the search for such a structure to be only a prolegomenon to Christian ethics, he believed that such an inquiry was indispensable for a proper understanding of the nature and the task of theological ethics. For him, moral experience is the primary object of ethics. In this connection, it must be noted, however, that it is Niebuhr's theistic point of view which enables--and, indeed, requires--that he make this the starting point of theological ethics.[63] Niebuhr elsewhere describes this point of view in terms of "radical monotheism." Such theocentric faith, he believes, is the fundamental Christian conviction.

Faith in God as the principle of being "relativizes" every particular historical expression of faith and keeps the latter from becoming idolatrous. As noted above, Niebuhr describes this underlying theological perspective both in Christian and in theistic terms. These two categories are not antithetical for him; on the contrary, the Christian has been taught through Jesus Christ to have faith in "God the Father, Almighty Maker of heaven and earth."[64] Thus Niebuhr uses the term "radical monotheism" to describe the fundamental conviction both of Jesus Christ and of the Christian community. Such faith means trust in the "One beyond all the many, whence all the many derive their being, and by participation in which they exist."65 Stated in its briefest form, it is faith in "the principle of being itself." It is this presupposition which fundamentally conditions all of Niebuhr's reflection on ethics. On the one hand, it leads him to reject the absolutizing of every historical form of faith, including Christianity, and every system of ethics based on a less inclusive faith. As an answer to the historical relativity of all forms of faith and ethics, however, it leads him to begin his analysis of the structure of the moral life at a different point and to incorporate into his ethic insights from general revelation (based on human reason) as well as from special revelation (Christology).

Niebuhr's understanding of the moral life rests upon a confessional base, namely Christian faith, which for him is most adequately described in theocentric terms. On the basis of this faith he adopts a dialogical method of relating to persons of other faiths who are also seeking to understand the moral life in other terms. In this quest the Christian moralist acknowledges the confessional character of all faith-claims. The Christian professes faith in the Father of the Lord Jesus Christ, faith in the One to whom Jesus Christ points all persons. In this sense, revelation through Christ is decisive, but revelation is not limited to the Christ-event. Radical monotheism thus provides the basis for affirming a particular confessional standpoint without absolutizing the latter. The decisive character of God's revelation through Christ for Niebuhr's own understanding of the moral life is evident, however, throughout his major ethical writings. It finds particular expression in his "conversionist" interpretation of the relationship of Christ to culture,66 in his analysis of radical faith as incarnate and revealed in history,67 and in his portrayal of Christ as symbolic form.68 Faith in the universality of the divine action and recognition of the idolatry of all claims to absolutism in faith and ethics prevent him, however, from basing Christian ethics exclusively upon Christology.

Does the foregoing analysis of H. Richard

Niebuhr's confessional faith stance and his method of ethical inquiry imply that "there is an implicit Christocentrism" in his thought?[69] While agreeing essentially with the interpretation of Niebuhr's theological position which has been developed above, Hoedemaker contends that there is such an implied Christocentrism in Niebuhr. Paul Ramsey reaches a similar conclusion when he describes the latter's ethics as "the ethics of Christocentric monotheism."[70] Both Hoedemaker and Ramsey appear to base their judgment upon the assumption that "Christocentrism" refers primarily to the view that, for Christians, God has revealed himself most fully in and through Jesus Christ. Anyone, therefore, who adopts this confessional standpoint is Christocentric by definition. For Niebuhr, however, at the most fundamental level this term means the substitution of faith in Jesus Christ for faith in the One to whom Jesus Christ points. It also means the restriction of revelation to its Christological sources. Understood in these two senses, "Christocentrism" appears to be inconsistent with "radical monotheism" as Niebuhr uses the latter.

To summarize, for Niebuhr "the starting point of all (ethical) inquiry lies in the recognition of that which is."[71] His method of ethical analysis is phenomenological in so far as he seeks to provide a structure by which human moral experience as a whole can be taken into account. At the same time, he seeks to understand the "is-ness" of moral existence as a Christian, not as a detached observer. His aim is to understand "what is going on" in human experience, including both its universal and its particular aspects, from the perspective of Christian faith. Stated in theological terms, the primary question of ethics is a question about the divine action: "What is God doing in the totality of his action toward men?" In Christian ethics, theological reflection and ethical reflection go hand in hand. Theology focuses upon the nature of the divine action; ethics, upon the human response to what God is doing. Both theology and ethics are human activities which take place in the context of a pattern of universal divine action. While recognizing the distinctiveness of Christian ethics, Niebuhr stresses the underlying continuities between Christian and other forms of morality. These continuities are found in moral experience.

Like Niebuhr, Gustafson also makes moral experience the starting point for theological ethics. The basic questions of ethics are embedded in moral experience. As such they are intrinsic to all ethical inquiry. According to Gustafson, these questions have to do with the nature and the locus of the good, the nature and character of the moral self, and the criteria of moral judgments.[72] Moreover, the method and procedure of theological ethics, including Christian ethics, are the same as those which are used in other types of ethics. Christian ethics differs from other forms of ethics only in content, not in form or method.

Since moral experience represents the primary datum of ethics, Gustafson begins his ethical inquiry with a critical analysis of the former. His approach to ethics, including theological ethics, is basically phenomenological. Such an analysis discloses certain patterns of moral activity and moral relationships.[73] Not only does it reveal the basic questions of ethics; it also discloses the conditions--the fundamental relationships and processes--which are prerequisite in order for moral judgments, moral choices, and moral actions to occur. Significantly, Gustafson does not attempt to construct on this basis a single normative structure of moral existence that is ontologically grounded. Rather, his aim is to provide an analytical framework for understanding the constituent elements in moral experience, the factors which shape these components, and the interrelationships among the latter.

For Gustafson, one of the most significant elements in morality is the character of the moral agent, and this in turn is shaped by the perspective, the disposition, the intentions, and the moral norms of the agent. All of these factors, in turn, are influenced by the faith of the latter. Since there are many forms of faith, including many perceptions of Christian faith, morality is influenced by religious faith in many different ways. At the level of descriptive analysis, the sources of theological ethics are seen to be broader than revelation; they also include natural affective and rational sources which significantly shape moral experience generally, including that of Christians.

Although different theological ethicists begin their moral analyses at different starting points, each inevitably turns to a number of other sources of insight and illumination.[74] The latter include social analysis, theological affirmations, moral principles, and a conception of Christian existence. Taken by itself, each of these "base points" proves inadequate, Gustafson believes, for understanding the moral experience of the Christian community. More significantly, each represents a construct--a theory, a belief, an idea--which is abstracted from the concrete experience which it is used to interpret. Hence, the only adequate starting point for ethics as well as for theology is human experience. The latter is "prior to reflection."[75] It is also social and historically conditioned.

Gustafson's method and procedure of moral inquiry resemble that of H. Richard Niebuhr at a number of important points. Both base their ethics fundamentally upon moral experience. For both, an analysis of experience provides a basis for the normative task of ethics. Both refuse to draw a sharp line between Christian moral philosophy and theological ethics. Both recognize many affinities between theological ethics and other forms of morality, and both point to common elements in experience to account for these commonalities. For both, Christian ethics represents a transformation--or a "qualification" (Gustafson)--of the moral life rather than the substitution of a new morality built exclusively upon revelation. For both, Christian ethics is fundamentally theocentric.[76]

Yet Gustafson's analysis of moral experience differs from that of Niebuhr in a number of important respects. For Niebuhr, it will be recalled, the primary question of ethics is, "What is God doing?" Lehmann and Barth also state the primary question similarly in terms of the divine action (Lehmann) or the divine command (Barth) although they attempt to answer it exclusively on the basis of Christological revelation. Gustafson believes that this way of posing the fundamental question of ethics is presumptuous since it is not humanly possible to say with specificity and certainty "what God is doing (or saying)"; moreover, it also implies an unwarranted passivity on the part of humanity that violates human agency.[77] In both instances Gustafson's appeal is to moral experience--the experience of the Christian community in the first case and a general recognition of greater human autonomy in the second. Hence, he reformulates the primary question as follows: "What is God enabling and requiring me (or us) to be and do?"[78] This way of restating the fundamental relationship of God to the events of nature and history suggests that the latter is more remote and indirect than the language of divine action or command implies.[79] It includes, for example, the creation of a moral order to which individuals and institutions ought to conform. The existence and nature of such an order are inferred on the basis of underlying religious beliefs, and the agent's discernment of God's will for present human conduct takes place in relationship to such an order. The concept of what God is enabling and requiring also implies a larger role for human agency than do images of divine action and deontology.

On the basis of the foregoing understanding of the relation of God to the world, Gustafson proposes "the imitation of God" as a central symbol of Christian ethics.[80] This image, he believes, is based upon the experience of God in biblical and Christian history. On the one hand, it focuses attention upon the <u>human</u> action which God makes possible and requires. It also reflects the fundamental motivation (gratitude) of religious persons for being moral and the basic direction (toward God) and intention (the well-being of creation) which guide them in this endeavor.[81]

Finally, this symbol exemplifies Gustafson's concern with virtue as the primary or integrative theme in moral experience rather than duty or the good or responsibility. "Virtue" points to the significance of character--of the "sort of person" one becomes--in the determination of moral conduct. Christian faith influences the character of believers in important ways, but here, too, such influence is most adequately described in terms of the "transformation" or the "redirection" of the self rather than a replacement of the latter. Faith works through the processes and the "stuff" of human self-hood; it does not create an ontologically new self on the basis of redemption.

3

THE NATURE OF THE GOOD

The previous chapter dealt with the question of the starting point of Christian ethics. There we were concerned primarily with the sources of human knowledge of the good, of moral agency, of the nature and function of social institutions, and of criteria of moral choices. We turn now to a consideration of the nature of the good. In theological ethics the good is defined abstractly as "the will of God." At the level of ethical analysis, however, the question must be raised whether it is possible to describe the content of the moral good in more concrete terms.

Some Protestants define the good in terms of obedience to known laws which are revealed in Scripture. In the Roman Catholic tradition of moral theology, on the other hand, the good is defined both in terms of natural law known through human reason and in terms of "divine law" known through special revelation. From the perspective of the ethicists included in the present study, however, such attempts to define the good either in terms of revealed or in terms of natural law appear legalistic and static. In contrast, these writers interpret the good in fundamentally relational terms. They define it first of all, in terms of the relationship of humanity to God and, secondarily, in terms of the relationships of persons to each other. Beyond their acceptance of a relational notion of the good, however, these authors differ in important ways concerning the nature of that good and the extent to which it can be specified. They differ also in their interpretations of how the good is perceived and the manner in which moral agents proceed from perception of the good to specific moral decisions. While the latter questions will be dealt with more fully in subsequent chapters, some consideration of them is necessary in the present context in so far as they help define the possibilities and the limits of speaking meaningfully about the <u>nature</u> of the good.

Obedience To The Command Of God:
Barth, Bonhoeffer, And Brunner

For Barth, Bonhoeffer, and Brunner, the norm of human conduct is obedience to the command of God. For Barth and Bonhoeffer, as we have seen, this command is known exclusively through Christ; for Brunner, it is disclosed concretely in the moment of decision through the Spirit, but it is also made known in a "fragmentary and indirect way" through the "orders of creation."[1] For each of these theologians, good human action is action which is done in obedience to the concrete command of God rather than in conformity with laws or principles or ideals. It includes both the <u>intention</u> of obedience to the divine command and <u>conduct</u> that conforms to the latter.

For Barth, as we have previously noted, theological ethics is based upon God's electing grace as this is made known in Jesus Christ. God's electing grace is sovereign grace; hence, it always confronts man also as commanding grace.[2] Not only is the command of God the starting point of theological ethics; the former constitutes the entire content of the latter, for theological ethics presupposes the <u>intention</u> of obedience to God's electing grace as this is known exclusively in Christ. "Man's action is good," Barth writes, "in so far as he is the obedient hearer of the Word and command of God."[3] Thus, the relationship of Christian ethics to Christian faith is tightly circular. This does not mean that God's will is never done outside of the Church; it means, rather, that God's will is done Christocratically outside of the community of faith through the kingship of Christ in the world. For Barth, such action is not "good" from the standpoint of theological ethics, because it lacks the intention of the agent to be obedient to the command of God.

Since God is sovereign and free, one cannot specify in advance of the moment of decision what particular acts of obedience will be required. One knows only that one is summoned to be obedient to the God who has revealed and continues to reveal himself in Christ. Yet Barth's ethics is neither individualistic nor intuitive. While Jesus Christ is the norm of conduct, he cannot be known apart from his witnesses, that is, apart from the witness of the apostles and the whole people of God, including both Israel and the Christian Church. "It is in their testimony that the divine command is always to be sought and will always be found as the sovereign divine decision."[4] Moreover, the God who has made himself known in Christ has revealed himself as Creator, Reconciler, and Redeemer. The God who confronts man as his Commander is the God who always meets man in and through this threefold activity. He is the One who has created man, who reconciles man to himself, and who wills to redeem man for eternal life. This is the persistent pattern, or direction, of the divine command. God's command will always meet man "at some point on the ways of this God--and to this extent not in empty space."[5]

Not only does God reveal the threefold form of his action toward man through his Word, but he also thereby reveals three basic characteristics of human existence which correspond to the threefold pattern of divine action. Over against the Word of the Creator, man knows that he has been created to be God's covenant-partner and finally to participate in eternal life. Over against the Word of the Reconciler, man knows himself to be a sinner to whom God has been gracious so that he may henceforth live on the basis of the divine forgiveness and hope in God's promise. And, finally, over against the Word of the Redeemer man knows himself to be even now a "child of the Father led by the Spirit."[6]

On the basis of this understanding of humankind in relationship to God, Barth proceeds to examine the great motifs in Christian ethics in relation to the major themes of the Church Dogmatics. This means that

51

his development of these motifs is Christological since his ethics is controlled by his dogmatics. These extensive sections on ethics show how Barth seeks to establish the identity and integrity of Christian ethics in contradistinction to all other forms of ethics, on the one hand, and how he attempts to give shape and structure to the discipline, on the other. In both of these endeavors Barth makes clear the extent to which he stands in the Reformed tradition of theological ethics.

For Barth the central question of ethics is the question of obedience to the Word of God. The Command of God differs from all other forms of obligation, however, in the fact that it is, first of all, a "permission." It is the gift of the freedom to live before God and with Him in peace and joy. The Command of God comes to sinful man as the promise of his lost freedom; hence, the divine command is now perceived to be the form of the divine grace.[7] Authority and freedom are united in Christ, for in him genuine obedience is seen to be "the obedience of the free man to the free God."[8]

Not only does the divine command differ from all other forms of obligation in its basis (God's electing grace) and its form (permission-obligation); it differs from the latter also in its content. Unlike any other claim, it demands a specific decision in relation to a particular person, Jesus Christ.[9] Obedience to the command of God means intentional obedience to Jesus Christ in and through every other form of obligation. Unless obedience to other authorities is "in the Lord," unless it is intended finally as a form of obedience to Christ, it is not obedience to the command of God. Hence, it has nothing to do with theological ethics or with a Christian understanding of the good.

The command of God confronts humanity, not as an ideal duty or freedom but as a reality in the person of Jesus Christ.[10] Obligation and freedom are united in Christ and only in him; hence, he is the source of true obedience and genuine freedom among men. In him there was a perfect correspondence between what he was permitted and what he was commanded to do. In his freedom he lived the life of "the first and basic and normative covenant-partner of God."[11] It is through him--the reality of the divine command which is present in him--that other persons may know what genuine obedience and authentic freedom are, and it is on the basis of this reality--as it elects and claims others--that they may also become covenant partners of God. This reality of grace present in Christ is the only source of genuine freedom and joy and power to be fully man. What God requires he gives before he requires, and what he both intends and effects through his grace is the restoration of humanity to the divine likeness--i.e., to conformity to his grace--and to fellowship with himself in eternal life.[12]

Barth's insistence upon the "reality" of God's electing grace in Jesus Christ and his insistence upon the fact that Christ cannot be known apart from the witness of the community of faith provide the basis for giving a more definite shape or structure to his ethics. The shape or form of his ethics is based upon his analysis of God's special revelation. God is completely free to command as he chooses to command; moreover, each demand is addressed to man in the form of a concrete claim. However, the divine command is neither casual nor arbitrary. As permission, it always sets man "free along a definite line."[13] One cannot tell in advance what the specific content of the divine claim will be, but we know that at "all times and places" it will be the command of the God who meets man in a threefold pattern of action as Creator, Reconciler, and Redeemer.[14] The command of God always comes to man in certain "spheres"--or patterns or structures of relationships--in which all historical human action takes place. These spheres correspond to the threefold form of the divine action; moreover, the former are recognizable or identifiable only on the basis of the latter. While the three spheres--creation, reconciliation, and redemption--may be separated for purposes of analysis of the structure of the ethical event, God always commands and man always acts in all three spheres simultaneously. On the basis of this self-characterization of God, which corresponds to his inner trinitarian being, Barth develops a number of "directives," which give general guidance for discernment of the divine command.

Such directives are necessary in order to provide "a formed reference" for understanding the ethical event in which man is confronted by the divine command. More particularly, they are necessary in order to avoid the pitfalls both of legalism and of intuitionism. They represent "generally discernible" patterns which the divine command has taken in the history of the covenant community of Israel and the Christian Church.[15] As such, they do not tell man what action will be required of him in any future moment of decision, but they do point him in the direction of the particular forms of obedience which will be required of him. Since they are based on historical revelation, they must be taken with utmost seriousness; yet the final answer must be left to God who is free to command as he wills.

Both the Ten Commandments and the Sermon on the Mount are to be understood as "directives" rather than as universally binding moral principles or duties.[16] They define the position of man in relationship to God, his need to hear the divine command, and the definite character of the claim which this command places upon him in every concrete moral choice. The Sermon on the Mount gives the requirements of the Old Testament commandments a new dimension and a radical depth by reason of its clearer Christological focus on grace; but it, too, is intended fundamentally as "a constant direction to new and particular obedience on the lines it lays down."[17]

Barth's most extensive treatment of directives in relation to specific ethical issues is found in Part Four of the third volume of _Church_ _Dogmatics_. Here he develops the implications of the theological principles underlying his ethics for such specific issues as marriage; the near and distant neighbors; respect for life; the protection of life--suicide, abortion, euthanasia, self-defense, capital punishment, and war; and vocation. Through the combination of the directives which he spells out with great sensitivity and detail and through the precisely structured way in which he provides for "the exceptional case" in relation to the general directives, Barth is able to give definite form and shape to his ethics.

In summary, Barth's conceptualization of the normative in Christian ethics is strongly biblical. The central question of ethics is the question of obedience. Yet, while Barth's ethics is deontological, the obligation rests ultimately upon the gift of a new relationship which God has established with humanity. This new relationship (election/grace) becomes the source of a covenant-ethic in which man is called, most fundamentally, to be the covenant partner of God and, secondarily, as God's covenant-partner to be wholly and genuinely free in relationship to the neighbor. Man is summoned to be in his action that which he already is on the basis of grace--viz., a new being, a child of God, a covenant-partner of God.[18] Barth also uses the concept of "responsibility" to define man's ethical situation as one who is continuously addressed by the command of God.[19] The good is always "a matter of command and prohibition, of exhortation, warning, precept and direction."[20] Ethics as a preparation for responsible action is essentially a matter of man himself being questioned by the Word of God in preparation for obedience to the command of God which comes in the moment of decision. The divine command is sovereign. It should be obeyed just because it is the divine command. Barth writes: "Nothing that we can do in fulfilment of the will of God is higher and deeper than to love Jesus and therefore to keep His commandments--just because they are His, just because we cannot love Him without keeping His commandments. We definitely fulfil the will of God when we do this."[21] Ostensibly, consequences are not to be taken into account in the determination of what the content of the divine command may be.

Although Barth strongly insists that the specific content of the divine command cannot be known in advance of the concrete summons to decision, he provides a mediating position between those ethicists who stress the significance of moral principles and those who stress the uniqueness of each moral situation. He also differs from those ethicists who locate the distinctive element in Christian ethics in _agape_. Barth locates the former in obedience to the divine command; moreover, the divine command includes the summons to many forms of obedience.[22] Among the qualities of Barth's ethics which are deeply rooted in the distinctively biblical understanding of man in relationship to God and to his fellowman are: the sovereignty of God's free grace; man as the covenant-partner of God; man's existence in fellowship with others (his co-humanity); the three-fold pattern of divine action in creation, reconciliation, and redemption; and the revealed will of God as the norm of human conduct.

For Emil Brunner, as for Barth, the norm of the good is the command of God; moreover, the specific content of this command can be known only through the hearing of the Word in each new moment of decision.[23] Brunner, however, reflecting the influence of Luther at this point, maintains that the content of the divine command can be described in a formal way as the unconditional requirement of love: "Love God--and your neighbor." God always wills that man shall love in this two-fold way. Like Barth, Brunner interprets Christian ethics essentially in terms of obedience. For both, the command of God is understood first of all as gift and only secondarily as demand. In each case, Christian ethics is deontological rather than teleological. Man ought to obey God simply because God commands obedience, not for some utilitarian reason. While the divine command always comes to man in the form of specific acts which are required of him, it always demands the obedience of the whole self.

Like Barth, Brunner also believes that the command of God will always be consistent with his self-disclosure in and through his historical activity.

But, whereas Barth describes the divine action in terms of a threefold pattern of creation, reconciliation, and redemption, Brunner speaks only of creation and redemption.[24] For Brunner there is a greater dualism between man's experience of God's work as Creator and his work as Redeemer than is true for Barth. As a consequence of this dualism, or tension, Brunner describes all Protestant ethics as "interim ethics"--that is, as a provisional ethic for the present time of decision between the Fall and Resurrection. The command of God comes to man in the midst of the "orders of creation"; moreover, God's will as Creator is revealed through these orders although the latter have been corrupted by sin. These natural forms of community--marriage and the family, labor, the state, culture, and the institutional church--are intended by the Creator as a training ground for true community based on love.[25] While they may be known in their empirical form on the basis of reason, their true meaning can be known only on the basis of special revelation. In obedience to the Creator, man is summoned to accept these existing orders, but in obedience to the Redeemer he is summoned to transform them by protesting against their injustice and lack of love.

For Brunner the basic problem of Christian ethics arises out of the antinomy between the natural forms of community which impose their own duties and claims and authentic community based on self-giving love. The answer which he gives to this problem, particularly in <u>Justice and the Social Order</u>, is essentially that of Luther, namely, the Christian lives in two different albeit interrelated "kingdoms" or "realms" governed by two different moralities. The "orders" are located essentially in the realm of law (the earthly kingdom), and justice rather than love is normative here.[26] In the realm of redemption, on the other hand, love is the norm--self-giving, neighbor-oriented love, which is the bond of true community. Such love is a possibility only in inter-personal relationships; hence, it always stands in tension with the institutional claims of culture. The origin of this contradiction is found in the Fall, and the contradiction itself will continue until it is finally overcome eschatologically.

While Brunner agrees with Barth in making "the command of God" the norm of Christian ethics, he tends (unlike Barth) to reduce the content of the latter to love. "Good," he writes, "is fully described by the one word: <u>Love</u>, and indeed, in the New Testament sense, as love of our neighbor."[27] Self-giving love is revealed in Jesus Christ to be the essential meaning of human existence. Moreover, Brunner limits Christian love as a possibility to inter-personal, I-thou relationships. To be sure, the Christian is motivated by love to seek justice in the social order, but justice in the sense of rendering each man his due remains normative in the latter sphere. Thus, for Brunner the dualism between ethics based on creation and ethics based on redemption remains unresolved.

Barth avoids this dualism through a greater concentration on the unity of the divine action in creation, reconciliation, and redemption and through the consistent employment of this pattern of interpretation (rather than love) as the norm of human conduct. For both Barth and Brunner, man exists in and for community. To be human is to live in responsibility for the neighbor. For both writers this means to be oriented toward the neighbor so that one seeks the good of the neighbor rather than the self. Brunner's conception of love appears, however, to be too largely abstracted from man's historical condition; hence, it tends to be ultimately individualistic and perfectionistic. Barth's conception of love, on the other hand, is more "intentional" and more communal; it is more directly related to the whole range of human need, including justice.[28]

Whereas the ethics of creation and that of redemption remain in antinomy with each other in Brunner, for Barth the entirety of ethics is subsumed under redemption--that is, under grace, under Christology and ultimately under a Christocratic conception of the relationship of Christ to secular culture. Barth has a more positive attitude toward secular culture, and he is more open to a radical transformation of the latter--for example, the state--than is Brunner, since for him culture is included within the order of grace. In so far as the internal structure of his ethics is concerned, Barth is more consistent than Brunner in his insistence that theological ethics be based exclusively on Christology. Barth's ethics is addressed exclusively to the Christian community since its authority rests upon the presuppositions of that community; Brunner's ethics is addressed both to the Christian community (love and justice) and to all men in so far as the orders and natural justice are concerned.

Bonhoeffer's understanding of the nature of the good resembles that of Barth more closely than that of Brunner. In Christian ethics the question of the good becomes for him, "the question of participation in the divine reality...revealed in Christ."[29] As "reality"-- as the concrete place where God and the world are reconciled--Jesus Christ is the embodiment of the will of God. As such he is both the form and the content of the good. Christian ethics, therefore, is essentially an ethics of formation, or conformation, in the likeness of the incarnate, crucified, and risen Christ.[30]

The good is not a quality of external behavior; rather, it involves a response by the whole person to the word of God which is addressed to man in Jesus Christ. Bonhoeffer uses the term "responsibility" to describe such a life of wholehearted response to Jesus Christ.[31] The responsible life is a life of obligation and also a life of freedom. The obligation is expressed in terms of deputyship and correspondence with reality; it is also expressed in terms of "the commandment of God." The concrete meaning of such obligation--and, therefore of the good--is disclosed from above through the word of Christ addressed to the agent. Like Barth, however, Bonhoeffer also seeks to describe a more structured form--or pattern--of the Christian life in terms of discipleship.[32] Like Barth also, Bonhoeffer seeks to avoid the dualism between personal and social ethics implicit in the traditional concept of "the two kingdoms"; but, whereas Barth used the term "spheres" to designate the historical-cultural relationships in which the command of God is addressed to man, Bonhoeffer called the latter "mandates."[33] Unlike the "orders of creation," the mandates, or spheres, are Christologically grounded; they are identifiable only on the basis of revelation.

Conformity To A Moral Principle (Agape): Reinhold Niebuhr And Ramsey

In contrast to those ethicists who make the command of God the basic norm of human conduct, Reinhold Niebuhr and Paul Ramsey define the latter in terms of a moral principle, viz., agape. While Ramsey differs from Barth, Brunner, and Bonhoeffer in this regard, he nevertheless resembles the latter in interpreting Christian ethics primarily in deontological terms; for Reinhold Niebuhr, on the other hand, Christian ethics is fundamentally teleological. For Ramsey, agape defines what is "right," or obligatory; it specifies "the meaning of obligation."[34] For Niebuhr, on the other hand, agape is an ideal which gives guidance toward the realization of the self. For Ramsey, "good" human action is action which is obedient to the requirements of agape; for Niebuhr, the former aims at the fulfilment of human life in community.

Reinhold Niebuhr stands in the tradition of liberal Protestantism and the Social Gospel in so far as these movements make love the one inclusive Christian virtue, but he differs radically from the former both in his conception of the meaning of agape and in his understanding of the manner in which the latter is related to the complex problems of social justice. Whereas Rauschenbusch had attempted to apply love immediately and directly to the social problems of his day, Niebuhr believed that such a strategy rested upon an inadequate understanding of human sinfulness and a moralistic conception of love. On the one hand, he agreed with the Social Gospel that love is the final norm for the institutions of culture; but, on the other hand, he differed radically from the former in his insistence that this relationship can be properly understood only in dialectical terms.

It has been previously noted that for Reinhold Niebuhr the ultimate norm of human life is love and that, particularly in his later writings, the meaning of <u>agape</u> is most fully disclosed in the Cross of Christ. Such love is essentially sacrificial; it is heedless of the interests of the self. While natural man has some knowledge of this norm on the basis of reason, he experiences the former as an unfulfilled obligation rather than as the power of grace. <u>Agape</u> is most clearly perceived to be the final law of life on the basis of faith, but this insight is partially confirmed by reason on the basis of man's created nature. For Niebuhr, moreover, <u>agape</u> is not only the distinctive norm of Christian ethics; it is the only ultimate and absolute requirement both of individuals and of groups.

In order to comprehend Niebuhr's concept of <u>agape</u> more fully, particularly its relationship to other virtues, it is necessary to consider the relationship of love to justice in his thought. Since God is the Creator and Sovereign over history as well as its Redeemer, in Christ <u>agape</u> is disclosed to be the law of both man's personal and his collective relationships. It is the only moral principle whereby the conflicting claims both of individuals and of groups can be finally harmonized and fulfilled. Yet, the Cross also reveals the universality and power of self-love in all men. <u>Agape</u> is thus revealed to be an impossible ethical ideal within history on account of human sinfulness.

How, then, is <u>agape</u> related to the decisions and choices which are the very stuff of human history? This, for Niebuhr, is the critical question of Christian ethics.[35] If ethical discussion stops short of taking this question seriously, it ends in irrelevance to the concrete decisions which we make from day to day. If this question is answered too simply, the result is increased moral confusion in dealing with such complex and morally ambiguous problems as those of economics, politics, and war. The answer which Niebuhr gives to this question is distinctive and differentiates his ethical methodology clearly from that of Barth, Brunner, and Bonhoeffer. In essence, Niebuhr argues that the relevance of <u>agape</u> for man's life in culture depends upon the maintenance of a strong dialectical relationship between <u>agape</u> and the struggle for social justice. This means that the purity of love as the law of man's essential nature must be understood in absolutist and perfectionist terms[36] in order to provide both proper direction toward man's true end (<u>telos</u>) and an adequate measure of his sinfulness. It means also that the <u>agape</u> which is disclosed in the Atonement of Christ must be related to the world of culture, that the God who revealed himself as Redeemer is also the Creator; therefore, his will toward the world and for the world cannot be separated into two spheres, one personal and one institutional, as Brunner tended to do in <u>Justice and the Social Order</u>. It means, in addition, that the struggle for social justice based on man's natural capacity for justice must be given a greater relative independence than Barth allows and at the same time less autonomy than it has either in traditional Roman Catholic theories of natural law or in Brunner's "orders of creation." The dialectical relationship between love and justice is grounded theologically, for Niebuhr, in his dialectical understanding of the relationship of the Atonement to creation, of revelation to reason.

Justice represents the form of community which is possible within the limits of history. It is an instrument of community; hence, it is an instrument of love under man's sinful condition. It does not, however, have an independent basis either in the "orders of creation" or in natural law. On the contrary, justice is rooted in love, and all historical forms of justice fall finally under the judgment of <u>agape</u>. "Love is both the fulfilment and the negation of all achievements of justice in history."[37] Or, again, Niebuhr writes: "There is no justice, even in a sinful world, which can be regarded as finally normative. The higher possibilities of love, which is at once the fulfilment and the negation of justice, always hover over every system of justice."[38]

For Niebuhr *agape* provides both the motivation to seek justice and the norm of justice. But the dialectic of love and justice implies something more, namely a more positive relationship of reason to the ethic of the gospel than Barth and Brunner were willing to allow. The dialectic of *agape* with reason is needed in Christian ethics for two reasons. In the first place, it is needed to provide a realistic understanding of man's historical situation--including the nature of power and the sources of social evil--to the end that Christian faith may be made relevant to actual human experience in culture. But such dialogue is also needed, in the second place, not only for the illumination and guidance of culture which *agape* provides, but also, conversely, for a fuller understanding of the meaning of the gospel itself.[39] Thus, the full meaning of the gospel in terms of its implications for the abolition of slavery, for the greater equality of women and men, and for greater economic justice has been clarified in part through the impact of secular movements in history. The contributions of such movements are, of course, provisional since the latter are also distorted by egoism and pride. For this reason, they, too, must be subjected to the final norm of *agape* which alone is absolute and which can be finally symbolized only by the Cross of Christ; yet, within the order of history they help Christians comprehend more fully the existential and the historical meanings of the gospel and *agape*.

Not only is love related dialectically to justice; the latter also involves the continuous interplay--or tension--between equality and liberty.[40] Niebuhr calls these the "regulative" principles of justice. Viewed from one perspective, they can be derived from love on the basis of revelation rather than reason; but, understood from the other pole of the dialectic, they may be said to be based on reason and to point beyond themselves to their harmonization and fulfilment in the law of love. Thus, in the order of justification or validation in Christian ethics, liberty and equality may be derived from <u>agape</u> as implications of the Christian doctrine of man. They may also be derived from reason; yet they cannot be adequately comprehended on the basis of reason, for sinful men use them ideologically to justify their own selfish interests. In any event, however, equality and liberty are regulative rather than constitutive principles of justice. The latter cannot be equated either with equality or with liberty since the two are frequently in conflict with each other. Hence, these principles point beyond themselves to <u>agape</u>, and the former are clarified, purified, and fulfilled by the latter.[41] <u>Agape</u> is the only constitutive principle of justice; justice is enhanced, however, as it moves toward greater approximation to equality and liberty.

What, finally, is the relation of <u>agape</u> to other moral criteria according to Reinhold Niebuhr? As we have seen, sacrificial love is the only absolute moral norm; it alone is grounded directly in man's essential nature as an unconditional requirement. Yet there are many other secondary standards of conduct which are validated by experience and which are tentative and provisional expressions of the law of love.[42] These include not only justice, equality, and liberty but also many more concrete embodiments of these norms in family and community life.

Taken together all such norms are included in the broad category of justice; together they constitute a limited, or historically qualified, form of natural law. Such norms are based upon the experiences of various human communities and as such reflect the contingencies and relativities of history. This "limited natural law" is less absolute than traditional Roman Catholic conceptions of the law of nature presuppose, but it is also more positively related to love as the final requirement of human freedom than traditional Catholicism perceives.[43]

There are thus many virtues and many moral norms

besides _agape_ for Niebuhr. All of these are related dialectically to _agape_ and to the Kingdom of God. The former are both affirmed and negated by love, for love alone is capable of harmonizing and fulfilling the claims of all competing selves in their essential nature, including the indeterminate possibilities of human freedom and transcendence over nature.[44] Other virtues are in fact virtuous only in so far as they are embodiments of love and brotherhood in the midst of the contingencies of history, i.e., only to the extent that they correspond to man's essential nature as a being who, while finite and free, is created for community. For Niebuhr, man's essential nature remains highly indeterminate, however, since his freedom and transcendence are a fundamental part of this nature.[45] Hence, it is impossible to equate any particular structures of human society with "the laws of nature." For this reason, also, all of the "many norms of conduct" and structures of justice which seem to be based on nature must "be finally subordinated to the law of love."[46]

Although Paul Ramsey resembles Reinhold Niebuhr in making love the fundamental, or controlling, norm of Christian ethics, these two writers differ in a number of important ways regarding both the meaning of love and the proper relationship of the latter to social ethics. For Ramsey, Christian love is "obedient love."[47] This is the primary principle of Christian ethics. While the full meaning of love (_agape_) is known Christologically, the idea itself is deeply rooted in the faith of Israel. Its two major sources are the righteousness of God and the Kingdom of God. Both of these ideas are united, in turn, at a still deeper level in the notion of covenant out of which both stem. While the Christian idea of love is thus grounded in the fundamental biblical conceptions of the will of God and the reign of God, its full meaning is decisively disclosed in the teachings and the life of Jesus.[48] Through Christ men are taught to love one another as God-in-Christ already loves them. Such love is unselfish; it seeks only the neighbor's good. It is "obedient love" since it is done in obedience to God.

For Ramsey, Christian ethics is fundamentally deontological rather than teleological. It is primarily concerned with the intentionality of the moral agent--with the question, <u>Whose</u> good is to be sought in cases of conflict between the good of the agent and that of others? <u>Agape</u> directs the agent toward the good of the neighbor, not that of the self in or through the neighbor.[49] Christian ethics is, thus, primarily concerned with "right relations" among persons rather than with the consequences of particular moral choices. Due to this strong deontological emphasis, Ramsey has sometimes been interpreted to mean that consequences are unimportant in so far as the moral quality of decisions is concerned. Even in his early writings, however, he acknowledged that consequences are a necessary object of inquiry in Christian ethics <u>for the sake of the neighbor</u>.[50] Yet, throughout his career he has insisted that they are sharply subordinated to deontological claims in Christian ethics.[51]

Ramsey has stated this position more clearly and developed it more fully in his later writings in relationship to biomedical ethics and the just war doctrine. For example, referring to the ethical issues involved in the attempt to control the quality of human life through genetic control of the reproductive process, he writes: "In fact there is nothing more important in the whole of ethics than the consequences for good or ill of man's actions and abstentions--<u>except</u> right relationships among men, justice, and fidelity one with another."[52] The moral quality of human action is determined, in short, both by the underlying intentionality of the agent and by the consequences which the agent's decisions have for the neighbor. Ramsey clearly emphasizes the former, and the reason he does so lies in his belief that the "humanity of man" is more fundamentally at stake in the protection of the relationships of trust and fidelity among persons than it is in the increase of technological knowledge or the biological improvement of the species.

Similarly, in his writings on the just war Ramsey

appeals to two main criteria governing the just conduct of war, viz., the principle of discrimination and that of proportion. Here the deontological principle of discrimination (non-combatant immunity) clearly limits the teleological principle of the proportionality between good and evil consequences. First, the principle of discrimination is to be applied to particular forms of proposed warfare, for the former has to do with the basic question as to whether the latter are permissible at all; only after it has been determined that the proposed forms of warfare are "morally tolerable," only then should the question of proportionality of good to evil consequences be raised relative to the range of permitted actions.[53] The latter question is necessary, however, even though it is secondary in the order of moral reasoning. It should be noted, moreover, that, unlike the principle of discrimination, the principle of proportionality does not yield exceptionless rules of conduct. Hence, the application of the latter to specific cases remains largely a work of prudence.[54]

The deontological character of Ramsey's ethics is indicated in more specific terms by the role which he assigns to "rules" and "principles" in moral reasoning. At first these terms were used interchangeably, but more recently he has attempted to distinguish between the two. "Principles," he writes, "are <u>directions</u> of action."[55] They may be either general (unexceptional) or summary in nature. In contrast to such governing or regulative principles, however, rules refer to "particular <u>directives</u> of an action"; they either prescribe or proscribe "a <u>definite</u> action."[56] Both principles (which have a higher level of generality) and rules (which are more action-specific) are needed, Ramsey believes, to provide direction and guidance to the moral agent in the movement from the ultimate norm (obedient <u>agape</u>) to concrete decisions. His own model of moral reasoning moves from this ultimate norm through a series of increasingly specific principles and rules specifying the "sorts" or "kinds" of action which "obedient <u>agape</u>" requires.[57] Such principles and rules define the right-making qualities of particular moral choices. On the one hand, they give expression to the continuities in human relationships; and, on the other hand, they focus attention upon the moral significance of means which are used to achieve even good ends. Both the choice of ends and that of means are limited by the claims of trust and fidelity.

While Ramsey was primarily concerned to define the basic component in Christian ethics in his earliest work, he nevertheless recognized that it was not sufficient to establish <u>agape</u> as the fundamental norm of Christian conduct. To describe Christian ethics in this manner is to raise immediately two issues that are critical, particularly in the field of social ethics, viz., the question of the unity of Christian virtue and the question of the relationship of that which is basic to that which is general in Christian ethics. Ramsey began to wrestle with both of these problems in <u>Basic Christian Ethics</u>, but the latter in particular has occupied a more central place in his later work where he has focused more sharply upon the issues and problems of social ethics. It has been a major concern, for example, in his writings on war, medical ethics, and the role of natural justice in Christian ethics. We shall return to this question momentarily. First, however, we need to attend to Ramsey's concept of virtue.

If <u>agape</u> is the primary norm of Christian conduct, may it also be described as a virtue? If so, is it the only Christian virtue, or is it the first among many such qualities of character? Are Christians to be only lovers in relationship to their fellowmen, or should they also exemplify patience, humility, truthfulness, and many other qualities which are more or less universally esteemed? If all of these virtues--and more--are included in Christian ethics, how are they related to love?

According to Ramsey, love is essentially a directional principle or norm of conduct. It points the moral agent not toward the self or toward God but toward the neighbor. It is "a relation by which one man exists for another."[58] It is always a "present decision" rather than a "habit" of moral behavior or a stable pattern of character. "Such obedient love," Ramsey declares, "is not a virtue; it has virtues."[59] Neighbor-love is the source of Christian virtues. Virtues arise out of, or are "elicited" by, love for the neighbor. Ramsey thus agrees with Augustine that love is the unifying principle of virtue, but unlike Augustine he locates this unity in love for the neighbor rather than in love for God. "Virtue," he writes, "is nothing else than the perfect love of the neighbor, and love of neighbor calls for virtues of character."[60] Thus, the virtues are "forms" of neighbor-love rather than "forms" of love for God. They represent patterns of behavior--patience, gentleness, loyalty, courage and the like--which are among the duties which each man owes to his neighbor.[61] Agape expresses itself in and through these forms, but in so doing it transforms them and directs them toward the neighbor, thus giving them their specifically Christian quality. Love, in short, is neither the only Christian virtue nor the chief among many in a pantheon of virtues. It cannot be defined but only described relationally. It is a directional response of the whole self toward the neighbor--a response which includes such qualities as those attributed to it by Paul in I Corinthians 13: "Love is patient and kind; love is not jealous or boastful; it is not arrogant or rude. Love does not insist on its own way; it is not irritable or resentful; it does not rejoice at wrong, but rejoices in the right. Love bears all things, believes all things, hopes all things, endures all things."[62]

Since Christian love is directed toward the neighbor, it must necessarily be concerned with the formation of social policy. In pursuit of this task, it draws upon the resources of faith--upon distinctively theological ethics itself, but it is also compelled to draw upon other resources as well. In Basic Christian Ethics, Ramsey emphasizes both the positive content which Christian love has for social ethics and the extent to which the former remains dominant and free. The Christian understanding of human sinfulness gives rise to a negative task of justice, viz., the restraint of sin.[63] The norm of "obedient love" also contains significant, positive content for social policy when compared with intuitionist and existentialist forms of ethics.[64] Moreover, for the sake of the neighbor *agape* must also enter into "alliances" with other social policies based upon other foundations. In particular, contemporary Christian ethics needs to make common cause with the ethics of philosophical idealism.[65] While Ramsey is critical of the natural law tradition in Catholic ethics, his treatment of the relationship of *agape* to ethics based upon reason may be aptly described even here as love "transforming natural law."

In his subsequent writings, Ramsey has sought to clarify and develop the role of natural justice in Christian social ethics. This concept has assumed increasing significance in his thought, but he has refused to incorporate it into basic Christian ethics.[66] It does not constitute an independent principle of Christian ethics alongside of *agape*. Rather, reason remains finally subject to revelation; natural justice remains finally subject to Christian love which transforms it and utilizes it in the service of the neighbor. This position may best be described as a "radical revision" of natural law rather than a synthesis after the manner of Aquinas. To say that natural law does not occupy part of the ground-floor of Christian ethics can only mean, in this context, that it is not a controlling principle of Christian conduct along with--i.e., on a par with--*agape*. Love reigns both in personal and in social ethics, but it reigns through the enlistment of natural justice and not apart from it. Like the virtues of patience, loyalty, and kindness, justice based on reason and directed toward the neighbor is a "form" of neighbor love.

Ramsey's continued effort to relate *agape* to the issues and problems of social ethics as well as his greater concern with continuity and stability in the moral life of individuals has led to a shift from *agape* to "covenant" in defining the primary norm of Christian ethics. Ramsey does not, however, perceive this shift to covenant-language as a substantive change but only as a different way of expressing the claims which are embedded in neighbor-love. Attention has already been called to the fact that in Basic Christian Ethics the notion of agape was rooted ultimately in the idea of covenant. In that early work Ramsey declared:

> In this book, the basic norm for Christian ethics has been called 'obedient love' because of its intimate association with the idea of 'covenant' and with the 'reign' of God....These two are, in fact, the same thing: obeying the covenant and doing justice, love for neighbor and fulfilling the law."[67]

During the sixties, when the debate over contextualist ethics was at its height in this country, Ramsey sought to overcome the individualism and pragmatism of that movement by emphasizing the inner thrust of agape itself toward the development of rules of practice which embody Christian love.[68] In The Patient as Person, however, the concept of covenant replaced agape as the basic norm of medical ethics.[69] Like agape, this concept defines the meaning of "righteousness between man and man," but it provides a stronger basis for affirming the claims of faithfulness and fidelity which are implicit in the practice of medicine as a profession. More particularly, "covenant" provides a more precise model for reconciling the welfare of the individual with the welfare of society; it also provides a stronger basis for appeal to the broadly human "community of moral discourse" because it is more directly related to justice.

In summary, the concept of covenant has always functioned in Ramsey's thought to symbolize both the range of human relationships (interpersonal and social) where God wills that agape should reign and also, particularly in his later writings, the moral qualities of fidelity and loyalty which are at the heart of Christian love. It is clear, moreover, that for him covenant fidelity, like _agape_, needs to be embodied both in principles and in rules of practice before it can provide adequate moral direction either for individuals or for social groups.

4

THE NATURE OF THE GOOD (Continued)

Pattern Of Response To God's Action:
Lehmann, H. Richard Niebuhr, And Gustafson

In contrast to Reinhold Niebuhr and Ramsey, for whom <u>agape</u> is the ultimate norm of Christian ethics, the three theologians to whom we now turn reject the tendency to define the will of God in terms of a single moral principle. For them, the relationship of God to the world is more complex. According to Lehmann and H. Richard Niebuhr, the divine will is disclosed in and through the divine action. Hence, for them the primary question of ethics is, "What is God doing?" Lehmann believes that this question is properly raised only within the <u>koinonia</u>; hence, the answer to it is found only within this context. The divine action is not limited to the <u>koinonia</u>, however; for whatever God does in and through this fellowship, he does also in the world. For Niebuhr, on the other hand, the answer to this question is given in human moral experience as a whole. Not only is the divine action universal, but there is more commonality between Christian and non-Christian forms of faith and morality than Lehmann allows. Like Niebuhr, Gustafson grounds his ethics in human moral experience rather than exclusively in the Christian community. But, unlike Niebuhr, Gustafson attempts to provide greater moral direction through the development of action-guiding values and principles based upon the religious beliefs of the Christian community. Such values and principles are not limited to love. Moreover, they must be understood in dynamic terms because they represent an on-going human response to a teleological pattern of divine action.

(1) Lehmann: Maturity

According to Lehmann, Christian ethics is concerned, not with the _good_, but with "what I as a believer in Jesus Christ and as a member of his church, am to do."[1] The answer to this question is given only in the _koinonia_. Moreover, it always takes the form of specific acts of obedience to God whose will is disclosed in and through his action in the world. For Lehmann, as for Barth, God's sovereign freedom means that his will cannot be comprehended in terms of principles or precepts. Hence, Christian ethics is "oriented toward revelation and not toward morality."[2] _Koinonia_ ethics is fundamentally indicative rather than imperative in character, for revelation points to the primacy of what God is doing in the behavioral situation out of which the ethical question arises. To be sure, an "ought" factor is present, but it is not the primary ethical reality. "What God is doing" implies an obligation on the part of members of the _koinonia_ to be obedient to the will of God, but this imperative claim is subordinated to the divine initiative and grace. From the perspective of the _koinonia_, the general answer to the question, "What am I to do?" is, "I am to do what I am!"[3] Because he knows himself to be forgiven and free in Christ, the believer is summoned to obedience in this freedom to the will of God.

Understood in terms of the biblical story, God's activity is essentially messianic--i.e., political--activity. God is always at work "doing what it takes to make and keep human life human."[4] This means that he is bringing into being "a new humanity." God wills that the _koinonia_ be expressive of this new humanity both in its own common life and in its relationships to the world.[5] Concrete acts of obedience are required even in morally ambiguous situations. This does not mean, however, that there is always a single right action.[6] Rather, the "rightness" of human acts consists in their bearing the "risk of obedience" and thus being "potentially instrumental" to the divine action. In view of God's sovereign freedom, however, there can be no assurance that such acts will in fact be instrumental to the fashioning of a new humanity in the world. Their primary significance lies, rather, in their symbolic meaning as "signs" of the presence of the new humanity. In any event, Lehmann fails to make clear whether such acts of human obedience constitute a <u>duplication</u> of the divine action or a qualitatively different <u>human response</u> to the latter. The reason for this ambiguity lies in the fact that he is not concerned with the moral quality of particular human acts but only with their parabolic significance.

Lehmann's ethics is primarily concerned with the basis, direction, and style of the Christian life rather than with the nature of the good or with an analysis and clarification of the process of decision-making. The <u>koinonia</u> constitutes the "ethical reality" which provides the basis both for Christian living and for thinking about Christian ethics. As a "fellowship of maturity in love," the church is a community in which the achievement of maturity is "always both a possibility and a fact."[7] It is both the context in which the Christian life is lived and also "the custodian of the secret of the maturity of humanity."[8] It is not only a fellowship of believers but also a "fellowship-creating" community.

<u>Koinonia</u> ethics is fundamentally teleological ethics. It aims, however, not toward morality, but toward maturity.[9] Morality is a "by-product of maturity." For Lehmann "maturity" is a social rather than an individualistic concept; it means "the integrity in and through inter-relatedness which makes it possible for each individual member of an organic whole to be himself in togetherness, and in togetherness to be himself."[10] Stated in a different way, <u>koinonia</u> ethics aims at the achievement of freedom. Freedom, however, is also understood in a social rather than an individualistic sense. Maturity and integrity are the proper expressions of human freedom since man is by nature a social being.

Lehmann thus describes the goal of Christian ethics in terms of maturity, integrity, and freedom;

but he does not deal with the question of how these goals are to be achieved. Nor does he deal with the critical question of how conflicts between community and freedom are to be resolved. We are told, instead, that the resolution of such problems "belongs to the possessor of the secret of maturity."[11] Koinonia ethics finds it quite "beside the point" to take up the question of the nature of specific acts and the relation of such acts to the good.[12] Although morality may be quite useful in supplying "rational clarification and guidance" for conduct, it nevertheless falls outside the scope of Christian ethics because the latter is not interested in the quality but only in the symbolic significance of Christian behavior.[13]

If the basis of Christian ethics is the koinonia and if its direction is toward maturity, its methodology of decision-making is contextualist. Christian ethics is contextualist in a double sense for Lehmann. In the first place, it presupposes the Christian community as its context; and, in the second place, its methodology of decision-making is concrete, relational, and intuitive.[14] The will of God is perceived immediately and directly through the sensitive conscience of the believer.[15] The ethical component in any concrete situation is that which makes it possible for human beings to be open *for* and *to* one another.[16] The style of koinonia ethics is thus the style of free, mature, whole persons who as members of the fellowship of believers are led by the Spirit to a fresh disclosure (act-revelation) of the will of God in each new ethical situation.

(2) H. Richard Niebuhr: The fitting

Like Lehmann, H. Richard Niebuhr also defines the will of God in terms of the divine action rather than in terms of principles or laws. Niebuhr differs sharply from Lehmann, however, in his understanding of both the nature of God's action in history and the normative implications of the latter for human moral decisions. Niebuhr's analysis of the pattern of divine action is more "realistic" in that it is more informed by an empirical understanding of the processes and structures of creation. The broader set of categories which he uses to describe what God is doing in his creative, ordering, and reconciling activity enables him to give a much fuller account of "what is happening" in human history than Lehmann provides. Similarly, the normative significance of the divine action for human conduct is interpreted in different ways by these two men. For Niebuhr, Christian ethics is an ethics of response, first, to the divine action and, secondly, to other human action; for Lehmann, it is an ethic of obedience to the will of God which is perceived in and through his concrete action.

Niebuhr's concept of "response" is rooted in his relational concept of value.[17] In contrast to all forms of Idealism and Rationalism which begin with conceptions of value in terms of an abstract good (Plato), and abstract ought (Kant), or an abstract essence (Nicolai Hartmann), Niebuhr affirms the primacy of being over ideas. Value, he declared, is "a function...of being in relation to being."[18] Thus, the worth of a particular being is defined, in any relational theory of value, "by reference to a being for which other beings are good."[19] Value is a social concept. As such, it has many dimensions because it is rooted in the manifold relations which beings have to each other. Moreover, these relationships are both reciprocal and dynamic.

Not only does Niebuhr's relational value theory provide a way of understanding value in social and dynamic terms; it also suggests an alternative way of understanding the "good" and the "right" in terms of the "fitting" response of the self to the needs, capacities, and potentialities of other selves to which it is related. This does not mean that the categories of "good" and "right" are no longer needed. It means, rather, that they are concretized and re-interpreted in relational terms. <u>Good</u> refers to that "which meets the needs, which fits the capacity, which corresponds to the potentialities of an existent being."[20] <u>Right</u> refers to that relation of being to being in which "their potentiality of being good for each other is realized."[21] Stated in terms of responsibility, the <u>fitting</u> act is that act which is conducive to the good of existent beings, and it alone is right.[22]

For Niebuhr, the fundamental structure of moral activity is most adequately defined in terms of responsibility. Moral experience is too complex, he believed, to be molded either practically or theoretically into consistent patterns of teleology or deontology. Hence there was need for an additional symbol which would do greater justice to those aspects of human agency which were obscured by the latter. The issue of human agency will be dealt with more fully in the following chapters. Here we are concerned primarily with the concept of responsibility as a norm, or criterion, of moral action. For Niebuhr, the image of responsibility served this function, both in relationship to a contemporary understanding of moral agency and in relationship to the biblical ethos, including that of both the Old and the New Testaments.[23] Through the aid of this symbol it is possible, he believed, to interpret the particularity--not just the distinctiveness--of biblical ethics more adequately than through aspiration or obedience. Understood in terms of this image, the formal criterion of Christian ethics is "the fitting."

As noted above, Niebuhr's analysis of moral experience in <u>The Responsible Self</u> is basically phenomenological in character. As such, it is first of all descriptive, but there is also a sense in which the four elements which he finds included in the idea--or pattern--of responsibility are also normative for moral action. Unlike "rules" of conduct, however, they refer not to particular acts but rather to certain general-- or formal--standards to which human action must conform in order to be "fitting" (or "right"or "good").

Stated in their most abstract form, these characteristics of responsible moral action represent "rules for ethical reasoning" rather than guides for concrete decision-making.[24] Thus Niebuhr writes:

> The idea or pattern of responsibility, then, may summarily and abstractly be defined as the idea of an agent's action as response to an action and with his expectation of response to his response; and all of this is in a continuing community of agents.²⁵

Responsible action is action which includes <u>response</u> to prior action, <u>interpretation</u> of that prior action, the recognition of the agent's <u>accountability</u> for his/her action, and the universality of the <u>community</u> of moral interaction. Understood even in their most formal sense, these principles do in a certain manner shape, or "inform," concrete moral choices; yet, the precise way in which they do so is affected both by the agent's center of value and by the former's understanding of the empirical situation in which the concrete moral choice is made. Interpreted in terms of this model, the primary question of theological ethics becomes, "What is God doing?"; accountability is understood in theocentric terms; and Jesus Christ becomes, for Christians, the indispensable "paradigm of responsibility."²⁶

In order to see how the formal norm of responsibility--or the fitting--is made more concrete in Niebuhr's ethics, one must turn to his more detailed description of "the virtues of Jesus Christ," his analysis of Christian ethics as response to the divine action, the role of Scripture--especially the covenant theme--in his thought, and the relations of the moral law to Christian ethics.²⁷ In <u>Christ and Culture</u> Niebuhr defines Jesus Christ in terms of his virtues.²⁸ The distinctiveness of Jesus' ethic, according to Niebuhr, lies in the radicality of his faith in God, including both his trust in and his loyalty to his Heavenly Father. Such heroic faith expressed itself in radically theocentric love, hope, obedience, and humility as well as in other virtues-in-relation-to-God. Moreover, Jesus Christ is the moral authority of Christians; as such he not only exemplified these excellencies but also communicates them to his followers by mediating to them a livelier, more

79

single-hearted trust and loyalty in relation to God. The virtues of Christ cannot be understood as abstract qualities of his character but only in relationship, first of all, to God, and, secondarily, to other persons. Moreover, the virtues of Jesus are best comprehended when they are viewed together as qualities of his whole-person-in-relationship-to-God rather than as isolated excellencies. Viewed as elements in such an inclusive pattern, these virtues along with many others have their fundamental unity in Jesus' radical trust in God, and each derives its distinctive quality from that trust.

When Niebuhr described the manner in which theocentric faith and the ethos of universal responsibility were expressed in the life of Israel, he did so in terms of covenant.[29] For the Israelites all human relationships were transformed into covenant relationships: "Promise-making and promise-keeping were the essential elements in every connection between persons." Not only religious observances, but also domestic, economic, and political relations were basically covenant relations between and among men based upon the fundamental covenant between God and man. Responsibility expressed in terms of covenant included law, but the former pointed beyond the latter to the basis of the law in underlying human relationships. Understood in terms of covenant, natural, historical, and cultural relationships among persons were similarly transformed by radically monotheistic faith. Niebuhr's description of the family is typical in this respect of all other human relationships: "The family, with all its natural basis in sex and parental love, was now given a sub-foundation as it were in promise and the keeping of faith between husbands and wives, parents and children."[30]

Radical faith understood in terms that include both trust and loyalty was expressed even more fully in Jesus Christ than it was in Israel, Niebuhr believed, for in Jesus such trust seems less qualified and such loyalty more single-minded. Hence, for Christians the most adequate way of describing Jesus' relationship to

God is to speak of him as the Son of God.³¹ Yet, the faith of Jesus cannot be understood apart from the faith of Israel, for both bear witness to the oneness of God and to the unity of the divine action in all events in nature and in history. Moreover, for both, faith includes loyalty within a universal community; it means the understanding of all human relationships in terms of covenant, in terms of faithfulness, in terms of the making and keeping of promises rather than primarily in terms of abstract or universal reason.³²

One of the major features of Niebuhr's ethics which distinguishes it from "act" forms of intuitionism (whether deontological or teleological) is his transformationist conception of the moral law.³³ In part, this law is known through special revelation in the Judeo-Christian community; in part, it is known through natural reason. While both forms of the moral law are included in Christian ethics, the distinctiveness of the latter implies that it is informed in its totality in a particular way by the Scriptures and by the community of believers. Both the Scriptures and the community point beyond themselves to God, but to be a Christian is to know God through participation in a particular historical community of faith. Christian ethics neither absolutizes the revealed moral law (imperatives and values) nor rejects it because it is culturally conditioned. Rather, Christian ethics results in "a great conversion of the power, spirit and content of the law."³⁴ The source and authority of the law are now perceived to be the living God whose will is both righteous and universal; hence, obedience to God means a radical extension and intensification in the application of the law. It means a rebirth and critique of the law in light of its relativity. Most importantly, however, it means the conversion of the imperative into an indicative. Since the content of the law is now perceived to be love, the law takes on the character of counsel, and bondage to the law is turned into the freedom of sonship.³⁵ Christian ethics is not bound by rules; yet "it knows all the rules." Within our human history, law and gospel--obedience and freedom--remain in tension (polarity) but not in duality (separation). Nevertheless, Christian ethics rests upon the conviction that the transformation of individuals and culture, including the moral law, is a present possibility of grace.

(3) Gustafson: The well-being of creation

In the previous chapter attention was called to the fact that Gustafson differs from Lehmann and H. Richard Niebuhr in his formulation of the primary question of ethics. For Lehmann and Niebuhr, this question is phrased specifically in terms of the divine action: "What is God doing?" Gustafson asks, instead, "What is God enabling and requiring me (or us) to be and to do?"[36] He prefers this way of stating the basic question because it focuses on our _human_ action and suggests a larger measure of human autonomy. In addition, it implies a more indirect relationship of God to the world, thus providing the basis for a more objective and rational understanding of the moral order based on fundamental religious beliefs. In a subsequent section attention will be given to the implications of these alternative ways of formulating the primary question for an understanding of moral agency. Here our concern is to compare the corresponding concepts of the good. To what extent does Gustafson's question imply a different conception of the good in human conduct?

It should be noted, in the first instance, that Gustafson agrees with Lehmann and Niebuhr in understanding God's relationship to the world in dynamic, historical terms. God's will for man can never be reduced to universal, absolute laws although there are discernible patterns of divine action. Moreover, his relationship to the world can never be comprehended finally in terms of moral principles or ideals. The very possibility of "good" human action presupposes the priority of the continuing divine initiative in salvation and the present sovereignty of God over creation. For Lehmann, God's action is understood Christologically in terms of redemption. For Niebuhr, on the other hand, the divine action always has a threefold but unified form: it is always creative, ordering, and reconciling activity. For Gustafson, also, God is dynamically related to the world as Creator, as Sustainer and Governor, as Judge, and as Redeemer.[37] Unlike Lehmann and Niebuhr, however, Gustafson interprets this relationship primarily in interactive, processual terms rather than in terms of divine agency.[38] God is that ultimate power which "bears down upon us, sustains us, sets an ordering of relationships, provides conditions of possibilities for human activity and even a sense of direction."[39] The religious person construes the creative, sustaining, ordering, and redemptive powers in human experience fundamentally in terms of piety, i.e., in terms of awe and respect.[40] From the perspective of theocentric piety, the primary moral question is "What is God enabling and requiring us to be and to do?" Stated in its most general terms, the answer to this question is that "we are to conduct life so as to relate to all things in a manner appropriate to their relations to God." In contrast to all forms of anthropocentric ethics, theocentric ethics requires that consideration be given to the "good of the whole (creation)."[41]

For all three ethicists, then, the divine will is revealed in and through the dynamic socio-historical processes of human history as well as through nature. In contrast to Lehmann and Niebuhr, however, Gustafson focuses upon the possibilities and requirements for <u>human</u> conduct--i.e., upon obedient, responsive human action rather than upon what God is immediately intending and doing in and through particular events. In comparison with Lehmann, Gustafson differentiates more clearly between the divine purposes and the intentions of human agents who are both finite and sinful. It is not only truer to moral experience, he believes, but also less presumptuous to say that the intention of the agent is the agent's own and that it is shaped "in response to his beliefs."[42] This does not mean that God's action is not purposive.[43] It means, rather, that our human understandings of what God wills are based upon religious beliefs about God rather than upon direct perceptions of his intentions in relationship to particular historical events. It means, in the second place, that our human intentions are oriented toward the particular possibilities and requirements which are present in concrete moral choices. Understood in these terms, the intentionality of moral agents is given greater objectivity; thus, it can be criticized and judged both by the self and by others in terms of the broader experience of the religious community.

In comparison with Lehmann and H. Richard Niebuhr, Gustafson attempts to give a more empirical, rational account of the way in which faith shapes and informs the moral life. His method of analysis, however, is similar to that of H. Richard Niebuhr. For both, the primary data of ethics are drawn from experience; both employ a method of analysis that may be characterized either as phenomenological or philosophical. Gustafson, however, seeks to identify the psychosocial aspects of selfhood more precisely, thus indicating the empirical processes whereby beliefs influence both character and action. He also gives greater attention to the normative task of ethics in providing moral direction. In comparison with Niebuhr, Gustafson's focus is more upon the character of the agent and upon moral discernment as a rational process of moral reasoning.[44] Through critical analysis of the experience of the Christian community, he attempts to identify the socio-historical sources of moral norms and values in that community. These sources include Scripture; but they also include the beliefs and the ethos of the Christian community as well as secular understandings of human nature and society.[45]

Critical analysis of moral experience thus provides an important basis for the normative task of Christian ethics. It offers a method for understanding the structures and processes of human life and for identifying fundamental religious beliefs that influence the formation of character. It also provides a basis for the development of action-guiding principles and values based on religious beliefs under the tutelage of a moral community that is informed by a common faith and loyalty, common worship, and shared

Scriptures. The development of such norms is a process which involves interpretation, including both theological interpretation of the meaning of Christian faith and interpretation of contemporary events in the light of this faith.[46] It is, moreover, a process which is corporate. It requires a recovery of "the third use of the law"--i.e., its pedagogical function--in order to give specificity to the good in human action. Like Calvin, Gustafson makes this use of the law the principal one.[47] Such action-guiding principles and values are inferences from the religious beliefs of Christians, in the first instance; but, for the most part, they can be stated in broadly human--that is, natural or rational--terms, and they can also be justified on rational grounds. Gustafson's quest for "almost absolute" and "almost universal" principles and values as inferences from moral experience resembles Ramsey's effort to spell out the meaning of agape in terms of general--or unexceptional--and summary rules. Unlike Ramsey, however, Gustafson does not derive such principles and values exclusively from agape. In his emphasis upon "the third use of the law" and the prescriptive task of ethics, Gustafson stands in sharp contrast to Lehmann. According to the latter the theonomous conscience of the believer is "governed and directed by the freedom of God alone."[48]

For Gustafson, the central theological norm of Christian ethics is Jesus Christ.[49] Christ becomes "the content-filled symbol" for human efforts "to discern what God is enabling and requiring in the world." He is "a particular paradigm" of what his followers "ought to be and do" in particular instances of moral action. While not their only norm, he is "the most important" norm for Christians in their interpretation of what God wills. He is the "central obligatory norm" for those who would be his disciples. Through his life, his words, and his deeds, as these are depicted in the New Testament, Christ provides "a source of illumination" and "a criterion of judgment" to his followers. The disposition and the intention, the virtues and character, of each agent as well as the moral decisions of the latter are all subject to Christ as their central norm. Stated in terms of Gustafson's more recent work, Jesus is the incarnation of theocentric piety and fidelity.[50] As such his life, his teachings, and his ministry are "a historical embodiment of what we are to be and to do."

For Gustafson Christian ethics may be described as "an ethics of the imitation of God."[51] This symbol does not mean that Christians are to do precisely what God is doing; rather, it points them to purposive, responsive human action that is directed toward "the well-being of creation." Since God seeks justice for the weak and liberation for the oppressed, those who put their trust in him should "do likewise." Christians should "imitate" God's love for humankind through human deeds of love toward the neighbor.

The "imitation of God" is essentially a teleological symbol. God wills "the well-being of the creation"; he "creates new possibilities for wellbeing" in the events of nature and history.[52] Just as God's relationship to the world is interpreted teleologically, so our human response to what God is enabling and requiring us to do should be teleologically directed toward the well-being of the whole. It is a major task of ethics to specify as fully and precisely as possible the qualities of that well-being. This task is, however, an on-going process since these qualities vary with changes that occur in the events of the natural world as well as in human history. Hence, the human effort to do what God enables and requires me (us) to do has a certain teleological open-endedness toward the "common good" that distinguishes Gustafson's ethics from Ramsey's deontological ethics.[53] The specification of those qualities which constitute "well-being" includes many values, and the latter are understood in relational terms. Significantly, this teleological orientation in Gustafson's conception of the good does not undercut his emphasis upon the prescriptive task of ethics. Indeed, the former demands the latter.

While Gustafson's ethics contains elements both of

teleology and of deontology, it is most adequately understood as an ethic of virtue. His primary concern is with the character of the moral agent--the beliefs, the perspective, the disposition, the intention, and the moral norms which, taken together, shape the moral action of selves in so far as the latter are free. For Gustafson, the normative task of Christian ethics includes the specification of those qualities of character which are not only "consonant with" but also "required of" members of the Christian community.[54] The role of virtue is particularly important in this regard, for virtues refer to "dispositions," i.e., to certain "persisting tendencies" to act in particular ways.[55] The language of virtue refers to a "readiness to act" in a particular manner, to what are called "habits" in classical Catholic moral theology.

In part, the virtues of Christian character--e.g., the so-called "theological virtues," faith, hope, and love--are based upon the distinctive religious beliefs and the moral experience of the Christian community. Others--e.g., the "moral virtues"--are based upon reason. In any event, however, there are many virtues in the Christian life as in our common human life. Even the distinctively Christian virtues do not rest exclusively upon special Christian beliefs; instead, they have a broader basis in human experience. Thus, Gustafson speaks of the "moral requisites" for personal human fulfilment. These include freedom, trust, love, hope, justice, order, joy, and opportunity for achievement.[56] Similarly, certain moral conditions are also necessary for the existence and construction of human community. Among these are trust, fidelity, forgiveness, reconciliation, hope, love, gratitude, joy, justice, courage, temperance, and prudence.[57] Obviously, there is a close relationship between the moral conditions and moral qualities which are necessary to nurture and sustain personal and community forms of human life. This interconnection between the personal and the communal forms of human existence is evident in experience; theologically, it is grounded in the unity of God's relation to the world as Creator, Sustainer and Governor, and Redeemer.[58]

5

THE NATURE OF THE MORAL AGENT

In the preceding two chapters attention was focused upon the meaning of the good, or the right, in human conduct. Each ethicist's interpretation of the moral good rested upon certain presuppositions concerning human nature and moral agency. In the present chapter we turn to an analysis of these underlying presuppositions. Here we will be concerned with the major symbols, or images, which are used to interpret the structure of moral agency. While each ethicist employs a variety of symbols in analyzing the latter, such images may be divided into three main types; moreover, one of these types tends to be predominant for each ethicist. The first two--the teleological symbol, man-the-maker, and the deontological symbol, man-the-citizen--represent traditional metaphors of human moral existence; the third--that of man-the-answerer--was proposed by H. Richard Niebuhr as an alternative, or additional, image for conceptualizing human moral activity.[1] Each of these symbols calls attention to important aspects of moral existence which remain obscured by the use of other images alone. Significantly, such symbols are not mere figures of speech which are used to describe the moral life. Rather, as Niebuhr observes, symbols and reality "participate in each other."[2] Symbols give "intelligibility and form" to human experience.[3] They perform an indispensable function in the apprehension and interpretation of all experience, including moral activity.

Different ethicists, then, use different symbols--obedience, aspiration, or response--to represent the fundamental structure of the moral life. They also use other images to interpret other aspects of moral existence which do not seem to be adequately comprehended in the master symbol. Such additional images are needed to account for elements in our experience which are not adequately perceived in terms of duty or value or response alone. The master image is important, however, for it points to the basic orientation of the agent toward the good or the right.

The Self As Obedient: Barth, Brunner, Bonhoeffer, And Ramsey

The question of the nature and structure of moral agency cannot be considered apart from the broader question of human nature. What qualities of selfhood and human existence constitute the basis, or ground, for moral choices? What kind of freedom do such agents have to choose between good and evil? Do they have an innate, natural capacity to know and choose the good? Or do knowledge of the good and the ability to choose the good rest exclusively upon grace? If the latter is the case, what is the role of the human agent in the realization of the good? How, in short, is human freedom, which is in some sense part of our humanity, actualized?

While Barth, Bonhoeffer, Brunner, and Ramsey view the fundamental structure of moral action in terms of obedience, they differ in important ways concerning their understandings both of the nature of the self and of moral agency. For the first three of these men, good--or right--human action is done in obedience to the command of God; for Ramsey, it is action which is obedient to the requirements of Christian love.[4] In each instance Christian ethics is deontological. It is oriented toward obedience to God rather than the pursuit of some goal. The differences have to do with the question how God's will is apprehended or perceived and also with the question of human agency in works of obedience.

Barth's anthropology is based exclusively upon Christology. Just as Jesus' divinity consisted in his being "man for God," so his humanity consisted in his being "man for man," i.e., man for his fellow men.[5] On the basis of this understanding of the human nature of Jesus, Barth concludes that the basic form of humanity is fellow-humanity. This means that the humanity of each and every person consists in being in relationship with other persons.[6] The basic structure of this relationship is the encounter of one person (I) with another (Thou). This is man's created, or creaturely, nature. As such it has not been lost as the result of sin.[7] While Jesus shared this basic form of our humanity, he alone--as the only "real" man--has fulfilled God's purpose in the creation of humanity to be his covenant-partner. Although it has been perverted by sin, the basic form of our creaturely existence remains. It establishes the continuity of the human subject as creature, as sinner, and as a sinner saved by grace.

Not only is man created <u>with</u> his fellowmen; he is created to be a covenant-partner of God through being <u>for</u> his fellows. There is thus a fundamental correspondence between man's created nature and his destiny as a covenant-partner of God.[8] It is important to note, however, that man is not created a covenant-partner of God, but only for this purpose. The actualization of real humanity, the achievement of man's destiny, depends solely upon God's sovereign grace. Man's existence as fellow-humanity is a sign of his creation for covenant; grace confirms and actualizes what he is by nature.

For Barth, the basic form of humanity is best typified in terms of the duality of I-Thou encounters in which the givenness and the particularity of each is disclosed. It is signified also in the interpersonal relationships in which the mutuality of interdependence is evident. It is typified most of all in the encounter of man with woman. Barth identifies four essential marks of "distinctively human" existence.[9] These criteria represent necessary elements in the encounters of I's with Thou's, which constitute the image of God in man. These marks of humanity are: one person looking the other in the eye, which symbolizes the openness of each to the other; mutual speech and hearing; mutual assistance; and encountering each other with gladness, which presupposes meeting each other in freedom. Freedom is "the secret of being in encounter and therefore the secret of humanity."[10]

To summarize, for Barth the humanity of man consists in his existence in relationship with his fellowmen. This understanding of human nature is grounded in Jesus' humanity and, finally, in the triune nature of God. As God exists in relationship (Trinity), so, too, he created man in his own likeness. The "image of God" is, therefore, an analogy of relationship, not an analogy of being.[11] It is indestructible because it is grounded in creation, and this means, for Barth, ultimately in redemption. Creation is the external basis for the covenant which God willed to establish with man.[12] It is the presupposition which creates the formal possibility of man's becoming a covenant-partner with God. Correspondingly, the covenant--man's existence as a covenant-partner in the service of God--is the internal basis, the inner meaning or goal, of creation.[13] Man is created fellow-man for the purpose of covenant-partnership with God. The realization of this relationship, however, rests exclusively upon grace.

Barth's exclusively Christological anthropology poses two fundamental questions for theological ethics, including in particular social ethics. The first has to do with the possibility and nature of moral evil; the second, with the role of man as moral agent. Viewed from the perspective of redemption and the present Lordship of Christ over the world, sin and evil are ontological impossibilities.[14] When the latter are denied ontological significance on the basis of an eschatological perspective that is grounded in the sovereignty of the divine grace, the question must be raised whether Barth has not also obscured the penultimate (Bonhoeffer) actuality and power of sin and evil in human history. To the extent that this happens, there is no adequate basis for moral discriminations between relative forms of evil and social injustice in particular historical and social situations.[15]

Not only does Barth's denial of any ontological status to evil undercut the seriousness of the latter in the struggle for social justice within history; his concept of the divine command implies that theological ethics is not concerned with good and evil, but only with obedience to the concrete command of God. This means that, particularly in the earlier portions of <u>Church Dogmatics</u> before he takes up the task of "special ethics,"[16] Barth does not allow any place for rational deliberation and the assessment of alternatives in moral decisions. The fundamental reason why Barth disallows such a role for the practical reason is his desire to protect the sovereign freedom of God. While he does allow a larger role for moral reason in the constructive task of special ethics, he nevertheless insists that human reflection about the specificity and continuity of the divine will must always terminate in a readiness to hear and obey the divine command which remains sovereign and free.[17] The most that can be expected from an analysis of the "spheres" in which obedience is required and from the "directives" which chart the past pattern of the divine command is "guidance," not prescription. "Ethics," he writes, "will still have to leave the final judgment to God."

The nature of moral agency in Barth's ethics can be further clarified by reference to his concept of responsibility. This idea will also provide an instructive point of comparison with other ethicists included in the present study, particularly Brunner, Bonhoeffer, and H. Richard Niebuhr. Barth writes:

> It is the idea of responsibility which gives us the most exact definition of the human situation in face of the absolute transcendence of the divine judgment. We live in responsibility, which means that our being and willing, what we do and what we do not do, is a continuous answer to the Word of God spoken to us as command. It takes place always in a relationship to the norm which confronts and transcends us in the divine command.[18]

For Barth, responsibility is fundamentally accountability, and accountability is understood in terms of obedience to the command of God. This is a theological definition of the concept. The idea of responsibility is correctly understood only by Christians, for it is grounded in the divine covenant with man.[19] Because God's covenant is universal, all men are in fact responsible even if they do not understand themselves in these terms. In contrast to H. Richard Niebuhr, for Barth both the form and the content of responsibility are Christologically determined. Responsibility means answerability of the whole person in terms of "a total divine claim to our obedience."[20] It means "our total responsibility," for God "intends and seeks and wills us in our totality." It means answerability to a claim based upon grace: Be what you in fact already are! In ethical terms, this means, you are free and also summoned to be obedient to the command of God in its given concreteness and particularity.

There is a necessary place for moral reflection in relation to responsibility in Barth's thought; such reflection differs sharply, however, from the role of reason in moral philosophy. According to Barth, moral reflection focuses properly upon an examination of our being, our willing, and our doing in relationship to the command of God; it concerns our readiness to receive the decision of God at every point of our existence. It continuously seeks to answer the question, "What ought we to do?", recognizing full well that this question can be finally anwered only by the command itself.[21] Such reflection, however, has no place for deliberation about means and ends, possible consequences, or rational conceptions of obligation and value. In the end, the agent does not determine the content of a responsible human act, for this is given in the divine command. The only good human action, the only responsible human action, is obedience to that command.

Brunner's understanding of human nature is more Lutheran and more dialectical than that of Barth. Whereas Barth includes creation within the order of redemption, these two modes of God's relationship to the world--and to man as creature--are more sharply differentiated in Brunner. For Brunner, the Christian doctrine of man includes two critical components, viz., the formal "image of God" and the law, both of which must be understood dialectically.[22] Both of these concepts point to the "contradiction" in man between his created nature and his existence after the Fall. Both point to the purpose for which humanity was created and also to the distorted, or perverted, nature of human existence under sin. The image of God in which man was created has been broken or defaced, but it has not been destroyed. Brunner thus distinguishes between the <u>form</u>, or structure, of distinctively human nature and the <u>content</u> of the latter.[23] The form of man's existence as a being who has the capacity to be addressed and to be responsible remains; but the content--i.e. the fulfilment of this formal capacity in love--has been lost.[24] Man was created for freedom-in-responsibility, for freedom-in-and-for-love; this is the <u>imago Dei</u> in its original form. But due to sin, there is a contradiction which runs throughout human nature, separating humanity from its true origin and its true destiny. This cleavage is present in all persons; it affects the whole self, not just particular capacities or acts of the self. At its most fundamental level, sin is unbelief.[25] In its origin and essence it is the severance of humanity from the true source of its being; the resulting alienation can be overcome only by grace.

Like Barth, Brunner also defines the distinctive element in human existence in terms of responsibility.[26] Although the true meaning of this concept is known only on the basis of Christian faith, all persons have some knowledge that they are responsible. This fact is evidenced by the universal experience of "a bad conscience."[27] The bad conscience is the accusing conscience; it represents knowledge of guilt at the place of responsibility. Like the law which it symbolizes in a negative way, the bad conscience points beyond our sinful existence to our true nature and destiny as beings who are accountable. "True responsibility is the same as true humanity." Yet only in Christian faith is this idea treated with full seriousness. Here man is declared to be responsible for the fact that he is a sinner.[28]

For Brunner, as for Barth, responsibility is interpreted fundamentally in terms of obedience to the command of God. For Brunner, however, the command comes both through creation and through the special grace of redemption. For both, Christian ethics is based upon the Reformation principle of justification by "grace alone." Brunner believes, however, that Barth undercuts human responsibility through his unqualified rejection of all general revelation.[29] Man has some knowledge of the will of the Creator through human reason. While knowledge of the "orders of creation" cannot be equated with the divine command, the former do provide some indication of the content of God's will. Indeed, obedience to these orders, which are intended for the preservation of that which God has created, is man's first duty.[30] Our second duty, however, is to obey the command of the Redeemer who "bids us ignore the existing orders, and inaugurate a new line of action in view of the coming Kingdom of God."[31] The important point in the present context is that on the basis of general revelation man has some fragmented understanding of God's will; such knowledge is rooted in his _humanum_. This knowledge constitutes an important basis for social ethics in general and for the task of social justice in particular.

The reality of evil and the role of the moral agent, at least in response to the Creator, are more clearly recognized by Brunner than they appear to be by Barth. Sin is a continuing activity for which man remains responsible.[32] Revolt and rebellion against God are very much a part of human history. In them God meets man through the law which condemns and drives him to despair; at the same time, however, the law prepares the way for the gospel. That man "_can_ be a sinner is due to his origin; that he _must_ be a sinner is due to his falling away from his origin."[33] For Brunner, the dialectical relationship of law to gospel continues even in the lives of believers, who are at the same time justified yet sinful (Luther). Knowledge of the law precedes the gospel, but the law also has a larger role in the life of believers than Luther perceived. For Brunner, the law always functions in a threefold way as the word of discipline, repentance, and guidance in "joyful childlike obedience."[34] At the same time, obedience to the Creator implies the need for man to use all of the resources of reason, including the biological and social sciences, to understand both the creaturely form and the fundamental structures of his historical existence.[35] Nevertheless, the work of the Creator and the work of the Redeemer are experienced as two sharply separate forms of God's relationship to the world. In this respect Brunner reflects a strong dualism which is lacking in Barth.

In his <u>Ethics</u> Bonhoeffer sought to overcome the dualistic interpretation of the Lutheran concept of the "two kingdoms" in terms of two spheres. The theological basis for this task, he believed, is found in the Incarnation, for Jesus Christ is the concrete place where God and the world are reconciled and thus become one.[36] The Incarnation means that there are "not two realities, but only one," viz., "the reality of God which has become manifest in Christ in the reality of the world."[37] The whole idea of two spheres is alien to biblical thought. Moreover, Jesus Christ--in his unique form as incarnate, crucified, and risen--is "real man"; to be conformed to him means to be oneself a "real man."[38] To be a real person is to live as a whole person before God in the world. Bonhoeffer calls such a life one of "responsibility": "We give the name of responsibility to this life in its aspect as a response to the life of Jesus Christ as the 'yes' and the 'no' to our life."[39] Responsibility is lived out in the totality of human relationships, both personal and societal, for all are included in the single reality of Christ.

At this point it will be helpful to compare Bonhoeffer's concept of responsibility with that of Barth and, more especially, with that of H. Richard

Niebuhr at two main points. First, we shall ask about the role of the agent in decision-making; secondly, we shall inquire whether tha basic structure of responsibility is the same in all three authors. On account of his inclusion of Creation within Redemption, his denial of the ontological possibility of sin and evil, and his emphasis upon the sovereignty of the divine grace, Barth tended to leave the role of the human agent in obeying the divine command in doubt. For Bonhoeffer, however, both the decisions and the actions of the moral agent are clearly his own. Responsible action involves observation, assessment, and decision; it includes consideration of motives, possibilities, and consequences. It also includes the risk of concrete decisions and a readiness to accept guilt.[40] It involves the use of reason in gaining knowledge of "the natural," i.e., the form in which life is preserved by God in the fallen world. In this respect Bonhoeffer's conception of moral agency resembles Niebuhr's notion of "the responsible self" more closely than does Barth's.

When attention is turned to "responsibility" as the structure of moral existence, however, it is evident that Bonhoeffer's understanding of this idea is fundamentally shaped by the law-and-gospel dialectic in Lutheran ethics. Consequently, his concept of responsibility remains basically deontological; in this respect it resembles that of Barth although Barth reverses the order of the relationship between law and gospel. Bonhoeffer develops the "structure of responsibility" in terms of man's obligations to God and his fellowmen and, more particularly, in terms of deputyship, the commandment of God, and the mandates.[41]

According to Bonhoeffer, the only "warrant"--or basis--for ethical discourse is the commandment of God.[42] The commandment of God lies beyond the ethical; yet, the former also includes the latter in the sense that it provides the ground for understanding the ethical, including man's experience under the law. The "ethical" is related to the commandment of God only in a formal and negative way; it defines the boundaries within which the latter comes to man. The commandment, on the other hand, is concerned with the positive contents of God's will and with human freedom. It always comes to man in clear, definite, and concrete terms; hence, it leaves "no room for application or interpretation," but only "for obedience or disobedience."[43] Unlike the "ethical," the commandment not only binds but also sets free; it not only demands but also grants permission.

The basic relationship between the "ethical" and the commandment of God is dialectical in character. According to Bonhoeffer, knowledge of good and evil stems from the Fall. It is a sign of man's estrangement from the Creator; moreover, knowledge of good and evil represents the false possibility that man can be autonomous and thus live in isolation from God. Such autonomy, however, is an impossibility; hence, natural--or fallen--man experiences the claim of conscience as the call of human existence to a recovery of its lost unity with itself.[44] Conscience is experienced as "bad conscience" which accuses man of the violation of his original unity with God. Fallen man thus experiences knowledge of good and evil as law; in contrast, the commandment of God addresses man from beyond the brokenness of his existence. On the one hand, it frees the ego from its quest for self-justification and autonomy; at the same time, it frees the self to bear responsibility through acceptance of guilt.[45] For the man of faith, conscience is set free in the service of Christ to obey the commandment of God which comes to man from beyond the conflicts between good and evil. Here the self finds unity with itself in Christ. The liberated conscience remains, like the natural conscience, a "warner" against transgression of the law of life; but now the finality of the law is overcome by Christ.[46]

The basic polarity in Bonhoeffer's ethics between the law and the commandment of God is grounded in the Lutheran dichotomy between God's work as Creator and his work as Redeemer. In contrast, H. Richard Niebuhr stands in the Reformed tradition. His conception of the divine action--and the divine will--is more unified in terms of an ongoing pattern of creative, ordering, and reconciling action. Human responsibility thus becomes, for Niebuhr, a more integrated pattern of response which cannot be so sharply divided into categories of law and gospel, of penultimate and ultimate. His concept of response implies a transformationist rather than a dialectical relationship of grace to culture. Moreover, the content of responsibility is defined less exclusively in terms of Christology and Scripture. Although conscience is experienced by natural man primarily as an accusing conscience, it also points to an underlying moral order that is grounded in the will of a beneficient Creator.[47]

Finally, for Bonhoeffer, the structure of responsibility--e.g., deputyship and the mandates--is derived from Christology. For Niebuhr, on the other hand, it is grounded in human moral experience. More specifically, it rests in the nature of man as a social being who lives in interaction with other selves. Although the categories of obedience and aspiration comprise important elements in moral experience, they do not exhaust the meaning of the latter; indeed, they do not adequately grasp the basic structure of selfhood as a being which is necessarily engaged in responsive interaction with other selves.

Like Barth, Brunner, and Bonhoeffer, Paul Ramsey also conceives of moral agency fundamentally in terms of obedience. However, Ramsey interprets obedience much more exclusively in terms of a single commandment of neighbor-love. His conception of the relationship of love to justice is also more unified than that of Brunner and Bonhoeffer. Major differences occur, however, with regard to the role of reason in the determination of what particular acts of obedience are required and also, especially in comparison with Barth, concerning the role of the human agent in the acts themselves.

Ramsey's concept of man is similar to that of

Barth in three important respects. First, both interpret the _humanum_ as the "image of God" understood in relational terms; secondly, both define the nature of man in terms of covenant existence; and, thirdly, Ramsey calls his own concept--like that of Barth--Christocentric. Man was created originally in the "image of God" in the sense that he stood within a relationship of responsive obedience to the Creator.[48] However, as a result of the Fall, the "image of God" in humanity has become distorted. As a consequence, man's whole nature has been corrupted, and the decisive meaning of the "image of God" as the expression of man's essential nature can be known only as it is disclosed through Christ. Although rationality is an essential part of man's dignity and created nature, it is not in itself the image of God in man; for it, too, participates in the Fall.

For Ramsey, a Christian understanding of man must be finally "Christocentric" in the sense that it is based fundamentally upon theological rather than upon independent philosophical or scientific conceptions of human nature. Unlike Barth, however, Ramsey does not entirely reject the latter, for to do so would exclude theology from any outside sources of illumination. Knowledge from these fields is needed as _a_ basis both for a fuller understanding of man and for Christian ethics, particularly social ethics. Such knowledge must always be given a subordinate place, however, in Christian anthropology; it needs to be transformed by being brought into relationship with Christ.

Ramsey agrees with Barth that "covenant-fideltiy is the inner meaning and purpose of our creation as human beings, while at the same time creation as a whole constitutes the external basis for covenant."[49] Man is created to be not only _with_ but also _for_ his fellowmen even as God chose to be with and for humankind. Being _with_ one's fellow-humanity is prerequisite to being _for_ the latter. Moreover, each person has certain rights--among them property, liberty, and justice--which are rooted in our common interdependence.[50] Such rights represent the promise and the possibility of covenantal fidelity. As such they are claims which are based in our creaturely human existence.

As noted above (Chapter 3), in his later writings Ramsey has made increasing use of the covenant image to define the primary norm of Christian ethics. On the one hand, this concept expresses the continuity in moral relationships more clearly and forcefully than does _agape_. This is true both of relationships between individuals (e.g., promises, marriage) and of relationships that are basically societal (e.g., justice). In The Patient as Person, on the other hand, it is also a more generalized concept which raises the ethical question in terms of the claims to loyalty, fidelity, and faithfulness which are rooted in the social nature of human existence. In this respect the function of "covenant" in Ramsey's ethics is similar to that of "responsibility" in the ethics of H. Richard Niebuhr. There are many kinds of covenant relationships in which all persons stand. Some are entered by birth; others, by choice; and perhaps others, by need.[51] In any event, the ethical implications of these relationships are known both by natural reason and by charity. One such covenant is that between the physician and the patient. The ethical implications of this bond have been spelled out in a striking manner, Ramsey believes, in the traditions and canons governing the professional practice of medicine.[52] While recognizing that criteria of medical ethics based upon the biblical norm of "fidelity to covenant" may differ in some respects from those based upon other notions of covenant, Ramsey's emphasis in this treatise is clearly upon the common ground between rational and charitable justice.

Whether he uses the language of _agape_ or that of covenant, Ramsey has been concerned throughout his writings with defending the equality of worth of all human beings on the basis of their relationship to God through creation and through the divine love disclosed in Christ. Measured by the standard of _agape_, or covenant fidelity, justice is tilted in favor of the weak and powerless. These have need for special protections on account of their special vulnerability. At the same time, however, the rights and integrity of all human beings are threatened by the ethos of modern culture--by its pragmatism and utilitarianism, by the erosion of the <u>human</u> meaning of sexuality and parenthood, and by the unfettered pursuit of technology. Against all such threats Ramsey affirms the equality of human rights and the claims for faithfulness and loyalty which are grounded in our fellow-humanity. Chief among these rights is the protection of life itself. This concern for the individual is evidenced in Ramsey's medical ethics in his treatment of such issues as abortion, experimentation, and care of the dying. It is also evidenced in his just war doctrine, both in his definition of what constitutes a justifiable war and in his use of the principle of dicrimination to limit the means by which war may be conducted.

The covenant symbol presupposes a concept of community based upon mutual faithfulness, or loyalty, to all members of that community. The obligations which arise out of the claims to faithfulness constitute the primary moral bonds of society; as such they have priority over any utilitarian calculus of the greatest good for the greatest number. Proportionality of good over evil by itself is not a sufficient justification of any moral act. In medical ethics, for example, the criterion of informed voluntary consent is based on the covenant relationship that exists between the physician and the patient, or between the researcher and the subject. On the basis of this claim of the patient/subject, Ramsey allows "no morally significant exception to the requirement of informed consent."[53]

A final aspect of Ramsey's concept of man should be noted. While his primary concern is to protect the rights of known individuals, he also believes that the humanity of all individuals--future as well as present--can be protected, secured, and nurtured only through fidelity to humans who are now alive. The concept of covenant is appealed to in order to protect known individuals, but the former also expresses the mutual interdependence of individuals and society and the bonding of human life through relationships of birth and choice. Protection of marriage and parenthood appear to be necessary not only for the sake of persons now alive but also for the sake of generations yet unborn. Both marriage and parenthood are covenants, and both are expressions of the image of God in human sexual relationships.[54] While at times in his polemic against utilitarianism Ramsey seems to exclude all concern with benefits for future generations, his basic point is that such concern can properly be expressed only in paying heed to the faithfulness claims of particular individuals--men, women, and children to be procreated in existing relationships of sexuality and marriage--rather than through an effort to control the future of human evolution. Faithfulness to known individuals constitutes the responsible creaturely way of safeguarding the <u>humanum</u> in all and in behalf of all. In contrast, cloning and positive eugenics rest upon false conceptions of the goodness and rationality of man; they represent arrogant attempts to overstep man's creaturely limits and shape the future in a manner that threatens his essential humanity. Instead of affording a possibility and a promise for a greater fulfilment of human life in fidelity and in trust, such technological manipulation of procreation threatens to destroy the image of God in which and for which man was created.

The Self As Purposive:
Lehmann, Reinhold Niebuhr, And Gustafson

In contrast to those ethicists who interpret moral agency primarily in terms of obedience, Lehmann and Reinhold Niebuhr understand the former primarily in terms of purposive, goal-oriented action. While Gustafson's ethics may be described as an ethic of virtue rather than duty or the good, his concept of moral agency is much closer akin to teleology than it is to deontology. Hence, for purposes of analysis and comparison with the other ethicists included in this study, it will be useful to include Gustafson among the teleologists. While he resembles Lehmann and Reinhold

Niebuhr in his conception of the self as purposive, his teleology differs in important respects from that of the other two. For Lehmann the self aims at maturity; for Reinhold Niebuhr, it seeks the fulfilment of the indeterminate possibilities of its creaturely existence (perfection); for Gustafson, it seeks--or should seek--the well-being of creation. Not only do these ethicists differ in their conceptions of the goal of human action; they also differ significantly in their interpretations of the nature of man (the _imago Dei_) and the roles of reason and law in providing moral direction for concrete decisions. Each of these issues has important consequences for social ethics. We turn first to Lehmann because he poses these questions in their sharpest form and attempts to answer them in exclusively Christological terms.

For Lehmann, as we have seen, the starting point for Christian reflection about ethics is the _koinonia_. The latter is that historical community in which the transformation of human life--including both human motivation and the structures of human relatedness--is accomplished. God's activity in the world is essentially political in character. The formative images which are used in the Bible to describe the divine action are _political_ images: people, covenant, land, kingship, law, and--above all--messiah.[55] The politics of God gives to theology a Christological focus, and at the same time and in precisely the same way it provides a Christological foundation for ethics. The messianic image is essentially Christological in character, and it is this image which holds theology and ethics together, thus giving to Christian ethics its distinctive quality.[56] Within the _koinonia_ the divine action is perceived to be aimed at the creation of a new order of humanity typified by Christ, the Second Adam.

Lehmann seeks to provide an exclusively Christological foundation for Christian ethics in order to counter every attempt, whether direct or indirect, to base the latter upon anthropology. As the "second Adam" Christ is "the norm of all anthropology."[57] He is the "real Adam"; it is he rather than the "first

Adam" who discloses what man is in his essential nature. Hence, he is the basis and norm of all Christian reflection about the nature of man.

According to Lehmann, the doctrine of the Second Adam has two main implications for Christian ethics. In the first place, it means that the new humanity to which this doctrine points is both the subject and the goal of ethical action. This new humanity is a present reality, brought into being in the life, death, and resurrection of Jesus Christ. Christian ethics is a reflection upon what this new humanity means; Christian behavior is action that stems out of, and points to, the presence of this reality in the world. In the second place, the Christological doctrine of the Second Adam effectively rules out every attempt to base Christian ethics upon anthropology. All such attempts--including those of Aquinas, Reinhold Niebuhr, and John Bennett--are based upon some form of natural law.[58] They presuppose the residual goodness of natural man and reduce the distinctively Christian quality of ethical behavior to "little more than an addendum" to man's natural goodness. Such appeals to theological anthropology are intended, Lehmann believes, to produce ethical guidance for moral behavior and also to provide a common ground between Christians and non-Christians. In contrast, a <u>koinonia</u> ethic seeks to resolve both of these problems Christologically. With regard to the first, a theology of messianism provides ethical guidance, Lehmann believes, by making human behavior "the parabolic bearer of a new humanity."[59] The reality of the new humanity itself gives shape to human behavior in the concrete situation. According to this interpretation, Christian ethics is fundamentally indicative rather than imperative. When the problem of the realtionship between believers and non-believers is understood Christologically, the common ground between the two is not a common core of ethical wisdom--what Bennett calls an "overlap"--but a "common ethical predicament" which both share vis-a-vis the "second Adam." Lehmann's answer to this question is, in effect, a restatement of the Reformation concept of "justification by grace alone," but it does not deal with the basic problem which Bennett raises, viz., that of providing a basis for a Christian social ethic in a pluralistic society.

Lehmann does, however, in fact acknowledge that Christians and non-Christians do on occasion reach moral judgements that are quite similar, but he prefers to account for such similarities on the basis of the Holy Spirit rather than anthropology.[60] He thus places the issue of the meeting ground of believers and non-believers exclusively under the doctrine of the Spirit rather than under the doctrine of Creation, including anthropology. Hence, he focuses on the new, open, dynamic dimensions of human life which are brought to light by the reality of the "new humanity." By refusing to deal with this question _also_ under the category of creation, Lehmann by-passes the whole question of the possibility of social ethics rooted in part in man's experience of mutual interdependence and common humanity which persists even in his sinful state.

Lehmann seeks to recover the distinctiveness of Christian ethics by focusing exclusively on the new order of humanity and the parabolic significance of behavior. "[T]he Christian interpretation of behavior starts with and stays within the context of the fact of the new humanity."[61] As a result, his _koinonia_ ethics tends to be abstract (parabolic) and perfectionistic. This "new order of humanity...has its own way of looking at things and its own way of living out what it sees."[62] In this order there is no place for prudential calculation or any motivational concern; on the contrary, Christian behavior arises out of that "purity of heart" which makes the rational clarification of moral action unnecessary and finally irrelevant. _Koinonia_ ethics is primarily concerned with the parabolic significance of human action as a sign of God's humanizing activity. Such meaning can be known only "by insight, not by calculation."[63] From the standpoint of _koinonia_ ethics, the attempt to employ moral principles in ethical analysis and decision-making is "unreal" because there is no rational way of "closing the gap between the abstract and the concrete."[64]

As noted in the previous chapter, koinonia ethics aims at the achievement of freedom. Such freedom does not mean fundamentally freedom to choose the good rather than the evil; it means, rather, freedom to be obedient to God's humanizing activity. In a word, it means "obedient freedom." Moreover, it is through the theonomous conscience that the concrete meaning of such freedom in obedience can be discerned.[65] Focusing as it does upon the priority of the divine action, the koinonia provides a context in which the conscience can be "theonomously free." Such a conscience is "governed and directed by the freedom of God alone."[66] Hence, it is able to do what it takes "to make and to keep human life human." Only the theonomous conscience is able to overcome the dual gaps in moral experience between the abstract and the concrete, on the one hand, and between the "ought" and the "is," on the other. In the koinonia conscience is transformed from a bad conscience into a good conscience, i.e., into "inward integrity of heart." In this context, conscience receives that "imaginative sensitivity" to God's messianic action which enables the believer, in the midst of the struggle between good and evil, to live and act "on the other side" of that ethical predicament.[67]

The irony of Lehmann's interpretation of Christian ethics lies in the fact that while he is primarily interested in constructive social ethics, he cuts himself off from the resources of Christian faith for precisely this task by his attempt to base his ethic exclusively upon Christology and, more particularly, upon the koinonia and the doctrine of the Second Adam. The result is an ethic which stresses the distinctive quality of Christian behavior and one which is dynamic and open toward the future. In its orientation toward the eschatological future, it does not deal adequately with the continuities in moral relationships grounded in man's created nature. Its basic weakness, in short, is that it does not include a theological anthropology--that is, any doctrine of natural (fallen) man--based either upon Creation or upon Christology. The result of this failure is two-fold. Not only is Lehmann unable to provide an adequate basis for constructive social ethics based partly in man's created nature; he also fails to provide rational moral direction for life even within the koinonia.

Whereas Lehmann's concept of man is based exclusively upon the Christological doctrine of the Second Adam, that of Reinhold Niebuhr is based upon reason and experience. For Niebuhr, both of these sources of understanding are dialectically united in the Atonement, which is at once the source both of man's judgment and his hope.

For Niebuhr, the meaning of the gospel is most fully comprehended in the Atonement, for it is here that the paradoxical relationship between the divine mercy and the divine justice is most clearly disclosed. "In the New Testament the Atonement is the significant content of the Incarnation."[68] In the Cross the relationship of God to the world is seen to be finally one of love in which he takes the consequences of man's sin upon himself. The Cross reveals both the depth of the divine mercy and the seriousness of sin. Only by taking the consequences of his judgment against sin upon himself could God show forth the full depth of his love without forsaking his demand for justice. But the Cross does not only reveal the nature of God as agape; it also represents the most profound disclosure both of man's essential nature and of his sin. In the Cross of Christ man sees both what he ought to be but also what he cannot be on account of his sin.[69] Moreover, it is the "image of God" in fallen man which is addressed by the divine word of judgment and grace; it is this sinful man which is led to repentance, which hears the word of forgiveness, and which is freed to participate in the ambiguities of human history as one who is "simul iustus et peccator."

The relationship between the Christological and natural, or rational, sources of Reinhold Niebuhr's anthropology can best be clarified by reference to his analysis of man's freedom, his finitude, and his sinfulness (evil). According to Niebuhr, the Christian conception of man is sharply distinguished from all other views by the manner in which it interprets and relates these three elements of human existence to each other.[70] First, the biblical doctrine that man was created in the image of God affirms man's freedom, i.e., his capacity for self-transcendence. While this ability is partially evidenced in the capacity of reason to transcend nature by means of rational inquiry and reflection upon the processes of nature, it is most decisively and profoundly evidenced in the human "capacity for and affinity with the divine."[71] The fundamental problem of human freedom is the spiritual problem of finding meaning for the totality of existence, including both the natural world and human transcendence. Reason by itself is unable to discover such a principle of coherence and meaning, for it remains part of the whole which it seeks to comprehend. Hence, the very fact of human self-trancendence points beyond reason to a God who transcends the world, to a God who can be known only through his own self-disclosure. Because he is made in "the image of God," man is both constantly tempted to idolatry and ultimately dissatisfied with his efforts to make God in his own image. Thus his experience points beyond itself to the perspective of biblical faith, which provides the only adequate ground for understanding both the heights and the depths, both the possibilities and the limits, of human freedom.

The effort to understand the ground and the limits of man's freedom leads, therefore, to a consideration of the second element in human existence, viz., man's finitude. In the biblical concept of man, this aspect of experience is interpreted in terms of man's creaturehood. It is his status as creature which determines the limits of his freedom. Christian faith teaches that the world was created by God and that the whole of creation is good. In so far as man is concerned, this means that his conditions of finitude, temporality, and dependence are good since they are part of God's plan for creation. Man is created free, (i.e., with the capacity for self-transcendence), but his freedom is set within the givenness of dependence and limitation imposed by his creaturely existence.

The limits of his freedom are indeterminate, but man is not autonomous. He remains finally man; he is unable to escape the bounds of his creaturehood and become God.

The biblical doctrines of man as made in the image of God and of man as creature constitute the context in which the Christian conception of sin must be understood. Sin is not determined either by man's freedom or by his creaturehood; rather, these characteristics of his existence provide the occasion for his sin.[72] The paradoxical combination of freedom and finiteness inevitably produces anxiety in man. Anxiety, however, is not itself sin. It is, rather, the precondition of sin, and it is also the basis of all human creativity. Anxiety is "a permanent concomitant of freedom." Since anxiety may be purged of any tendency toward self-assertion on the basis of faith, sin is not necessary. If such faith is not present, however, anxiety issues in sin. It is for this reason that in orthodox Christianity unbelief is defined as "the root of sin." In the absence of perfect faith, anxiety brings forth sin either in the form of pride or in the form of sensuality. For Niebuhr, pride is the more basic of the two, and sensuality is indeed rooted in pride. Pride (or self-love) is man's tendency to deny the contingent character of his existence. It expresses itself in the following four forms: pride of power, pride of knowledge, pride of virtue, and spiritual pride or self-deification.[73] Sensuality, on the other hand, represents an effort to escape from the unlimited possibilities of freedom through idolatrous devotion to limited, "mutable" goods and the effort to lose oneself in the natural vitalities of human existence.[74]

Niebuhr further distinguishes between individual and collective forms of pride. This distinction is critical for social ethics. To be sure, group pride is rooted in that of individuals since, strictly speaking, only individuals are moral agents. Yet, the pride of groups achieves a greater authority over its members than do the claims and pretensions of individuals. Moreover, groups are more arrogant, hypocritical, self-centered, and ruthless in the pursuit of their goals.[75] Hence, collective egotism is the final form of sin. While it finds its most consistent expression in the national state, it is also found in the pretensions and idolatrous claims of religious groups. Just as sin is universal, so pride as the basic form of sin is universal. In the social order collective pride leads inevitably to injustice, both within states and among nations. There is, therefore, no realistic possibility of achieving genuine justice in history. This does not mean, however, that there are no significant differences in degrees of pride and approximations to justice in history. As Niebuhr puts it, there is "equality of sin" among men but "inequality of guilt."[76] Guilt means "the objective consequence of sin, the actual corruption of the plan of creation and providence in the historical world."[77] Biblical faith provides the basis both for ultimate religious judgment before God and for provisional ethical discriminations among moral choices. Religiously speaking, the <u>agape</u> of Christ is the standard by which the unrighteousness of all men is revealed; ethically speaking, it is the standard in terms of which the relative, proximate possibilities and choices of history are measured. To obscure the latter insight of biblical faith by a too exclusive concern with the former is to remove faith from history and deny the significance of man's self-transcendence and freedom within history.

Thus far we have been describing the three basic elements in Reinhold Niebuhr's anthropology: man as image of God, man as creature, and man as sinner. From the standpoint of Christian faith, these doctrines both describe and account for man's freedom, his finitude, and the origin of evil in human history. The question which concerns us at this point is the question of how these concepts give shape to Niebuhr's social ethics. To what extent, and in what ways do they, taken together, provide limits and direction in the making of moral choices? This is, indeed, Niebuhr's major concern throughout his writings, and this is--on his own terms--the test of the adequacy of his own doctrine of man.

In the first place, in his account of freedom and creatureliness as the constitutive elements of essential human nature, Niebuhr grounds ethics in the universal moral experience of humanity.[78] Not only are all men involved in the making of moral choices in freedom, but all dimly discern that love is the final claim to which their freedom in a community of selves points. Love is dimly perceived to be the law of their creaturely existence as free beings although it is experienced as a claim, or a lack, rather than as an achievement. Human freedom means the capacity for indeterminate levels of moral achievement and ever new forms of self-determination within the limits of creaturely existence. Man has the capacity, for example, for ever higher levels of justice, and the claims upon him to achieve the latter are the requirements of his essential nature as man.

In the second place, Niebuhr's doctrine of man as sinner provides the basis for his realism in ethics. Attention to man's essential nature alone leads to the illusions of idealism and utopianism which fail to take into account the depth and the pervasiveness of human sin. As previously noted, the collective forms of sin are much more demonic and destructive than its individualistic expressions. Since all social groups have power and since all are tempted to use this power in pursuit of their selfish goals, they inevitably become agents of injustice in history. Justice is, however, a requirement of man's created nature as a precondition for the actualization of his freedom. In his sinful state the claim for justice is experienced as a claim of _agape_. Niebuhr's concept of sin thus provides the basis for the struggle for social justice as a work of _agape_ while at the same time it points to the sources of injustice in all struggles to achieve greater justice within history. Because the tendency to use power selfishly is universal, all forms of power need to be placed under restraint of countervailing forms of power. As Niebuhr put the matter in epigrammatic form, "Man's capacity for justice makes democracy possible; but man's inclination to injustice makes democracy necessary."[79]

Finally, Niebuhr's anthropology preserves a dialectical tension in ethics between the claims of man's essential nature (as finite and free) and the realities of his sinful socio-historical existence. The dialectical relation of the gospel to history cuts across all levels of human experience. It is grounded ultimately in man's essential nature. The gospel thus illuminates the meaning of common human experience, and the former is in turn validated by the latter.[80] Man's nature as "image of God" points finally toward _agape_ as the inescapable requirement of his freedom, but man's nature as sinner points to the need for realism in estimating the possibilities and the limits of historical justice. The dialectical relationship between _agape_, on the one hand, and the possibilities and requirements of history, on the other, provides the basis for taking moral judgments seriously while at the same time relativizing the latter by relating them to a norm that transcends the possibilities of history. The gospel thus discloses the meaning of history and points to its final eschatological fulfilment. Meanwhile, history as we know it is an "interim" which moves toward its full realization in the coming Kingdom of God and yet stands under the judgment of God until the end.[81]

We shall return in a subsequent chapter to Niebuhr's analysis of the struggle for social justice in relationship to the Kingdom of God. It should be clear by now that this struggle is grounded in his concept of man. As we have seen, the latter is based theologically in the Atonement, but it is also verified by common human experience. At this point, however, an additional word is needed in order to indicate more precisely the basis and nature of Niebuhr's teleological conception of moral agency. Fundamentally, man is a being who seeks the realization of the indeterminate possibilities of his created nature in a community based on love. The meaning of human life consists essentially of a future-oriented quest for the fulfilment--or perfection--of selves in community rather than obedience to law or covenant obligations. Niebuhr's teleological conception of moral agency has two important consequences for the methodology of

Christian ethics. The first has to do with the issue of contintuity in the moral life; the second, with the role of consequences in human decisions. As Gustafson suggests, stress upon the indeterminate possibilities of human freedom leads to an emphasis upon discontinuity in the moral life.[82] The law of love stands in judgment upon all past achievements of the self; it also points to higher possibilities for its embodiment in each future act. Moreover, since the full meaning of *agape* can never be expressed in terms of any other principle or law, love is always related dialectically to the latter so that these are both judged and affirmed by *agape*. The principal uses of the law are its political (ordering) and theological (repentance) rather than its pedagogical (didactic) function. In contrast, Gustafson's concept of moral agency leads to stress upon the didactic use of the law as primary.

The question of continuity in ethics is closely related to that of consequences. While deontological forms of ethics generally include some concern for the latter as a secondary consideration in moral decisions, consequences serve a more intentional role in moral judgments based primarily upon ends rather than duties. In this sense, the teleological character of Reinhold Niebuhr's ethics is expressed not only in the quest for the realization of the indeterminate possibilities of human existence but also in his adoption of pragmatism as the most responsible method of decision-making. Such pragmatism, it must be made clear, is limited by *agape* as its controlling norm; hence, it can be adequately described only as "Christian pragmatism" in contrast to all other forms of pragmatism.[83] Niebuhr describes the basis for such an ethic when he writes:

> But to know both the law of love as the final standard and the law of self-love as a persistent force is to enable Christians to have a foundation for a pragmatic ethic in which power and self-interest are used, beguiled, harnassed, and deflected for the ultimate end of establishing the highest and most inclu-

sive possible community of justice and order.[84]

The purpose of pragmatism as a strategy of social justice is to recognize both the possibilities and the limits of love and justice in each particular historical situation. Within the context of the latter, however, it is *agape* which defines both the direction and the limits of Christian pragmatism.

In contrast to the stress upon discontinuity and the use of pragmatism in Reinhold Niebuhr's ethics, Gustafson emphasizes the regularities in moral experience, the didactic function of the moral law, and the role of character in ethics. These differences between Niebuhr and Gustafson are rooted fundamentally in their different conceptions of human nature. For Niebuhr, man is essentially a creature with indeterminate capacities for self-transcendence; for Gustafson, on the other hand, the continuities in human experience outweigh the discontintuties.[85] Unlike Ramsey, however, Gustafson places such regularities within a teleological rather than a deontological conception of moral agency. His interpretation of the moral life in terms of goals and ends is grounded, in turn, in a teleological conception of God's relationship to the world. Ramsey's deontological ethics, on the other hand, is based upon a covenantal understanding of this relationship. Moreover, Ramsey interprets the covenant primarily in terms of known obligations to known individuals. Gustafson's concept of creation is teleologically oriented toward the achievement of a divine goal through the processes of the natural world and the events of history; hence, he places greater emphasis upon human autonomy in the shaping of the historical future.

Gustafson's formulation of the primary question of ethics and his adoption of "the imitation of God" as a central symbol of Christian ethics rest upon his perception of the nature and role of the human agent in moral experience. Since all human experience of God is mediated rather than direct, it is presumptuous on the part of finite beings to attempt to say precisely what God is doing and what he intends in the midst of historical events. Hence, Gustafson restates the primary question to focus attention upon the human task of rational deliberation in determining "what God is enabling and requiring me (or us) to be and to do." The object of such deliberation is the clarification and specification of human action that is both responsive and obedient to God. Criteria of such human action can be rationally adduced from the shared beliefs and moral insights of a religious community. Gustafson's concept of moral agency presupposes both the fundamental integrity of human reason and a large measure of human autonomy. Human response to the divine action focuses attention upon the intentionality of the human subject; it implies a human determination of what God wills for the latter to do in the light of Christian faith; it also implies the freedom on the part of persons and communities to initiate new directions in moral action and freedom on the part of humanity to shape and control the historical future. In this sense, human agents are called to be "co-actors" with God; they are summoned to imitate God by willing what he wills, viz., the well-being of creation.[86] Viewed from a theocentric perspective, the vocation of the human community is to consent to the divine governance of nature and society and to cooperate with God in the pursuit of those divine ends which can be discerned.[87]

Whereas H. Richard Niebuhr began his ethical inquiry with an effort to understand the divine action as the ultimate context of human action, Gustafson begins with an analysis of the perspective, the disposition, and the intentionality of the self and the ways in which the latter are influenced by religious experience and beliefs. For H. Richard Niebuhr, the action of the self is fundamentally responsive; for Gustafson, it is basically purposive. Thus Gustafson writes: "Persons are agents; they exercise capacities and powers in accordance with purposes.... They can reflect upon these purposes and govern their exercise of capacities...."[88] Moreover, this purposiveness is an essential part of created human nature, for the self seeks its fulfilment through the pursuit of ends or goals. The search for the good leads both to the development of a disposition toward the good (virtue) and to a rational willing of the good (intentionality) in moral decisions. Moral agency includes the perspective, the disposition, and the intentionality of the self. All of these are consitutive elements in selfhood, and all are interrelated in moral experience. Each is--or may be--shaped or informed by the distinctively Christian beliefs of the agent, but they are characteristic of human agents generally. Fundamentally, Christian faith affects the moral life of believers through the transformation of the perspective, dispositions, intentions, and norms of the latter. This transformation is mediated to individuals, moreover, through their participation and nurture in the church as a moral community.

Of the ethicists whom we have examined, Gustafson is most closely akin to Catholic moral theology in his concept of moral agency. Human nature is inclined by creation toward the realization of its good, i.e., its potentialities. Moreover, the self is social; it participates in communities and can find its good only in community. Hence, there is an implicit notion of the "common good" as a rational or natural end of human action. In contrast to the traditional usage of this concept, however, Gustafson interprets it to include the common good of creation as a whole instead of limiting it to the human community.[89] Gustafson also differs from the traditional Catholic conception of human nature in his understanding of sin and the consequences of the latter for man's natural capacity to know and fulfil the moral law. Hence, his conception of the relationship of nature to grace in the moral life is more clearly transformationist than is traditional Catholic thought. Significantly, however, Gustafson finds a strong affinity between a number of contemporary Catholic writers, including Karl Rahner and Bernard Haering, and himself in this regard.[90] These more recent interpretations of the Catholic tradition lend support and theological undergirding to his perception of the nature of the moral agent at the points of the agent's teleological orientation toward self-fulfilment, its capacity for moral reasoning, its freedom, and the basic continuities of human existence.

The Self As Responsible: H. Richard Niebuhr

H. Richard Niebuhr's concept of responsibility is rooted in his relational idea of value and, more fundamentally, in his concept of the social self. While the idea of response is a recurrent theme throughout his ethical writings, it is most fully and systematically developed in <u>The Responsible Self</u>. Here Niebuhr analyzes three major types of ethics based upon three fundamentally different conceptions of the moral agent. Two of these--the teleological and the deontological--represent long and fruitful traditions in moral philosophy; the third--the ethics of responsibility--is relatively recent and has arisen out of a new perception of the self.[91] Teleological interpretations of the moral life rest upon the image of man-the-maker, acting for the attainment of some end or goal. In all of its actions the self is like an artisan, or craftsman, who shapes or constructs things in accordance with some idea of the good and for the sake of some end. As moral agents we seek the fulfilment both of ourselves and of society. Aristotle and Aquinas are classical representatives of the teleological tradition in ethics; both understood the moral life in terms of aspiration after some good and also in terms of the primacy of human agency in the actualization, or the realization, of the good. The symbol of man-the-maker accents the purposive nature of moral action; it also implies an understanding of human freedom as self-determination by final causes. Such causes constitute goods or ends which are under human control as are also the means for the attainment of these goals. Human freedom means the capacity of the self to seek the realization of the self and society through the pursuit of such ends.

Deontological ethics, on the other hand, rests upon the image of the agent as citizen, living under law. Kant is the classical representative of this tradition in philosophical ethics, but Kant has had his counterparts in Christian ethics from New Testament times until the present. Bultmann, Barth, and Brunner represent this position among contemporary Protestant theologians. Such thinkers understand the moral life fundamentally in terms of obedience to some law, whether it be the law of reason, the divine law contained either in Scripture or in tradition, or the concrete command of the Word of God. For them human existence comes into being amid an order or structure of reality that is apprehended primarily in terms of obligation, duty, and law. Hence, moral agency is more adequately symbolized by the political image of man-the-citizen whose life is bounded and structured by mores, commandments, and laws rather than by an image drawn from art and the crafts. Neither individuals nor communities have the freedom to choose either their final ends or means for the attainment of these ends apart from an underlying moral order. Viewed from this perspective the self in its moral agency is primarily obedient, legislative, and administrative. In all of its actions the primary question of the agent becomes: "To what law shall I consent, against what law rebel? By what law or system of laws shall I govern myself and others? How shall I administer the domain of which I am the ruler or in which I participate in rule?"[92]

For Niebuhr both of the foregoing images of the moral agent were synecdochic.[93] That is to say, each symbol--man-the-maker and man-the-citizen--represents an image which is drawn from a part of moral experience and which is used to describe and interpret the whole. Thus, while each represents important aspects of moral agency, each by itself is inadequate even though it remains useful, perhaps even indispensable, for the self-understanding of the agent. By itself each image leads to the necessity of compromising or adjusting an ideal goal or law to the possibilities and requirements of a present that is morally ambiguous. Not only is each symbol inadequate by itself, but efforts to combine the two result in a double theory of the right and the good. Hence, the problem of compromise and adjustment to an ideal goal or law is left unresolved.

Hence, Niebuhr is led to suggest a third metaphor which, he believes, corresponds more closely with human moral existence. This is the symbol of responsibility, of man-the-answerer, of the self engaged in dialogue. Like the others it also is a synecdochic image drawn from a part of the agent's experience and used to characterize the whole. The emergence of this symbol has resulted in large part from a new understanding of the self in the contemporary social sciences as well as in biology. In these disciplines human existence has come to be understood predominantly in terms of interaction, in terms of challenges in man's natural and social environments to which he responds. Although the symbol of man-the-answerer is a contemporary image of moral agency, it was prefigured in Aristotle and the Stoics. More fundamentally, it typifies our moral experience in the face of crises, including both social emergencies and personal suffering.[94] Here human beings define themselves in terms of their relationships to that upon which they and all of their actions are contingent--in terms of possibilities and limits which are given, not primarily in terms of human autonomy. Here the primary question of ethics becomes, "What is going on?"; and the action of the agent is understood as a response to that prior action. Whereas teleological approaches to ethics interpret the moral life primarily in terms of the <u>good</u>, and whereas deontological approaches understand morality fundamentally in terms of the <u>right</u>, the ethics of responsibility focuses attention upon the <u>fitting</u> action.[95]

Stated in theological terms, the primary question of ethics for Niebuhr is, "What is God doing?" The ethics of responsibility affirms: "God is acting in all action upon you. So respond to all actions upon you as to respond to his action."[96] The question concerning the divine action is primary for Niebuhr because it places the question of human action in its ultimate context. Human freedom and human responsibility are set finally within the context of "absolute dependence" upon God as the source, the governor, and the savior of the universal community. Teleological interpretations of moral experience do not give adequate attention, he believed, to the conditioned character of all human activity; deontological interpretations, on the other hand, do not give adequate attention to the role of the agent in the determination of its own response. Radically monotheistic faith affirms the unity and universality of the divine action in creation, in judgment, and in salvation. For Niebuhr, such faith is eschatological; it affirms that the divine sovereignty, which is a present--although oftentimes hidden--reality, will in the end become fully manifest. In this ultimate (not primarily futuristic) sense Niebuhr speaks of God as the "Determiner of our Destiny" and even as "the all-doer." Such divine determination, however, is neither fatalistic not mechanistic. It is more aptly symbolized in terms of covenant, the kingdom of God, and the family. Not only are these images more faithful to Scripture; they are also more consonant with our actual human experience.[97] While these metaphors point, in the first instance, to action that is prior to all human action, they also assume the reality of human freedom to act in response to the divine action. Understood in these terms, human action is self-action, but human freedom both presupposes and anticipates action that is not subject to human control.

For Niebuhr divine action and human freedom are inseparably bound together in moral experience. Moreover, the relationship between the two must always be understood in terms of the experience of the Christian community as part of the human community "in time and history." Thus, there is an openness in Niebuhr's understanding of freedom as a present reality--"of freedom in the now"--which has not received adequate attention. Niebuhr writes:

> Yet something like that freedom of which teleological and deontological thinkers speak in their different ways also comes into appearance when we analyze ourselves as responsive, time-full beings. The question of freedom arises in this connection as the question of the self's ability in its present

to change its past and future and to achieve or receive a new understanding of its ultimate historical context. If these two modifications are possible, then reinterpretation of present action upon the self must result, and a new kind of reaction, a response that fits into another lifetime and another history, can and will take place.[98]

Human freedom, for Niebuhr, is not a static or fixed entity; on the contrary, it is a dynamic reality, the dimensions and meaning of which are shaped in part by the agent's interpretation--and reinterpretation--of its past and its future, including its ultimate historical context. The model of responsibility would seem to be open-ended toward the discovery of newer horizons of freedom than Niebuhr himself perceived; but the model itself would become transformed into teleology if the question of autonomous human goals and values replaced the question of the nature of the moral order which is given through the divine action as the primary question of ethics.[99]

The basic issue raised by Niebuhr's ethics of response is this: Is man more adequately understood as responder and answerer, or is he better understood as maker and/or as citizen? For Niebuhr the answer to this question was grounded fundamentally in common human experience rather than in particular theological doctrines. The fundamental structure of human life is that of response rather than seeking after goals or obedience to law. It has to do with the question of how men interpret and react/respond to those things which are not in their power.[100] Response ethics, therefore, begins with an effort to understand the totality of human existence and history in terms of a unified pattern of divine action of creation, ordering, and reconciliation. Responsible action is action which is "fitting"--which corresponds to, is consistent with, and affirms the divine will for the fulfilment of creation. To be human is to exercise <u>creaturely freedom</u> and responsibility in faith. As noted above, an ethic of responsibility does not make the metaphors of aspiration and obedience unnecessary; it does, however, subordinate the latter to the former. Indeed, both man-the-citizen and man-the-maker are responders. Responsibility as the primary synecdochic symbol, however, interprets human action as response of the whole person to many kinds of action in an inclusive community of interaction, and it understands value in relational terms. It holds together freedom and limitation, gospel and law, human action and the limitations upon human achievement in a distinctive way.

The adequacy of the model of responsibility will, of course, be determined on the basis of experience. As an <u>alternative</u>, it differs in important respects from Gustafson's ethics of virtue, which seems increasingly akin to teleological ethics; from his theological teleology, which places proportionally greater emphasis upon God as the Creator of new possibilities for the well-being of creation; and from his conception of man as "co-actor" with God. To a certain extent these differences are matters of emphasis; yet, the fundamental structure of Gustafson's ethics seems increasingly to be teleological rather than responsiblist. To make the seeking after goals/values the primary model of ethics is to prompt the query as to whether this model takes sufficient account of the limitations of human life (the restrictions imposed by limited natural resources, by the creaturely limits of technology, by the moral order, by human sinfulness) and of human <u>accountability</u> to God <u>for all that is given concretely in creation</u>.

Niebuhr's ethics of response differs also from Paul Ramsey's basically deontological ethic in so far as the latter focuses primarily upon obedience to principles and rules which are intended to give concrete expression to <u>agape</u>. In contrast to Ramsey, Niebuhr recognizes more clearly the relativity of the moral law; he interprets Christian ethics fundamentally in terms of response rather than obedience--even "obedient love"; and he understands obligation and duty in more consistently relational terms.

THE STRUCTURE OF COMMUNITY: CONTINUITY AND CHANGE

All of the major theologians under consideration in this study understand Christian ethics to include both the personal and the societal dimensions of the life of believers. None of these writers restricts Christian morality either to I-Thou relationships between individuals or to a sectarian community which attempts to live in isolation from secular culture. In Augustinian language the Christian lives both in the "heavenly city" (<u>civitas coelestis</u>) and in the "earthly city"(<u>civitas terrena</u>). The fundamental problem of Christian social ethics is that of understanding the proper relationship between the two.

While the term "structures" has been used in the heading for this chapter, it is not intended to refer only to institutions but also to less formal structures of community life and relationships. As used in the present context, it refers to the societal "forms" through which the life of a community is expressed, including marriage and the family, economic and political structures, religion, education, art, and health care. In a word, we are here concerned with the forms and the relationships in which and through which the common life which Christians share with non-Christians is expressed.

The effort to understand these structures and the relationships which are mediated through them raises a number of important issues for theological ethics. First, how are these societal forms grounded? What is the basis or source of their authority? What fundamental purposes do they serve? How are they related to human fulfilment? Secondly, how is a theological interpretation of the basis and function of these struc-

125

tures related to an empirical, socio-scientific understanding of the latter? How, in other words, are faith and ethics related to empirical knowledge of these structures? In the third place, to what extent do these forms function, on the one hand, as instruments of conservation and stability, and to what extent, on the other hand, as mediators of social change? Finally, how is social justice related to a theological understanding of the divine will? What are the criteria of justice, and upon what are these criteria based in a secular, pluralistic society? Consideration of these questions involves an understanding of the nature and the forms of power and the ways in which the latter may be used both for good and for evil ends.

While all of the writers whom we have been examining include responsibility for society within Christian ethics, they differ in fundamental respects regarding both the bases and the functions of social institutions; they differ also regarding the relationship of an empirical knowledge of these structures to theological ethics. For Barth and Lehmann, society is viewed from the perspective of redemption. That is to say, it is viewed Christocratically in terms of the Lordship of Christ over the world (Barth) or in terms of the messianic action of God in the world (Lehmann). For Brunner, Bonhoeffer, and Reinhold Niebuhr, on the other hand, there is a basic dualism between life in culture and the claims and requirements of the gospel. This dualism is rooted theologically in the tension, or polarity, between creation and redemption. In contrast to both of these groups, H. Richard Niebuhr, Ramsey, and Gustafson interpret the relationship of faith to culture fundamentally in transformationist terms.

Structures Of Redemption: Barth And Lehmann

Barth attempts to avoid the dualism in traditional Lutheran ethics between the religious and the secular "realms" by including the totality of human relationships within the order of redemption. For him, the meaning and purpose of creation can be properly understood only when the latter is viewed Christologically. This means, moreover, that creation can be understood only as it is seen in relationship to the three-fold pattern of divine action in creation, reconciliation, and redemption.[1] The God who confronts man in Christ as Commander is one; he is also sovereign. Electing grace is commanding grace. Even now Christ rules over all that is, for all is included within his sovereign grace. Hence, there is no possibility of dividing human life into two realms or "two kingdoms"--one based upon nature, reason, and law, and the other based upon grace, revelation, and liberty.

Through the Word God rules Christocratically over all and through the divine command his purpose in creation is related positively to his purposes in reconciliation and redemption. Thus, the state, for example, becomes an order of redemption rather than an order of creation. It can be properly understood only when it is viewed Christologically. From the perspective of redemption the state, like the church, is an order of the covenant and thus one of the forms in which the meaning of our humanity is expressed within history.

As part of his doctrine of creation Barth develops four characteristics which define human nature as creature.[2] Briefly stated, these are: (1) man is a creature in history, elected and called by God, and summoned and enabled to be responsible before him; (2) the humanity of man consists in his existence as fellow-humanity, i.e., in the encounter between a human I and a human thou; (3) man is the soul of his body, both joined together in inseparable unity and indestructible order; and (4) man is a being who lives in a span of time which has been allotted him by God, his creator and the hope of his existence. On the basis of these Christological affirmations about man as creature, Barth proceeds to develop his "special ethics" within the framework of the doctrine of creation as one of three spheres in which the divine command encounters man.[3] While God always commands and man always acts in all three spheres at the same time, man's nature as creature defines the basic relationships in which every human stands. As creature man stands, first of all, in relationship to God. Here the command of the Creator means the freedom to be responsible before God in worship, confession, and prayer. Secondly, every person is created in the form of fellow-humanity--as man with woman, as parents with children, and as beings in relationship to near and distant neighbors. In the midst of these relationships <u>with</u> one's fellow-humanity, the command of the creator means freedom to be <u>for</u> one's fellow-humankind. In the third place, every human being has the gift of life. Here the Creator calls man to respect and protect this gift. Finally, human existence is existence with creaturely limits in space and time. Within the particularity of these limits the Creator calls each person to a life of specific responsibility and obedience to the divine command (vocation).

For Barth the Command of God comes to man within the relationships that define his creaturely existence, but neither these relationships nor the Command itself can be known apart from revelation. The creatureliness and the humanity of man can be comprehended, in short, only in the incarnation in Jesus Christ as the true, or real, man. The relational structure of human existence as co-humanity--man and woman, parents and children, near and distant neighbors--belongs to every man as creature, but this structure of relationships is truly known only as it is known Christologically. Thus, while Barth clearly defines human nature as social and while he also defines it in terms of man's creaturely relationships, such common humanity does not provide a basis for genuine knowledge either of man or of society. As in the case of philosophical ethics, Barth does not so much reject scientific and socio-scientific accounts of man; rather, he finds that they are all not only inadequate but also misleading because they rest upon false presuppositions. They have to do finally with "phantom man" rather than with man's true nature.[4] Nevertheless, they have a practical value for Christological anthropology, for they provide the "language, categories and framework" of self-understanding in terms of which the latter must be explicated.[5] They do not, however, provide positive knowledge about human existence or society. They do not, for example, provide the basis for knowledge of any "orders of creation" based upon reason and natural law.

Barth's ethics is intended primarily for the Christian community. Within this context his "special ethics" appeals to Scripture and to the Christian tradition to provide a structure for understanding the moral life on the basis of revelation. As we have seen, Christian ethics is, for him, fundamentally a matter of obedience to the command of God. Since the latter is known only by revelation, theological ethics precludes any significant role for the empirical investigation of man and society. In so far as Christian ethics is a matter of simple obedience, the former also precludes the weighing of the consequences of alternative choices in the field of social policy.

Yet there is a fundamental ambiguity in Barth's theological ethics which leads to a basic inconsistency when he turns to social ethics. As West observes, Barth understands human existence primarily in personal terms, i.e., in terms of the I-Thou encounter.[6] Just as the humanity of Jesus consisted in his being "man for other men," so the humanity of every person consists in his/her encounter with other persons in one-to-one relationships.[7] For Barth the most fundamental forms of such encounter are those between man and woman and also between parents and children. Relationships with broader social groups—with "near" and "distant" neighbors—are secondary and dependent upon the primary relationships between individuals. Thus, when he turns to a discussion of the problems of society on the basis of (a) the sovereignty—i.e., the freedom—of the divine command and (b) his Christological anthropology, Barth lacks the necessary tools for empirical analysis. The responsibility of Christians in society is subsumed under theological ethics since the civil community is under the reign of Christ. On the one hand, the command of God frees man from dependence upon all ideological efforts at self-understanding—frees him to be completely dependent upon divine grace; and, on the other hand, it frees him _for_ full identification with the neighbor and full participation in secular culture. This freedom of the Christian stems out of the sovereignty of the divine grace over the totality of human life; however, the inclusion of creation within redemption undercuts the seriousness of the struggle for relative forms of social justice within human history.[8] Thus, while Barth affirms the freedom and the responsibility of Christians for participation in secular life, his analysis of what such responsibility means in relation to specific problems in politics and economics tends to be ambiguous, oversimplified, and frequently inconsistent with his basic ethical methodology.

In addition to the "spheres" and "prominent lines" which Barth employs to give structure to the Christian life in his special ethics, he also uses the method of analogy in the development of his political ethics. As Barth uses this concept, it refers not to an analogy of being but to the similarity of relationships between life in the Christian community (the Church) and the civil community (the state).[9] These analogies provide specific examples of Christian decisions and action in the political sphere. As such they indicate "constant directions" in which Christian politics should move. As citizens, Christians will belong to different political parties; yet they will be united in the church, and on the basis of this unity they will "make the same distinctions and judgments" and work for a single cause.[10] As Barth's own use of analogy makes clear, however, this method of decision-making is much too imprecise to insure such consistency in moral judgments and action.[11]

In addition to the problem of continuity, or consistency, Barth's attempt to base Christian political ethics on an analogy between the Kingdom of God and the civil community poses a second major difficulty for social ethics. Although Christians may know that Christ is the center of both the church and the state, the question must be raised, On what basis should the former make its appeal to the latter? According to Barth, it must do so through the action of "anonymous"

Christians, whose proposals "can be made intelligible and brought to victory" in the political sphere only as they are shown to be "politically better and more calculated to preserve and develop the common life."[12] However, Barth fails to provide criteria in terms of which some decisions may be adjudged to be "better" than others and more conducive to the general welfare. Such criteria are essential both in the church and in secular society.

In the Christian community the final criterion is the will of God; in the civil community, appeal is made finally to the common welfare. In the Church, obedience to the divine command is required; in the state, particular choices and actions are to be defended pragmatically on the ground that they are most conducive to the common good. If the general welfare is made the common criterion of political policy, the relationship of this norm to the divine command needs to be clarified, and criteria of relative justice need to be specified on the basis of empirical analyses of the forms of power, order, and justice in human history. The need for such analyses and criteria is particularly apparent in Barth's political writings on Fascism, Communism, and the totalitarian state. Here secular thought would, if taken seriously, show the extent to which Barth neglects the reality and power of evil in his understanding of politics and political responsibility.

Like Barth, Lehmann also views the world and secular society from the perspective of redemption. "Protestant theology," he writes, "has never sufficiently regarded the world in the light of the victory of Christ."[13] Even the Reformers need to be corrected at this point. "Judgment and grace in Christ belong to the humanity which is common to all men in him."[14] Hence the difference between believers and unbelievers is "the difference between being in a situation which is hidden and being in one which is open." Viewed from the perspective of the _koinonia_, Christian ethics is concerned primarily with the perception of parabolic signs of redemption in the world at the point where the new humanity is becoming actualized.

Despite the fact that Lehmann makes the messianic image the primary symbol of the divine action in the world, when he turns to issues of social policy--segregation, war, and violence, he treats these exclusively from the standpoint of the individual rather than as questions of social justice.[15] In so far as the individual agent is concerned, the ethical issue, for Lehmann, is focused on the potentiality of particular decisions and actions to serve the humanizing purposes of God. Amid the ambiguities of human history, there is "never any <u>one right action</u>."[16] Rather, always there are "acts to be done"--actions which "bear the risk of obedience" and are potential instruments of the divine action in the world. There are, however, no objective criteria for judging what such acts of obedience and humanization might be. Indeed, it is a matter of indifference that "some Christians support desegregation and others disavow it."[17] What does matter is the interpretation of the behavior of Christians-- namely, that their action points to the humanizing action of God in the world. Because he rejects all moral principles, including middle axioms, as being abstract, Lehmann similarly refuses to deal with war and violence as moral issues which demand choices between conflicting moral claims with radically different social consequences. The fact that God overrules <u>wrong</u> human action makes the moral character of human decisions quite irrelevant.[18] In the last analysis, ethical action is never a matter of "having really done the good"; rather, it is a matter of bearing in "trust the risk of trust," in the confidence that God will forgive our ethical failures and that he will "pick up the pieces" of our broken human action through the divine activity.[19]

Since for Lehmann the ethical character of behavior is determined by its symbolic significance, the objective dimension of ethical analysis and decisions lies outside of his concern. This is particularly true with regard to the empirical structures and processes of society. From the perspective of the <u>koinonia</u>, the sociological problem of community is perceived as the problem of the relationship of the head to the body.[20] This means that community is understood essentially in organic terms rather than in sociological terms of institutions, order, and power. Moreover, the resolution of conflicts both among members of the koinonia and in the participation of believers in the world "belongs to the possessor of the secret of maturity."[21] Here the prudential calculation and weighing of empirical consequences of moral choices is ruled out both because the latter are ethically irrelevant and because Christian behavior, like the divine action, cannot be generalized.

Lehmann's scorn for the empirical dimensions of moral analysis and decision-making undercuts the basis of human accountability in social ethics. A more biblical and historical understanding of "what God is doing in the world" would lead to a more prophetic perception of the divine judgment which falls upon all forms of political and economic injustice in human affairs. Although the God of the Bible is sovereign and therefore is not defeated by the evil which humans do, the latter are nevertheless accountable for the consequences of their disobedience--for unfaithfulness in oppression of the poor and for the destruction wrought by violence and warfare. In a biblical perspective, divine forgiveness does not mean divine indifference to the results of human choices; it means, rather, God's acceptance of sinners and his initiative in reconciling them unto himself and with each other.

As in the case of Barth, Lehmann's phenomenology of the human is inadequate because he also fails to take seriously the importance of the empirical, societal dimensions of our humanity. Lehmann describes the formative biblical images of the divine action as "political images, both in the phenomenological and in the fundamental senses of the word."[22] He proceeds, however, to interpret politics symbolically in terms of its capacity to serve as the bearer of parabolic meaning rather than as the historical form of our humanity. Lehmann is primarily concerned with "the politics of

God" rather than with politics as a sphere of human responsibility. The controlling images which he uses to describe the political sphere are Christological. God's humanizing activity is messianic activity. The meaning of biblical politics is centered finally in the Transfiguration of Jesus.[23] This means that politics is removed from the context of moral assessment and responsibility.

Revolutionary violence is, for Lehmann, a paradigmatic instance of the transfiguration of politics when the former is viewed from an apocalyptic rather than an ethical perspective. He writes as follows:

> At the level of revolutionary politics, violence is unveiled not as the endemic nemesis of revolution but as a sign that politics have arrived at an apocalyptic moment of truth and point of no return.... In short, the apocalyptic significance of violence is the talisman of its transfiguration.[24]

This means that violence is not understood and assessed "in primarily ethical (moral), or legal, or even sociological terms" but rather as "an apocalyptic phenomenon."[25] An ethics of good and evil is transfigured by the dynamic in breaking of a new order over against an established order in and through such a moment of truth. When violence is placed in an apocalyptic context, it lies "beyond good and evil," and ethical justification for the use of violent means is no longer required. Such a "phenomenology" of violence obscures the role of human agency, on the one hand, and the tragedy and horror which are the result of violence, on the other.[26]

The Dualism Between Creation And Redemption: Brunner, Bonhoeffer, And Reinhold Niebuhr

In contrast to Barth and Lehmann, for whom Christian ethics is subsumed in its entirety under redemption, Brunner, Bonhoeffer, and Reinhold Niebuhr interpret the former in terms of a polarity between revelation and natural reason. This double rootage of theological ethics is particularly necessary, they believe, for social ethics. All three theologians, however, seek to avoid a static separatism, or dualism, between ethics based on creation (law) and ethics based on redemption (grace); and they attempt to do so on Christological grounds. Brunner describes the problem of the relationship between these two forms of the divine will in terms of "the command and the orders"; Bonhoeffer speaks of it in terms of "the concrete commandment and the divine mandates"; Reinhold Niebuhr defines it as "the kingdom of God and the struggle for social justice." For Brunner and Reinhold Niebuhr some knowledge of the divine will is available to man on the basis of reason grounded in creation; for Bonhoeffer, on the other hand, the mandates are known only Christologically--i.e., "from above" through revelation. For all three, however, social ethics is an arena of moral conflict between good and evil and of human decisions that are morally ambiguous. The struggle for social justice belongs to the sphere of the penultimate rather than to the time of reconciliation and/or redemption. This eschatological perspective constitutes the basis for the polarity between law and gospel, justice and love, in human history. This polarity is rooted in human sin; hence, it will remain so long as sin endures--i.e., until the end of the present historical order.

For Brunner, as we have seen, Christian ethics is an ethic of obedience to the command of God. While the content of the latter can be described formally as the unconditional requirement of love for God and neighbor, the concrete meaning of the command is known only as it is disclosed through the Spirit in the moment of decision. Since this command is always concrete, its content cannot be formulated in general terms. Nevertheless, since the God who demands obedience is both the Creator and the Redeemer, his will is also made known in a "fragmentary and indirect way" through the orders of creation.[27] As Creator, God demands that we accept these orders--that we adjust ourselves to the world and its concrete tasks; as Redeemer, he wills the transformation of the orders in so far as the latter are distorted by sin.

For Brunner <u>human</u> existence is existence in community and in responsibility. Strictly speaking, there is only one form of true community, viz., the union of a single <u>I</u> and a single <u>Thou</u> based on love. Genuine community is based upon personal relationships between individuals. The orders of creation, however, represent certain "natural forms of community."[28] Brunner lists five of these: marriage and the family, labor, the state, culture, and the institutional church. Each represents a definite form of collective life, or social organization, which is grounded finally in the ordering work of the Creator. Thus, while such societal forms--including institutions--are the products of natural and rational human impulses, they are also fundamentally divine creations and divine gifts. This means that they are sacred tasks and thus part of one's vocation. Through them God wills the preservation of that which he has created.

In their fundamental forms the orders of creation are the unalterable presuppositions of all historical life; yet, the concrete forms in which they appear in history are constantly changing. Such changes are due primarily to sin.[29] Hence the existing orders are not God's orders, and they do not in themselves constitute the command of the Creator. Yet the will of the Creator remains hidden within them as the concrete form of our humanity. Despite their distortion in their historical forms by sin, they are nevertheless fragmentary forms of community which are rooted in creation. They are not so much analogies of true community as the means of divine training for the latter, for in them persons are placed within society and confronted with the claims of group life. Viewed from the perspective of faith, the orders are instruments of service to the collective neighbor; they also point to the meaning of our humanity, viz., co-existence, dependence on others, and the fact that we owe our existence to others.

In and through them God preserves the created world from destruction.

Brunner's concept of society in terms of "orders of creation" leads to a strongly conservative attitude toward culture and social change. To a certain extent, this conservatism is balanced by the demand for the transformation of the orders in <u>The Divine Imperative</u>. Here it is said that the Christian will be both "conservative" and "revolutionary"; however, the changes the believer seeks to effect are to be accomplished largely through individual acts of love.[30] In <u>Justice and the Social Order</u>, however, the "dualism" between justice and love becomes more pronounced. Yet the basis for this development was present in his earlier work, particularly in his existentialist understanding of human nature and in the "insoluble dualism" between the requirements of the orders and the commandment of love.[31]

Despite his insistence that individuals exist only in community, Brunner's concept of human nature is fundamentally individualistic. True community exists only between a single <u>I</u> and a single <u>Thou</u>. Persons are finally abstracted from the more inclusive social relationships of actual life. Such an individualistic concept of humanity leads to a serious misunderstanding of the pervasiveness and ambiguity of power in all human relationships.

For Brunner, genuine community is interpersonal, based on love. In contrast, the orders of creation define the structures of human life in organizations and institutions based upon justice as their moral norm. Brunner's concept of justice is modelled, essentially, after Aristotle's notion of justice as rendering to each person his due.[32] Unlike love, justice is impersonal and even-handed. It "belongs to the world of systems"; in that world it is supreme.[33] Justice cannot make use of love, not does it need to do so; for justice is not concerned with the human beings as such, but only with the latter in relationships. Love, on the other hand, "knows nought of systems." If it is found in institutions, it exists only "between the lines" where individuals meet each other as persons.³⁴ The command of the Creator which meets man in the orders is the demand for justice and obedience; the command of the Redeemer which meets man in personal relationships is the command to love the neighbor. Moreover, the work of justice is essentially a work of human reason; the capacity to love is a gift of grace. Thus, the dualism between the interpersonal and societal forms of human life remains unresolved. Theologically, this dualism is grounded in the polarity between the divine action as Creator and Redeemer; anthropologically, it is grounded in the dualism between Brunner's existential conception of human nature and his concept of society, i.e., between his concept of true community and the natural forms of community. For Brunner, true community is limited to I-Thou relationships; society, on the other hand, is limited to fragmentary forms of community with a radically different norm. The former rests fundamentally upon faith; the latter is fundamentally a work of human reason.

Like Brunner, Bonhoeffer also sought to overcome the static (spatial) dualism of the traditional Lutheran concept of the two spheres, one temporal and one spiritual; but he attempted to do so on more exclusively Christological and eschatological grounds. Through the concept of the "mandates" he affirmed the relative autonomy of the world in relationship to Christ. Bonhoeffer used the term "mandates" rather than orders of creation to refer more clearly to a divinely given task rather than a determination of being.³⁵ Moreover, unlike the orders, the mandates are known only through the revelation of Christ. They cannot be understood in any sense as the products of human history, but only in relationship to their Christological origin and goal. Bonhoeffer lists four such mandates: church, marriage and the family, culture, and government.³⁶ All four are disclosed and attested by Scripture.

Since these forms of human life are grounded in the reality of Christ, there is no possibility of retreating from a secular into a spiritual realm. God wills that there shall be marriage, labor, government, and church in the world; and he wills that all of these--each in its particular way--shall be grounded in Christ and directed toward him. All of the mandates are intended for all persons. In them and through them each individual stands as a whole person before God. While two of the mandates--marriage and labor--were present before the Fall, all four define the form and the concrete meaning of human life as a life of obedience. Marriage and labor are presupposed by government; it is the function of the latter to order and protect the former. Through the establishment of law and through force, government preserves the world for Christ; hence, all persons owe obedience to the governing authorities for the sake of Christ.[37] While the mandate of the church differs from the other three, it similarly extends to all humanity; and--most significantly--it does so only in relationship to marriage, labor, and government. All four mandates are "conjoined," and it is only in their interrelatedness--only in their mutual support and mutual limitation--that together they express the commandment of God.[38] Only as they exist together are they divine commissions.

The mandates belong to the social structure of human life in the world. Although apart from revelation they are not perceived as mandates, they nonetheless extend to all humanity. They include the development of institutional forms of human life, but they do not provide divine sanction for institutions in their existing forms. Having grounded human existence in the secular world in the divine mandates, Bonhoeffer seeks to maintain the unity and sovereignty of the divine will over the totality of human life dialectically, i.e., eschatologically. The world is thus given a place of relative autonomy by assigning it penultimate significance in preparing the way for the coming of Christ.[39] While the estrangement between humanity and God resulting form the Fall can be finally overcome only through the justification of sinners by grace, nevertheless the way for the coming of justification is prepared through the penultimate. Created human life must be preserved for the sake of the coming of Christ. Concretely, this means that being man (personhood) and being good (moral goodness) are prior to justification.[40] It is in our broken humanity and the contradiction of our efforts to be morally good that the word of justification and redemption is given to us. Expressed in negative terms, preparing the way means repentance; in positive terms, it means being man and being good--respecting the conditions and demands of the penultimate and removing those obstacles such as hunger and injustice, which impede the hearing of the gospel.

While life in the secular world is thus prevented from being either absolutized or separated from faith through the relation which it bears to the ultimate, Bonhoeffer--like Brunner--remains fundamentally a dualist in his ethics. Though he affirms the unity of human life, including its social dimensions, in the reality of Christ, the implications of this unity for ethical reflection and for obedience to the single divine commandment in the world remain unclear. To bridge this gap Bonhoeffer introduces the concept of "the natural" which, he believes, has been neglected in Protestant ethics. "The natural," he writes, "is the form of life preserved by God for the fallen world and directed towards justification, redemption and renewal through Christ."[41] Fundamentally, the contents of the natural--including the rights of natural life--are known through reason, and it is the duty of man on the basis of reason to acknowledge and protect the claims of the natural. Yet Bonhoeffer fails to specify--either on the basis of reason or of revelation--what the protection of such rights means in concrete cases. In the end, the answers which are given to this question seem to be based finally either upon consensus or upon an appeal to necessity. As James T. Laney points out, such answers do not provide an adequate ethical basis either for adjudication or for the guarantee of human rights.[42] Moreover, to attempt to resolve the problem of conflicting moral claims by arguing that the natural will sooner or later vindicate itself if basic rights are violated is to abdicate _human_ responsibility for social justice.

In sum, in affirming the relative autonomy of secular society, Bonhoeffer fails to show how the penultimate may be given moral direction by the ultimate except as the individual is addressed by the concrete commandment of God. The mandates do not in themselves provide such direction although they point to the concrete place where the commandment is heard and where persons are summoned to deputyship and freedom, including the freedom to bear guilt. The mandates point to certain forms (orders, structures, or spheres) of human life, all understood in dynamic and interrelated ways; but they do not resolve moral conflicts in themselves. Ostensibly, the "commandment of God" gives people "warrant" for ethical discourse although the former lies beyond the latter and is indeed the final answer to the latter. But the possibility and value of ethical discourse at the level of the penultimate remains problematic both because the will of God is known finally only on the basis of revelation and also because it is always revealed concretely in relation to specific choices and decisions.

In comparison with Brunner and Bonhoeffer, Reinhold Niebuhr's understanding of society is more historical, more empirical, and more dialectical in terms of the relationship of faith to natural reason. Like Bonhoeffer, Niebuhr also rejected Brunner's attempt to ground social justice in certain orders of creation, and he did so for two main reasons. In the first place, this notion represented an excessively static--or fixed--conception of social institutions which failed to take adequate account of the dynamics of human freedom and human history; in the second place, it resulted in too radical a separation between justice and _agape_ as the ultimate norm of historical justice. For Reinhold Niebuhr, the relationship between justice and love is dialectical; theologically, this dialectic is grounded in the Atonement. From the perspective of faith, the crucifixion of Christ is the decisive event in which the relationship of God to the world is disclosed and both "the possibilities and the limits" of human history are made manifest. Here the divine love revealed in the Cross is perceived to be the norm of human freedom and also to stand in judgment upon all human action, collective as well as individual.

For Reinhold Niebuhr the Christian doctrine of the Atonement is a symbol of the paradoxical relationship of the divine mercy to the divine wrath in God's relationship to the world. As such, it constitutes the final key to the meaning of history.[43] It points both to the meaning of history--to the seriousness of distinctions between good and evil, to the importance of human decisions and achievements--and to the impossibility of the fulfilment of history within history. But because it has meaning, history points beyond itself to the judgment and mercy of God for its final fulfilment. Thus the grace revealed in the Cross becomes the ground both of forgiveness (justification) and of "the release of the soul into action."[44] In its positive dimension, grace is the freedom, the awareness of the obligation, and the power to seek new and higher forms of justice amid the moral ambiguities and the perplexities of history in the confidence that the meaning of the latter will be finally fulfilled. As "interim" between the first and the second coming of Christ, history is the sphere of human responsibility for the achievement of the highest possible measure of order, freedom, and justice out of obedience to God and love for the neighbor.

To affirm the seriousness of history is to understand the latter as the work of human freedom in both its creative and its destructive aspects. History is grounded in human freedom and human transcendence. It is the story of humanity's quest for community, of human life in the "earthly city." In terms of social ethics, the fundamental question is how the "earthly city" is to be understood. What is the basis of human life in secular society? What are the norms of the latter, and how are such norms related both to the necessities and to the possibilities of historical existence? Unlike Barth and Lehmann, who attempt to derive answers to these questions exclusively from revelation, Niebuhr's starting point is the reality of human experience, and the method which he employs to analyze this social reality is a dialectic of empirical reason and faith.[45]

For Reinhold Niebuhr, human beings are social by nature. Community is rooted in the freedom and the mutual dependence of selves, both for their existence and for their fulfilment. "(T)he community is as primordial as the individual."[46] The family is the most primitive and the most persistent form of community. It is rooted in human sexuality and provides both for sexual partnership and for the rearing children.[47] The family, in turn, is the basis for the creation of larger and more powerful communities as civilization develops. In part, the latter are the product of natural and unconscious forces of cohesion and authority; in part, they are the consequence of rational and intentional efforts to achieve union and integration. Thus, every community is "both organism and artifact."[48] The bonds of community are both voluntary and involuntary, both natural and rational. Community is both the basis and the goal of individual life. Yet the relationship of the individual to the community is more complex than the foregoing analysis implies. Hence this relationship must be understood in terms of its vertical as well as its horizontal dimensions. Viewed in this perspective, the community represents not only the fulfilment but also the frustration of each individual member.[49] This dialectical relation of the individual to the group is characteristic of all human communities; it is the source of the conflicts and limitations as well as the harmonies and partial fulfilments of all collective life.

For Niebuhr, the fundamental task of Christian social ethics is that of achieving a clear understanding of the realities of our common social life while at the same time preserving a sense of responsibility for the achievement of the highest possible forms of social justice. In the pursuit of this task the empirical cultural disciplines are just as essential as revelation. Without them theology becomes obscurantist, and the gospel is emptied of meaning. By themselves, however, these disciplines lead inevitably to illusions about human nature and to an ideological distortion of the truth which they contain. Only the Christian doctrine of man--as creature and as sinner--is able to provide a perspective in terms of which both the truth and the limits of scientific conceptions of human nature can be discerned. Thus the relationship between theology, on the one hand, and socio-scientific and historical studies, on the other hand, is basically dialectical. Niebuhr writes:

> There is, in short, no possibility of fully validating the truth in the foolishness of the Gospel if every cultural discipline is not taken seriously up to the point where it becomes conscious of its own limits and the point where the insights of various disciplines stand in contradiction to each other, signifying that the total of reality is more complex than any scheme of rational meaning which may be invented to comprehend it.[50]

The cultural disciplines, in a word, point beyond themselves to revelation as the ground of the final meaning of human life, and the truth of revelation is, in turn, confirmed by reason.

If the realities of our common social life cannot be adequately comprehended apart from revelation, neither can they be understood apart from an empirical knowledge of the concrete historical forms and processes of collective life. These forms and processes differ in fundamental ways from those which are involved in interpersonal (I-Thou) relationships. Moreover, the former cannot be adequately understood on the basis of analogies and paradigms drawn from the realm of redemption. Collective forms of human life are related to the individual members of such groups in both positive and negative ways. The need for community is grounded in human freedom and human finitude; but, since sin is universal, all historical forms of community are distorted and corrupted by pride, or self-love. Further, collective forms of pride cannot be reduced simply to the pride and egotism of individuals even though the former are rooted in the latter. Groups exercise greater authority over their members; moreover, the former are more arrogant, hypocritical, self-centered, and ruthless than individuals in the pursuit of their ends.[51] For Niebuhr, in short, collective pride is the final form of sin, and the former differs in significant ways from individualistic forms of egotism.

Although it is most consistently expressed in the national state, collective egotism extends to every form of group life. This insight constitutes the basis for Niebuhr's realism in assessing the possibilities and limits of the struggle for social justice. The universality and the persistence of sin does not mean that there are no significant moral discriminations and choices within human history; it does mean, however, that there is no realistic possibility of achieving complete justice in history. Understood from the perspective of Christian faith, the _agape_ of Christ is both the norm by which the sinfulness of all human achievements is judged and the standard in terms of which the relative possibilities of historical forms of justice are measured.

According to Reinhold Niebuhr, Augustine was "the first great 'realist' in western history."[52] In his picture of life in the earthly city, the latter was the first to give an adequate account of the conflicts, tensions, and competitions of interest, which are characteristic of all human community. Augustine's insight was derived from his biblical conception of human selfhood, including the concept of evil as rooted in the self. This perspective on human nature enabled him to see both the limitations and the distortions in the rationalistic notions of selfhood and history espoused by the classical philosophers. Although Niebuhr considered Augustine's realism somewhat excessive, resulting in an indiscriminate criticism of historical forms of community, he nevertheless believed that the latter's account of life in the earthly city was fundamentally correct. On the one hand, it was realistic without being either cynical or relativistic. Although egoism is universal, it is not normative, for it does not conform to humanity's essential nature as a being who is created for community based on love. Moreover, Augustine's concept of social reality was realistic without being cynical in so far as it represented the comingling of the earthly city with the heavenly city throughout human history. Thus, while the peace, the order, and the justice of all historical forms of community are distorted by egoism and pride because sin is universal, the former also represent relative forms of peace, order, and justice based upon created human nature; at the same time, the contradictions--the conflicts and tensions--in such historical communities point beyond themselves to the possibilities and claims of love. Niebuhr also considered it a major strength of Augustine that he defined the normative dimensions of life in the earthly city in terms of love rather than in terms of natural law. In its classical and medieval forms, natural law assumed an order of history based upon an underlying order of nature which failed to do justice to the human capacity to transcend nature. Not only does love as a norm do greater justice to the endless variety of historical forms of community; it also provides more adequate resources than law for the modification of human behavior.[53]

Niebuhr's realism is the product both of empirical reason and of revelation. It is the result of a dialectical interplay between "political realism," as understood in political science, and "Christian realism" about human nature. Harland identifies the following elements as consistent ingredients in Niebuhr's political realism: "a clear recognition of the limits of morality and reason in politics; the acceptance of the fact that political realities are power realities and that power must be countered by power; that self-interest is the primary datum in the actions of all groups and nations."[54] Harland then suggests four ways in which Christian faith is related to political realism in Niebuhr. First, the former can prevent the political realist from defining the national interest too narrowly. Secondly, it prods the political realist to find those points of coincidence between the interests of nations and those values which transcend national interests. Thirdly, Christian faith can help prevent the political realist from falling into moral cynicism concerning the possibilities of justice among nations. Finally, the former can expose the moral pretensions in all groups in so far as they idealize and absolutize their own self-interests. By unmasking the self-interest in all competing groups, Christian faith may moderate the conflicts among groups.[55]

If Reinhold Niebuhr's concept of human nature provides the basis for realism in his ethics, it also provides the basis for the struggle for social justice in history. As we have seen, his anthropology points both to the sinfulness of humanity and to *agape* as the final law of human life in both its interpersonal and its communal dimensions. For Niebuhr, community is both an individual and a social necessity.[56] Man's nature as "image of God" points finally toward *agape* as the inescapable requirement of his freedom, but man's nature as sinner points to the need for "realism" in estimating the possibilities and the limits of historical justice as an instrument of neighbor-love. Hence, the relationship of *agape* to the struggle for social justice must always be conceived dialectically. On the one hand, historical forms of justice are a necessary work of love in communal life; and, on the other hand, all such systems of justice fall short of the requirements of love and therefore stand under the judgment of love. Here as elsewhere the relationship of the gospel to history must be applied dialectically "to the experience of life from top to bottom." On the one hand, there are "no complex relations of social justice to which the love of the Kingdom of God is not relevant"; yet, on the other hand, there are "no areas or experiences where historical insecurity and anxiety are completely transcended, except in principle."[57]

For Niebuhr, systems and structures of social justice represent "*ad hoc* efforts to strike a balance between the final moral possibilities of life and the immediate and given realities" of historical existence.[58] For him, the "realities" of social existence are relational and dynamic rather than static and fixed. They refer fundamentally to the forms of power and interest underlying the development of structures of justice and order rather than to such structures themselves.[59] These forces are rooted finally in human freedom and transcendence; in their historical form they have been perverted by sin, which is universal.

The contributions of the social sciences are indispensable for understanding the nature, the forms, and the requirements of human life in community; yet the latter can not be adequately comprehended apart from a knowledge of human life and community which is derived from the biblical conception of man and history. As we have seen, these two sources of insight are related dialectically.

Phenomenologically, both interest and power are natural forms of social cohesion; they are present in every community. By itself, interest does not constitute a sufficient basis for community because it is unable to provide an adequate ground for order. Hence, collective power is needed both for the establishment and for the maintenance of community. Such power is expressed in two forms, viz., the central organizing power of government and the equilibrium--or balance--of the forms of power which are present in any given social situation. Both forms of power are "essential and perennial aspects of community organization; and no moral or social advance can redeem society from its dependence upon these two principles."[60] Hence, a balance of power is prerequisite for the achievement both of order and of justice in history.

Order and justice are both presuppositions of communal life; and while they are not in themselves embodiments of brotherhood, both are approximations of brotherhood under the conditions imposed by human sinfulness. Every system of justice stands under final judgment of the law of love, but within the limits of history justice not only provides for the restraint of evil; it also represents a more positive expression of community than individuals are able to achieve on the basis of natural inclination and interest. Niebuhr describes three ways in which principles and systems of justice become instruments of brotherhood by extending the sense of obligation toward the neighbor: (a) from an obligation which is immediately felt to a continued obligation expressed in fixed principles of mutual support, (b) from a simple I-Thou relation to the complex relations of the self to "others," and (c) from "obligations, discerned by the individual self, to the wider obligations which the community defines from its more impartial perspective."[61]

For Reinhold Niebuhr, all historical communities have some general principles of justice by which their own embodiments of justice are measured. While the former are more historically conditioned than traditional Catholic conceptions of natural law assume, they do nevertheless constitute a limited form of natural law; as such they represent partial expressions of love within the contingencies of history. Such norms rest upon the experience of human communities. They are the products of reason and experience. As such they represent "rational efforts to apply the moral obligation, implied in the love commandment, to the complexities of life and the fact of sin" more than they do fixed standards of reason.[62] Just as reason is necessary in the application of natural forms of justice to concrete community relationships, so it also performs a necessary role in relating agape to the demands of collective life through justice. In this task conceptions of justice based on natural reason are related both positively and negatively to the work of justice as an expression of agape.

The historical--or relational--notion of justice which informs Niebuhr's concept of natural law is also present in his "Christian pragmatism." While Niebuhr did not generally associate his own ethics with pragmatism until the period following World War II, the latter had been implicit in his dialectical method of relating love to the struggle for social justice throughout most of his career.[63] During his earlier years he had vigorously rejected pragmatism as a philosophy because it denied the reality of any moral absolute. While he continued to reject its moral relativism, he increasingly adopted pragmatism as a strategy for relating <u>agape</u> as the final absolute norm of history to the complexities and ambiguities of collective life. Thus, his pragmatism can be properly understood only as "Christian pragmatism."[64] In an article appearing in <u>The Ecumenical Review</u> in 1957, Niebuhr described the gradual development of pragmatism in his own thought and reflected on its double rootage in Christian faith and in his own engagement in the struggle for economic and social justice:

> Christian thought must not pretend that what we have described as its growing pragmatism has not been influenced by this general history in Western thought and life. But we must also recognize that what has been wrought out has actually been a view of life and the establishment of justice in a community which could have been elaborated originally if we had had a clear biblical insight into the nature of history, the freedom of man, and the corruption of sin in that freedom, and had therefore realized that history cannot be equated with nature; nor can the political judgments which we make about our and each other's interest be equated with the judgments which a scientist makes about natural phenomena. In other words the process we have described has been the gradual extrication of our thought from the baneful effects of heresies about man and God which have infected it ever since the French Enlightenment.[65]

Niebuhr's pragmatism has been strongly criticized in recent years on the ground that it represents an essentially conservative stance toward the prevailing social system. While contemporary pragmatism in this country has been progressive in its design and teleological in its ethical orientation toward future goals and consequences, it has in practice been relatively conservative since it has taken for granted the root values of the existing, functioning social system. It has been progressive within the context of this system, but it does not provide an adequate base for a radical critique of the system itself. Marxism had proved more adequate in this regard for Niebuhr during the early and mid-thirties; but, as he later recognized, the former also rested upon ideological assumptions that made it "worse than the disease which it was meant to cure."[66] Despite his "realism" and "pragmatism," Niebuhr sought to provide a transcendent perspective in terms of which the ideological character of all schemes of historical justice could be laid bare through such theological concepts as *agape*, the Kingdom of God, and eschatology. Taken together, these theological referents constitute the normative pole of his dialectic with all systems of justice. Within this perspective, pragmatism became a method for making choices between competing possibilities of social justice in human history.

The Transformation Of Community:
H. Richard Niebuhr, Ramsey, And Gustafson

In comparison with the ethicists whom we have just been considering, H. Richard Niebuhr, Paul Ramsey, and James M. Gustafson place greater stress upon the continuity between human historical existence, on the one hand, and the possibilities and demands of grace, on the other. While sin is also universal for this group, it presupposes a human nature that is fundamentally good. Hence, the resources of natural justice are more positively related to normative ethics. Moral norms and values are understood in relational rather than abstract or perfectionist terms. Hence there are greater possibilities for the transformation both of individuals and of communities. For H. Richard Niebuhr such transformation is made possible by a conversion from social or pluralistic faith to radical monotheism. For Ramsey it is basically a transformation of natural justice by Christian love. For Gustafson, the fundamental change which faith makes possible is the transformation of character, including a commitment to the well-being of creation and the common good.

For H. Richard Niebuhr, the self is fundamentally social; hence, selves and communities always exist together. The self is never simply an I-Thou self but always an I-You self; the Thou's to which it responds are members of an interacting community.[67] The basic form of human sociality is interpersonal community rather than contractual society. Contract theories of society are essentially atomistic and voluntaristic; they presuppose the existence of selves prior to social relationships since the latter are entered into by choice. For Niebuhr, on the other hand, the self is born "in the womb of society as a sentient, thinking, needful being ... and with the possibility of experience of a common world."[68]

The root metaphor which Niebuhr uses to describe the activity of the self is "response." While the responses of the self are fundamentally interpersonal, they are nevertheless inseparable from the communities and the society to which it belongs. Niebuhr's concept of the social self and its communities had many sources. On the one hand, he was influenced by the social psychology of George Horton Cooley and George Herbert Mead. The behavioristic and evolutionary character of their thought tended to be offset, however, by the influence of existentialists such as Martin Buber. Niebuhr was also influenced by sociological and anthropological theories of the priority of communities in comparison with contract societies as well as by the still longer tradition of moral philosophy, including a social understanding of conscience.[69] In contrast to teleological and deontological conceptions of moral agency in which other selves are secondary, "responsibility" points to the dialogic, interactional, and social nature of the self at every stage of its existence.

Not only are selves social in that they always exist in community with other selves; the bonds by which they are united in community are moral bonds of trust and loyalty to a common cause. Since both selves and communities exist in time, past and future are joined together in the interpersonal and communal relationships of the present. Through these relationships the members of a community are united by shared objects of trust and loyalty and by a common memory and hope. These--rather than interest or power--constitute the most fundamental sources of social cohesion. Faith as trust in and loyalty to a common center of value determines the ways in which interest and force are understood and utilized in particular societies. In this sense faith is both a source of unity and a source of cohesion; but in relationship to other competing groups it is a source of conflict in society. Henotheism-- faith in a particular social order as the center of value and object of loyalty--issues in "closed societies." Viewed internally to a particular social group (e.g., a nation) it is a source of cohesion; but in relationship to other competing groups it is a source of conflict.[70] In contrast, polytheism--faith in many sources of value--leads to a pluralistic conception of selves and society. Historically, polytheism tends to follow the disintegration of social faith. It issues in partial devotion to many limited causes; it fails, however, to provide a meaningful basis for order, unity, and purpose that transcends the conflicting interests and causes of particular groups. In contrast both to henotheism and to polytheism, radical monotheism-- faith in the One beyond all the many finite centers of value--provides the basis for universal community. All three forms of faith exist together in particular societies and are in continual conflict with each other. Radical monotheism has existed in human history primarily as a hope rather than as an actuality; yet it has contributed to the shaping of Western culture in many significant ways. While it has always been in conflict with social and pluralistic faith, it has nevertheless affected the religious, political, and scientific developments of the West by its protests against idolatry and by its conviction that society is part of a universal moral order.[71] Such transformation always remains incomplete, but it is nonetheless real.

Human communities, then, are fundamentally faith communities.[72] In so far as they are human, all communities are bound together by bonds of trust and loyalty. Such ties of faith are more basic than ties of love. Thus the family, for example, is founded on the pledge of mutual fidelity between husband and wife, rather than on love alone. Similarly, the existence and authority of the state rest upon the allegiance of its subjects, upon their oath of obedience to its laws and their promise to defend it against its enemies. Significantly, however, the structures of faith--of trust and of loyalty--appear in human community largely in negative form as distrust and unfaithfulness to one another.[73] Such negative manifestations do not, however, point to the absence of faith, but rather to the distorted forms in which the latter is present even in broken community. Thus treason, for example, presupposes faith. Treason is not the mere absence of trust and fidelity; rather, it is distrust and disloyalty, which reflect the brokenness of community rather than the absence of the latter. Just as the love of the earthly city was perverted love rather than the absence of love for Augustine, so the faith that is present in fragmented human communities is faith in perverted forms. Moreover, just as the earthly city was a corrupted form of society representing a relative order of justice and peace, so, for Niebuhr, historical communities are largely distorted or broken forms of community. As such, however, they point in a negative way to the underlying faith-structure of all human relationships, including those of society.

H. Richard Niebuhr's concept of community rests fundamentally on his idea of the social self. Selves are bound together with others by loyalty to a transcendent cause. While Niebuhr was deeply indebted to Royce for his understanding of the role of loyalty in the creation of community, he differed sharply from the latter in his perception of the object of common loyalty which binds the community together. For Royce, this cause is always the community itself. For Niebuhr, on the other hand, the former always transcends the latter.[74] Such a transcendent cause not only gives meaning to the community; it also calls forth loyalty from the members of the latter. Such loyalty involves a two-fold commitment both to the community itself and also to the cause which the latter represents.

For Niebuhr, this notion of community based upon loyalty to a transcendent cause was expressed concretely in the history of Israel in the idea of the covenant. Among the Israelites all human relationships were fundamentally covenant relationships.[75] The making and keeping of promises were the essential elements in all relationships between persons. Domestic, economic, and political relations, as well as religious observances, were basically covenant relations among and between persons based upon the fundamental covenant between God and humanity. Such an understanding of community contained a place for law, but the covenant pointed beyond the law to the basis of the latter in underlying human relationships. Natural, historical, and cultural relations were transformed into covenant relations without losing their natural bases in history and in culture. In this regard Niebuhr's description of the family is typical of all other human relationships: "The family, with all of its natural basis in sex and parental love, was now given a sub-foundation as it were in promise and the keeping of faith between husbands and wives, parents and children."[76]

Not only did this covenant conception of community inform and shape the life of Israel. It has also been a continuing force in the shaping of Western culture, including the growth of democracy and the development of science, for it is rooted fundamentally in human moral experience. It is based in the experience of the self as a responsible moral agent, in the perception of trust and faithfulness as the basic moral bonds in human relationships, and in the apprehension of a transcendent moral order which makes human moral life intelligible. Thus understood, human community is grounded theologically in the covenant between God and man. Such covenant relationships among persons and between persons and God constitute the structure of our humanity within history. They provide a basis both for social realism and for social transformation, for they are the arena both of monotheistic faith and of idolatry, of faithfulness and of unfaithfulness, of community which is broken and of community which is being reconciled and transformed.

Like Barth and H. Richard Niebuhr, Paul Ramsey also defines the fundamental nature and meaning of human existence in terms of covenant. For all three writers, the symbol of covenant points to the relational nature of good and duty; it also points to the continuity in moral bonds which cut across time and bind the present both to the past and to the future. In each case, created human nature provides the ground--what Barth calls "the external basis"--for covenant relationships as the fundamental meaning, or purpose, of creation. Despite these similarities, however, there are important differences among these authors regarding both the meaning of this concept and its implications for an understanding of community.

For Barth covenant is a Christological category, and the possibility of such partnership with God rests exclusively upon grace. Humanity as existence _with_ the fellowman constitutes the formal possibility of existence _for_ the fellowman, i.e., of covenant. The former is grounded in creation and thus applies to all persons; humanity as the realization of the promise of covenant rests exclusively upon man's being addressed by the command of God. Both the actualization of covenant and knowledge of the moral content of the latter depend exclusively upon grace. For H. Richard Niebuhr, on the other hand, the concept of covenant is a more general anthropological category. It refers to the social nature of the self as a being which exists in relationships of responsibility with other selves; moreover, these relationships are most profoundly understood in terms of the making and keeping of promises. In so far as they rest upon bonds of fidelity and loyalty, natural forms of society--such as the family and political and economic groups--constitute covenant communities. In this respect Ramsey's concept of covenant resembles that of Niebuhr more closely than it does that of Barth since, for him, covenantal relationships are also characteristic of human life generally. For Ramsey, these relationships--and not just their formal possibility--are grounded fundamentally in creation. This is true both of those covenants which are entered by birth and those which are entered by choice. Although knowledge of the full meaning of covenant is dependent upon revelation in Christ, these natural human relationships are an expression of the essential humanity of all persons.[77]

Since human nature is fundamentally covenantal by creation for Ramsey, the most basic bonds of community are obligations of faithfulness and loyalty which all persons owe to each other by reason of our common humanity. In part such duties are implicit in the tacit covenants into which we are born; in part they are explicit in the voluntary covenants which we enter through mutual commitments. In either case these obligations are the basis of the claims of justice, whether the latter is based on reason or love. Natural justice is the form in which our humanity is preserved; as such it is a partial embodiment of covenant although it always stands in need of transformation by love.

For Ramsey, Christian ethics as obedient *agape* has many fundamental resources for the development of social policy, but it must necessarily form alliances, or coalitions, with other systems of ethics and other forms of social thought in order to fulfil its obligations of neighbor-love. Christian social ethics, in short, has two sources, one based upon natural reason and the other based upon revelation. While *agape* is free to enter into alliances and coalitions with all forms of philosophy or social science which provide insight into human need and the empirical conditions which determine such needs, love exercises a sovereign role in relationship to all such knowledge.

Like his concept of human nature, Ramsey's concept of community also rests fundamentally upon the biblical notion of covenant. Human beings are created in and for covenant relationships with their fellow-humanity.

This means that they are created for community based upon obedient love. Because human nature has been corrupted by the Fall, however, all persons are self-centered apart from grace, and all natural forms of community are broken and distorted by sin. Nevertheless, man still lives in community, and the work of natural justice is a work of reason rooted in created albeit fallen nature. Since the task of Christian social ethics is to meet the societal needs of the neighbor in particular historical communities, obedient-love necessarily turns to rational and empirical analyses of these needs and the conditions for their fulfilment. The strategy of Christian ethics--viz., neighbor-love--is determined on the basis of revelation; the tactics of love, on the other hand, are limited, or conditioned, by available societal options. Not only is natural justice essential for the concrete embodiment of agape in the institutions and structures of community; it also sheds light upon the biblical notions of covenant and justice through its focus upon the historical relationships out of which the biblical concepts arose.

On the basis of the biblical idea of the covenant, Christian social ethics affirms the equality of worth and rights of all members of the community based upon creation. At the same time, it directs the individual bearers of such rights toward the creation of a community based on obedient love--i.e., upon a love which is obedient to God and directed toward the neighbor. Since the sinfulness of all persons is presupposed, there is strong emphasis upon the restraint of evil (sin) in the biblical understanding of justice. This negative task of justice is prerequisite to the attainment of more positive forms of community based on equality, freedom, and love.

Since obedience to the covenant does not in itself contain all that is needed for the development of a social ethic, Christian ethics must turn to rational and empirical analyses of society in order to learn concretely what the neighbor-in-community needs and also how these needs can best be met. Hence, in Basic

<u>Christian Ethics</u> Ramsey turns to Rousseau for a clearer understanding of the need for the restraint of evil and the source of obligation in political society.[78] Rousseau's notion of the "general will" rested upon the assumption that an originally good human nature had become corrupted through egoism and that this corruption was perpetuated through unjust and tyrannical social institutions. The primary purpose of his <u>Social Contract</u> was to explain why political restraint is legitimate. The answer to this question, Rousseau believed, rests both in the nature of society and in corrupted human nature. Society, he declared, came into existence when free individuals first contracted together to form an association based upon the "general will." The purposes of such an association were to provide protection against injustice and foster the attainment of the common good. In order to achieve these ends, coercion was needed to restrain evil; moreover, such coercion was justified both by the consent of the governed and by the selfishness, or partiality, of particular wills.

While Ramsey rejects the voluntarism in Rousseau's concept of society, he nevertheless finds it more compatible with the biblical notion of covenant than concepts of community based upon the utilitarianism of Bentham and Mill. Two elements in Rousseau's contract theory of society, in particular, are important for Ramsey, viz., the notion of sovereignty as the source of authority and the notion of generality as the criterion of just law. Although Christian ethics must reject the idea of self-obligation--obedience of each member of the association to the self alone--as idolatrous, the notion of the authority of the general will confirms the primacy of obedience and obligation as the basic bonds of society. These bonds, Ramsey believes, represent the fundamental relationships in the biblical concept of society. Moreover, Rousseau's appeal to the principle of generality both in the derivation and in the application of just law constitutes a political expression of the biblical principle of human equality. It also provides the basis for the social grounding of civil rights in the general rule of law and in the priority of the common good rather than individualistically in autonomous selves.[79]

In addition, the idealistic social philosophy of Rousseau and Josiah Royce provides a necessary corrective to existentialist conceptions of sin through its insights both into the social roots and into the institutionalized forms of sin. In short, Ramsey writes, "Idealistic as well as Christian democratic theory is ... grounded in the proposition, 'Man's capacity for justice makes democracy possible; but man's inclination to injustice makes democracy necessary.'"[80] In both, man's capacity for justice and a regard for the common good are combined with a recognition of human sinfulness. In this way idealistic political theory, through its concept of the general will, provides a ready ally for Christian love as the latter goes about its task of developing a political ethic. More particularly, Rousseau's notion of the general will provides a rational justification of democracy that is confirmed by a religious understanding of contemporary political community in terms of covenant relationships.

As noted above, however, in whatever alliance love makes with this or any other social philosophy the former always remains sovereign; hence, it criticizes and corrects the latter where their conceptions of human nature, of justice, and of the final source of authority run counter to the biblical notions of man as creature and as sinner, of the sovereignty of God, and of the requirements of justice based on love. Moreover, love is not forever wedded to idealistic social philosophy; it is free to form similar alliances with other forms of social and political theory which may offer more adequate understandings of political reality, provided only that the biblical understanding of humanity-in-community is not subverted.

Since the appearance of <u>Basic Christian Ethics</u>, Ramsey has refined and developed his concept of community in the context of his treatment of a variety of pressing social issues, including racial desegregation, war, and medical ethics. In his analysis of moral problems in these fields, he has given increased attention to the social and moral bonds of community. In particular, he has stressed the notion of covenant as the basic form of our humanity, and he has used this concept as a basis for elaborating the relationships of love to natural justice in the field of Christian social ethics. Generally speaking, during this period natural justice has assumed a larger role in his ethics, and he has moved increasingly toward a transformationist conception of Christian ethics, viz., "Christ transforming natural law."[81]

According to Ramsey, the most critical moral problem which contemporary man faces is the problem of community.[82] This, rather than the lack of agreement concerning specific moral criteria, constitutes the most fundamental problem of our age; for in the absence of community there is no common source of moral authority. In some respects the answer which Ramsey gives to this question is similar to that of Augustine in The City of God. Man has both a temporal and an eternal end, and it is only his citizenship in the eternal city which prevents the earthly commonwealth from being absolutized. It is his destiny for an eternal end that prevents the reduction of man to his contribution to the common good of the earthly city. In other respects, however, Ramsey's concept of community differs sharply from that of Augustine and is more nearly akin to that of Hobbes and Rousseau.[83] Like the contractualists, Ramsey holds that society is based upon the agreement of individuals to be a people, i.e., a covenant community based upon a common commitment to a common future. Sovereignty and society--the acceptance of a common authority and community--come into being simultaneously. Such a contract--or covenant--becomes the basis of law and obligation among the members of society. For Augustine, on the other hand, society is an association of people joined together by an object of common love. Such a concept of community is fundamentally teleological rather than deontological; it is oriented toward the pursuit of a common good rather than toward the fulfilment of obligations into which people have entered in the very constitution of community. According to Ramsey, the basic bond which holds society together is the mutual commitment (covenant) to be with and for one's fellowmen, not an agreement to be with the latter for the sake of the pursuit of some other good. In the biblical understanding of community, such commitment or agreement is based upon a recognition of the sovereignty of God; in contract theories of society, it is based upon the will of the people and presupposes a prior sovereign autonomy on the part of individuals.

Insofar as Ramsey's concept of community is based upon the biblical idea of covenant, it is essentially a Christological, eschatological idea. For him the basic problem of Christian social ethics is how this normative conception of community is related to historical communities. "As long as God's covenant endures," he writes, "human community cannot rightly be grounded in anything else (than obedient love)."[84] When Ramsey moves from this normative Christological statement to an analysis of historical communities, however, he is forced to deal more concretely with the relationships of love to natural forms of justice. In this context, Augustine's notion of the "two cities" expressing two radically different claims upon man aptly describes human life in its historical form. Significantly, however, unlike H. Richard Niebuhr, Ramsey does not interpret Augustine as a "transformationist" but rather as a "dualist" in his understanding of the relationship between Christ and culture.[85]

Brief reference to two social problems which Ramsey discusses will indicate the way in which he attempts to address the problems of community and moral authority in contemporary society. These problems are war and medical ethics. In <u>War and the Christian Conscience</u> Ramsey argues that the primary source of the just war doctrine in the Christian tradition is neighbor-love. As the size and influence of the church increased after the time of Constantine, Christians came to see that resistance to evil for the sake of justice might sometimes be required of them as a service of love. The just war doctrine, which was developed over the succeeding centuries, represented an effort on the part of the church to spell out both the requirements and the limitations governing Christian participation in warfare as an expression of Christ-like love. While the development of this theory was influenced by the just-war tradition in classical thought, neighbor-love provided the final justification and requirement for participation in military service; it also constituted the main source of the carefully circumscribed limits which were placed upon Christians in combat. As a result of this effort on the part of Christians to define the moral limits of warfare in terms of agape, even the secular just war tradition was infused and partially transformed by "new perspectives, limits, and principles" based on love. Such transformation is particularly evidenced by the general acceptance of the prohibitions of indiscriminate killing and of direct killing of the innocent as requirements of justice in the conduct of war.[86] While there is some movement toward a conversionist ethic in this work, Ramsey sees too much "dualism" between charity and natural justice to adopt the former position as his own. "It is difficult to speak with sobriety," he writes, "about 'Christ transforming culture' and converting the works of men."[87] Hence, he opts for a basically Lutheran conception of polarity between loyalty to Christ and responsibility to uphold the orders of society. Ramsey traces this polarity to a basic duality between God's relationship to the world as Creator and his relationship as Redeemer.

In The Patient as Person Ramsey seeks to address a number of problems in medical ethics through use of the concept of covenant. While he describes this study as "a book about ethics written by a Christian ethicist," it is addressed primarily to the broader human community rather than to those who share the Christian faith.[88] In the context of the pluralism of contemporary society, Ramsey finds the idea of "covenant" to be a key concept which provides a basis for "fundamental dialogue" between Christian and rational forms of ethics without surrendering the distinctively Christian concern of charity. Thus, it is a key mediating term which raises the ethical question in terms of the claims to loyalty, fidelity, and faithfulness which human life places upon human life by reason of our common humanity.

The chief task of medical ethics, according to Ramsey, is that of reconciling the welfare of the individual with the welfare of mankind.[89] In this task both general and theological ethics are joined together in a common endeavor. Both seek to identify the requirements--the actions and the abstentions--of justice which are rooted in the covenant relationships that are inherent in the practice of medicine. Both seek to humanize the relationships between the physician and the patient, the researcher and the subject; at critical points of difference, however, "the biblical norm of <u>fidelity to covenant</u>" is finally normative.[90] Both rational justice and charity make it necessary to spell out the faithfulness claims which are implicit in the relationships of human life with human life at various stages from conception to death. Since these relationships are defined in terms of covenant-fidelity, Ramsey's medical ethics is also fundamentally deontological. It is primarily concerned with the fulfilment of obligations to known individuals. Here, again, teleological concern for future-directed goods, either of present neighbors or of future generations, is strongly subordinated to the equal protection of each individual member of the human community. Not only is the humanity of each individual at stake in the honoring of such claims to fidelity; the humanity of all future generations is at stake as well.

Both in his use of natural justice and in his appeal to the covenantal nature of community, Ramsey has attempted to provide a more adequate foundation for Christian social ethics, and he has done so essentially on Christological grounds. In <u>Basic Christian Ethics</u> he indicated the need for such development because <u>agape</u> does not by itself contain sufficient resources for this task. In that work he turned to philosophical idealism; in his subsequent writings he has made increasing use of natural law and covenant ethics. As justification for the use of these resources, he has appealed to the concept of creation, but this idea has remained undeveloped in relationship to his ethics as a whole. More fundamentally, the basic Christological structure of his ethics in the earlier book appears to preclude the development of a transformationist ethic grounded both in creation and in redemption.[91] Yet this is precisely the direction in which Ramsey has attempted to move.

While Ramsey has drawn upon the natural law tradition in Roman Catholicism in relationship both to his political and his medical ethics, he has not developed a theory of natural law upon which to base the latter.[92] In Catholic thought natural law is grounded in creation; as such it points to the moral conditions which are necessary for the attainment of the common good. Natural law is, therefore, a resource not only for human preservation but also for human fulfilment. In his attempt to provide a theological base for the work of natural justice, Ramsey has, however, turned to Barth's doctrine of the relationship between creation and covenant.[93] For Barth this relationship is formal; for Ramsey, on the other hand, it is more dialectical. Thus, in actuality, in his attempt to base the work of natural justice upon creation, Ramsey resembles Brunner much more closely than he resembles Barth. For Brunner and Ramsey, our created human nature remains a partial albeit broken expression of our humanity.

To say that creation is the external basis of the possibility of covenant means, for Ramsey, that natural justice is the form in which our humanity is preserved and partially embodied. Natural justice includes both those systemic relationships into which we are born and those which we enter by choice. It includes familial, professional, economic, and political structures and relationships through which human life is sustained and preserved. Understood in these terms, the relationship of natural justice to the fulfilment of human life is viewed primarily in terms of the preservation of creation for redemption through Christ. Participation in this task is a necessary part of Christian ethics, but it remains in fundamental tension with the demands of _agape_. The motivation for Christian participation in the work of natural justice is that of neighbor-love; given the reality of human sinfulness, love expresses itself primarily in the restraint of evil (order, law, protection). Love does not, however, find many resources for positive justice--i.e., the fulfilment of the promise of covenant--in the continuing work of creation.

At times Ramsey clearly intends a more positive relationship between natural justice and _agape_ than the foregoing analysis implies. Indeed, he describes the position which he develops in Christian Ethics and the Sit-In as "love-transformed-justice";[94] and in Nine Modern Moralists he adopts the position of "Christ transforming natural law" as normative for Christian ethics.[95] In these writings as elsewhere love remains the controlling norm in his ethics, but now he intends it to reign by "redirecting," "reshaping," "renewing," and "reinvigorating" the natural justice which is already present and which shows love "the way to the action that should be done or not done."[96] Nevertheless, both the basis and the role of natural justice remain ambiguous in his ethics.

Like his concept of obedient love, Ramsey's notion of natural justice is basically deontological. While he recognizes a place for the "common good" in theological ethics, the idea itself is subordinated to deontology. It is rooted more in covenant than in an inclination toward the highest good grounded in created human nature. Concern for consequences and future-oriented goods--even the common good--is subordinated to fidelity to present individuals. In his social ethics, the emphasis falls upon order rather than freedom, upon the preserving work of justice rather than upon the fulfilment of the possibilities and potentialities in created human nature. Not only is preservation of our created human nature prerequisite for covenant; preservation remains the primary work (and aim) of Christian love in the field of social ethics.

In contrast to Ramsey, Gustafson's concept of community is grounded fundamentally in an analysis of human experience. Whereas Ramsey begins with a Christological concept of community based upon covenant (obedient love) and supplements this idea with resources based on reason, Gustafson moves from a phenomenological-sociological analysis of the empirical structures, or patterns, of community to a theological interpretation of the latter based on Christian faith. Viewed in the context of human experience, the patterns of personhood and those of community are seen to be interdependent. Moreover, the moral conditions which are necessary for the fulfilment of the community are essentially the same as those which are prerequisite for the fulfilment of persons. In both instances, Gustafson's approach to ethics is basically teleological rather than deontological. Moreover, his analysis of morality is more comprehensive and more richly textured in terms of the whole range of goods, virtues, and obligations which are imbedded in moral experience than is true of most Protestant ethicists.

Not only is Gustafson's empirical analysis of the historical forms of personal and community life based in experience; so also is his theological interpretation of both. Moreover, the relationship between these two approaches is basically dialogical. Each informs the other, although theology provides the ultimate normative framework for understanding the meaning of our humanity and our common life. The truth and the adequacy of theological claims about human life and community are tested in part by their capacity to account for available empirical data; value judgments about the latter based upon reason are, in turn, tested by insights drawn from theology and more ultimately from the faith of a historical community of believers. Gustafson's dialogical method of relating the empirical and theological approaches to community is essentially conversionist. It presupposes a basic unity between the on-going action of God as Creator in nature and in the processes of human history, on the one hand, and his work as Redeemer in the renewing, reordering, and redirection of these processes, on the other.

Gustafson's concept of God is fundamentally teleological; the divine teleology is even now evident in the actualization of goods and values in history and in the emergence of new possibilities for the well-being of creation.[97]

This dialogical approach to community has been present throughout Gustafson's writings. It informs both his understanding of the church as a community of faith and his interpretation of secular community.[98] In each instance, both sociological and theological analysis confirm the interdependence of individuals and the community. Neither of the latter is reducible to the other, but neither exists apart from the other. Reference to the essay, "A Theology of Christian Community," will serve to illustrate the manner in which Gustafson bases his interpretation of community upon both sociological and theological perspectives.[99] This essay is particularly important in the context of the present study because it approaches the question of community from the standpoint of the social mission of the church.

A sociological analysis of community reveals three important aspects of group life: cultural ethos, interpersonal relationships, and institutions.[100] Not only do these constitute forms of collective life; they also constitute the forms in which and through which human existence as persons is sustained and nurtured. Interpreted theologically, they define the social patterns of God's relationship to the world, the forms through which his purposes in creation are accomplished in human history. Moreover, God is related to the common life in essentially the same ways in all three aspects of community. That is to say, his purposes and activity cannot be reduced to a single mode in any one aspect of community, for the structures which he uses for the realization of his creative purposes are the same as those which he uses in the ordering and redemption of humanity. It is through these forms that the potentiality for creative human achievements is both given and realized; it is also through these patterns of community that human life is sustained and evil is restrained; it is likewise through them that God creates possibilities for new and better qualities of life, both for individuals and for groups.

Not only do the cultural ethos, interpersonal relationships, and institutions define the empirical, social patterns of divine activity; they also define the social forms of human moral activity as well.[101] They constitute the patterns of mutual service, responsibility, and obligation in which and through which moral action takes place. In view of the interdependence between individuals and the community, it is impossible to distinguish sharply between personal and impersonal relationships and to reduce moral action to the former. A sociological understanding of the nature and function of institutions also makes clear the place of duty in the life of the community. In institutions laws and rules are needed to define the obligations which individuals have toward each other and the duties which they owe to institutions. For Gustafson, this does not mean, however, that the Christian has an unconditional obligation to obey the rules and laws of a particular institution; it means, rather, an understanding of the needs which are served by the latter and the obligation to accept responsibility for political and economic institutions as a form of obedience to God and service to the neighbor.

Implicit in Gustafson's analysis of community from the double perspective of sociology and theology is a comprehensive conception of human life and moral action. The divine will is related both to the individual and to the institutional, both to the personal and to the impersonal, dimensions of culture; it includes both the creative impulses of humanity and the need for preservation of that which is given in creation. While institutions are essential to the on-going life of communities, the "private" and personal spheres must be protected not only for the enrichment and sustenance of individuals as persons, but also for the sake of society itself. Like his concept of the moral agent, Gustafson's concept of community is fundamentally teleological. Like the moral life of individuals, the moral relationships of communities are most adequately understood in terms of virtue rather than in terms of obligation.

Gustafson's approach to community resembles that of H. Richard Niebuhr more than that of Ramsey in at least two important respects. First, both Niebuhr and Gustafson ground their analyses concretely in the experience of human sociality. Ramsey, on the other hand, begins with a distinctively Christian conception of community based upon the biblical idea of covenant as obligation. Hence, for Niebuhr and for Gustafson there is more room for human freedom and a larger role for goods, virtue, and responsibility in the moral relationships of community life. In the second place, in their writings both Niebuhr and Gustafson have given primary attention to the moral relationships upon which community is based rather than to particular moral issues in politics, economics, and the family.[102] Ramsey, on the other hand, has dealt more directly with a wide range of social problems; in this context he has been primarily concerned to develop and defend a morality of right means. Gustafson has extended and deepened Niebuhr's analysis of community by his greater use of the sociology of institutions, whereas Niebuhr was primarily concerned with interpersonal relationships. Ramsey, on the other hand, has given more attention to politics and war. Thus he has dealt more concretely with justice and power as issues in social ethics.

While the basis for a social ethic is present in the work of all three of these men, the former has remained largely undeveloped in Niebuhr and Gustafson. For Gustafson, the most basic task of theological ethics is the development of a framework and a method of moral deliberation. This is the ethicist's primary contribution to the community's effort to resolve the more immediate problems of society. To be sure, the responsibility of the ethicist does not end with the construction of theory; however, in the formation of public policy the primary role of the ethicist is that of moral analyst rather than social strategist. A number of factors have contributed to Gustafson's more analytic approach to social ethics. Among these are the plurality of goods, obligations, and virtues which he sees in moral experience and the priority which he gives to virtue over obligation in ethics. This pluralism of values and claims often issues in irreconcilable conflicts in daily life, thus making the existence of single answers to such conflicts uncertain.

In his effort to develop a more systematic structure for Protestant ethics, Gustafson has been strongly influenced by the tradition of Roman Catholic moral theology. This influence is particularly evident in his teleology, in his emphasis upon virtue, and in the role which he assigns to reason in the work of culture. As previously noted, Gustafson has focused upon the values and virtues which are requisite for the moral life both of persons and of communities. Just as faith, hope, and love are necessary for the sustenance and fulfilment of human life in interpersonal relationships, so they are also--along with many other moral and spiritual conditions--essential for the maintenance and enrichment of human community. Other moral conditions which are requisite for human life in both its personal and its communal forms include freedom, justice, and order.[103] In part, these virtues point the moral agent toward other individuals; in part, they define qualities of the common life in both its personal and its impersonal forms. They define attitudes and dispositions of the moral agent both toward other individuals and toward the common life in society.

The place which Gustafson assigns to reason in culture, including its role in ethics, is similar to that which it has in Thomistic ethics.[104] The work of culture is fundamentally a work of human reason. While Gustafson does not himself adopt the terminology of natural law, he believes that certain generalizations can be made about "moral values and principles" which provide the necessary conditions for both personal and social forms of human life.[105] Such generalizations differ from classic natural law theory, however, in that they are inferences based upon experience rather than deductions from an ontological order of being.

Although natural reason has a larger and more integral function in Gustafson's ethics than is true of Protestant ethicists generally, there is a certain ambiguity concerning the relationships of nature to grace in his thought. Gustafson provides a strong basis for natural reason in his concept of creation; what remains unclear, however, is the extent to which his ethics is finally conversionist rather than synthesist. Like Karl Rahner, he rejects the tendency in traditional Catholic thought to locate the work of grace hierarchically above nature so that the former had no significant impact on human moral activity.[106] Gustafson interprets Rahner as a conversionist; and, while he differs theologically with the latter at a number of points, he finds Rahner's developmental view of natural law, his inclusion of nature (creation) within grace (redemption), and his inclusion of the natural *telos* of human life within its supernatural *telos* generally consistent with his own teleological, transformationist position.[107]

Yet a fundamental ambivalence regarding the relationship of nature to grace in Gustafson's ethics remains. Presumably, he would demur from Rahner's suggestion that all persons who act morally--on the basis of a natural law that is itself an expression of grace and can be known and acted upon by all--are anonymous Christians; yet the extent and manner in which the moral action of such persons would be further transformed by Christian faith and discipleship remain problematic, particularly in the area of social ethics. When Gustafson has addressed the question of the distinctiveness of Christian ethics, he has done so primarily in terms of virtue, i.e., the character of the moral agent. In Can Ethics Be Christian? he sought to articulate a transformationist conception of Christian ethics in which the latter is in certain respects distinctive without being exclusive. In that study he noted three major aspects of morality which are qualified by religious experience and belief: the reasons for being moral, the character of the moral agent, and the points of reference (religious symbols and moral principles and values, for example) used to determine conduct.[108]

In his analysis of the moral life of individual Christians in the foregoing essay, Gustafson has made a strong case for a conversionist interpretation of Christian ethics. The case for such a conversionist interpretation of culture is not so clear, however; for here one is dealing not just with the impact of religious beliefs upon those who hold them but with the participation of all members of a community in its common life. Here the values and decisions of Christians are--or should be--shaped by their ultimate religious beliefs--by the convictions which they hold about "what God is enabling and requiring them to be and to do," by their ultimate loyalty to God, and by their moral heritage. What remains unclear, however, is the basis and significance of the similarity--or coincidence--between a theocentric ethic and an ethic based upon reason (nature). At times, the former appears to differ substantially from the latter; at other times, the differences between the two appear quite minimal.[109] Despite the universality of human sinfulness, for Gustafson human nature remains fundamentally oriented toward the good. The work of culture as the natural end of human life is included within the divine teleology. Culture is fundamentally a task of reason, and man is free and able to participate in the creation of a new and better future. Christians do this intentionally as those who are "co-actors" with God--as "imitators" of God--and as those who are accountable to him.[110] Others do so on the basis of the divine ordering of creation and providence. In both instances the external form of action may be the same; however, from the perspective of an ethic of virtue, the moral quality of the latter differs significantly in respect to the underlying motivation and intentionality of the agents.

Whereas Ramsey sought to reconcile the claims of the individual with those of the community through a deontological interpretation of covenant, Gustafson appeals to the notion of "the common good" to establish a harmony between the well-being of the individual and that of the community. As noted above, Gustafson extends this concept to include the fulfilment of creation as a whole. The common good also includes the well-being of future generations. This means, for example, that Gustafson is more open to medical experimentation with human subjects than is Ramsey, who is primarily concerned with the protection of individuals now alive. For Gustafson, on the other hand, the weight is upon human initiative and the freedom "to explore, develop, expand, alter, initiate, (and) intervene in the course of life in the world."[111] Such teleology is grounded theologically in Gustafson's conception of God as the Creator who wills and actively seeks the well-being of all that he has created. While Gustafson recognizes that the notion of the "common good" is both a relational and a distributive concept, it serves a largely directional function in his ethics rather than providing a precise way of harmonizing the well-being of the individual with that of the community.

In so far as the notion of the common good is basically a teleological concept, the former aptly symbolizes the distinctiveness of Gustafson's conception of the relationship of the individual to the community in contradistinction to Ramsey's deontological conception of covenant and H. Richard Niebuhr's interpretation of the latter in terms of responsibility. Although Gustafson's teleological emphasis upon the well-being of creation does not in itself rule out the development of general moral rules and principles in social ethics, he has not himself generally moved in this direction. Indeed, he clearly recognizes the need for such development in view of the divine governance and the reality of human sin.[112] For him, however, the work of social justice is essentially an on-going task which involves the weighing of values as well as obligations in the light of the dynamic nature of human history. Hence, his method of moral reasoning does not allow the same degree of certainty and universalization as that of a person such as Ramsey.

7

TOWARD A CHRISTIAN SOCIAL ETHIC

The primary purpose of the present essay has been to analyze and compare the approaches of representative Protestant ethicists to the task of social ethics. Based upon Gibson Winter's phenomenological study of human sociality, the following three elements were identified as essential components for any social ethic: a conception of the good (criteria of moral judgment), some notion of human agency, and some conception of the role and function of social institutions. Phenomenologically, these elements define the empirical structure, or form, of human moral experience in relationship to society. Taken together, they provide a useful framework for testing the relevance and adequacy of particular forms of social ethics.

The present study has been concerned with the debate in contemporary Protestant ethics between those writers who have attempted to base their social ethics exclusively upon Christology and those who have attempted to base the latter upon broader theological foundations. Our primary aim has been to examine the relationship between the ethical thought of these persons and their underlying theological assumptions. In particular, we have examined the extent to which the latter have determined the openness of individual ethicists to empirical analyses of human nature and social institutions.

In this concluding chapter an attempt will be made to compare and evaluate the strengths and weaknesses of Christological and theistic forms of ethics. Such an evaluation will be made in terms of the adequacy and coherence of their respective accounts of reason and revelation, the nature of the good (moral criteria), human agency, and social institutions. Special attention will also be given to the problem of social justice and to the manner in which the various writers move from theory to practice.

The Role Of Empirical Reason In Social Ethics

Ethics is a critical study of morality. It includes both the personal and the social forms in which our humanity is experienced or expressed. As a critical discipline its aim is to provide a normative evaluation of moral experience. Such evaluation presupposes moral criteria which rest ultimately upon certain fundamentally religious beliefs about human nature, the world, and ultimate reality.

Our purpose in drawing upon Winter's phenomenology of sociality was to identify the basic structures of human existence in society. The latter is fundamentally a task for the social sciences. Although Winter defines social ethics in essentially teleological terms as "the expression of ultimate commitments in the shaping of man's future," the structures which he identifies can also be interpreted either in deontological or in responsibilist terms or in a combination of all three images. In its empirical quest, social ethics is a search for the structures, or forms, of human existence in community. In itself such empirical investigation is not social ethics; yet the former is prerequisite for the latter. In addition to a description of the fundamental structures of human sociality, social ethics includes a critique of the concrete forms in which the latter appear based upon a normative conception of human nature. Such a normative concept is grounded ultimately in faith. Empirical form and normative criteria are united in moral experience. The one cannot be reduced to the other; yet the two are inseparable. Methodologically speaking, the most fundamental problem of ethics is how the relationship between the descriptive and normative dimensions of morality can be most adequately understood.

Debate concerning the proper starting point for theological ethics is essentially a debate about the question of authority in the moral life of Christians. For Barth, Lehmann, and Bonhoeffer this question is decisive. For them Christian ethics rests exclusively upon God's revelation in Jesus Christ. This revelation determines both the structure and the content of Christian ethics as well as the method of decision making which the latter employs. Insofar as these writers are consistent, their social ethics depends entirely upon revelation--through the command of God (Barth), through the activity of the Holy Spirit discerned in the <u>koinonia</u> (Lehmann), or through the reality of God in Christ (Bonhoeffer). While there are observable patterns of human life in culture--forms of fellow-humanity (Barth), mandates (Bonhoeffer), and events which have symbolic meaning as signs of God's redemptive action in the world (Lehmann), these patterns are known Christologically rather than through philosophical reflection and empirical investigation. For these theologians, the fundamental structure of Christian ethics precludes any significant role either for moral philosophy or for the social sciences in Christian ethics. This is true both of their conceptions of human nature and of their conceptions of social institutions.

Brunner and Reinhold Niebuhr, on the other hand, base their ethics upon the joint foundations of reason and revelation in Christ. For them God's will is disclosed most fully in his redemptive action in Christ; but since the God who reveals himself in Christ is also the Creator, his will is also manifest in his works of creation, and natural man has some capacity for justice. As we have seen, however, Brunner's concept of human nature is essentially personalistic (I-thou) rather than social; love as the norm of personal relationships stands in sharp antinomy to justice as the requirement of human life in community. In short, both the structures and the law of man's natural communities--"the orders of creation"--remain finally alien to Christian love although Christians are summoned to participate in the former in obedience to the command of the Creator. For Reinhold Niebuhr, particularly in his later writings, the antimony between love and justice is less sharp than it is for Brunner. The norm both of man's individual and of his collective life is the sacrificial love of Christ revealed on the Cross. While there are partial embodiments of such love in human history, particularly in interpersonal relationships, agape remains an impossibility for social groups. In collective human life justice represents the highest possible approximation to agape, but the former always stands under the judgment of the latter. For both Brunner and Reinhold Niebuhr, there is a strong polarity between justice and love. For Brunner this relationship is conceived in basically dualistic terms; for Niebuhr, the relation is more dialectical.

Like Brunner and Reinhold Niebuhr, Ramsey also constructs his ethics upon the double foundations of Christology and reason. For him that which is basic in Christian ethics rests upon the love revealed in Christ; that which is secondary rests upon natural reason. Ramsey attempts to overcome the dualism in Brunner and Niebuhr by providing a more positive role for justice, including natural justice, in relationship to agape. Christian love includes justice measured by the standard of God's righteousness. In contrast to Reinhold Niebuhr, Ramsey maintains that agape is neighbor-centered rather than sacrificial; hence, it can be more fully embodied in history than Niebuhr perceived. Such embodiment, moreover, entails the development of rules and moral principles which express the concrete meaning of agape in practice. These rules, or principles, are derived deductively from agape; hence, Christian ethics is fundamentally an ethic of obedience to known obligations.

In contrast to all of the foregoing writers, H. Richard Niebuhr and Gustafson make moral experience the starting point for ethics. For both, the choice of this starting point is critical; it determines the fundamental structure of their ethical analysis. It provides a basis for understanding both the continuity and the discontinuity between Christian and non-

Christian forms of morality. It provides a basis in experience for distinguishing between the totality and the particularity of Christian ethics, between the roles of reason and revelation in theological ethics. Christian ethics begins with an analysis of moral experience as a whole because it is here that the constituent parts of morality are seen together in their concreteness and in their interrelationships--faith and human action, the individual and the communal dimensions of human existence, creation and salvation, law and liberty, power and justice. Such analysis is not itself ethics, however; rather, the former is a preparation for the normative task of the latter. Not only does such analysis reveal the fundamental structure of moral existence and moral activity; it also poses the basic issues which are the proper subject for ethical reflection. Niebuhr considered <u>The Responsible Self</u> a prolegomenon to Christian ethics and described it as "an essay in Christian moral philosophy."[1]

In order to comprehend the significance of Niebuhr's claim that the proper starting point for ethics is moral experience, it will be useful to compare his "philosophical" approach to ethics with a phenomenological mode of inquiry broadly conceived.[2] Such a comparison will serve to clarify the structure of Niebuhr's own thought and assist in differentiating the latter from that of the other writers whom we have been considering. It may also suggest ways in which Niebuhr's ethics can be extended and developed with a more intentional focus on the special task of social ethics.

<u>The Responsible Self</u> is neither philosophical nor phenomenological in the narrower, professionalized senses of these terms; yet, in the broader sense it is intentionally philosophical and implicitly phenomenological. Both as regards its aim and also its approach it may be compared with Maurice Mandelbaum's <u>Phenomenology of Moral Experience</u>. The aim of both authors is to analyze human moral experience. According to Mandelbaum, "The essential conviction of a phenomenological approach [to ethics] is ... the insistence that

an adequate moral theory must be based upon, and remain faithful to, the facts of moral experience."[3] This is a fundamental conviction which informed Niebuhr's approach to ethics as a whole. It was expressed precisely in his formulation of the prior question of ethics, viz., "What is going on?"[4] In Niebuhr's case commitment to the primacy of experience was derived more from such thinkers as William James, George Herbert Mead, Troeltsch, Weber, Bergson, and what Niebuhr called "the theologians of experience" than it was from any school of phenomenology.[5] Like James and also like Mead, Niebuhr was concerned with the structure of the self as a fundamental form of human experience. Like them he also believed that the primary data for understanding the structure of selfhood are to be found in experience. For Niebuhr, experience includes both moral and religious experience as well as those psychological and sociological patterns of behavior which are empirically observable.

This concern for the fundamental structures of human existence is basic to H. Richard Niebuhr's approach both to theology and to ethics. It is expressed not only in his understanding of the self as social but also in his relational concept of value, in his idea of the triadic form of faith (self-other-cause), in his understanding of faith as trust and fidelity, and in his concept of responsibility as the underlying structure of moral experience. Niebuhr's search for structures is akin to the phenomenological search for general essences (or universals) in so far as both are concerned with the universal rather than the particularistic aspects of selfhood, faith, value, and responsibility. These forms of relationships are fundamental for Niebuhr because they are grounded in being. Special revelation and ethics based upon the faith which such revelation calls forth may transform, or re-direct, the natural forms of faith and morality that are rooted in these structures, but revelation does not negate the latter. In an address entitled "The Triad of Faith," Niebuhr quotes Jonathan Edwards with approval: "Love is a structure, it appears, and when I inquire into the meaning of love the structure of human existence also comes into my view though that structure of existence appears in broken and somewhat negative form."[6] This reference of Niebuhr to Edwards is particularly significant in view of their common recognition of the goodness of universal being and the role of the aesthetic, or the fitting, in ethics. For both theologians the search for the structures of human existence is integrally related to the search for the structures of true virtue and/or responsibility.[7]

While descriptive analysis of human moral experience is fundamental to the task of ethics for Niebuhr, he does not use such analysis to establish universal moral standards on empirical and rational grounds. Rather, this approach provides a way of dealing with relativism in ethics through the disclosure of objectively relational structures of being in which moral values and claims are grounded. Viewed in light of the historical character of human existence, the quest for universal definitions of the good and obligation is finally abstract and idealistic. At the same time, however, viewed in terms of our common human interdependence moral goods and duties are seen to be objective rather than subjective, relational rather than idealistic, concrete rather than abstract. In so far as the historical and social nature of human existence is recognized, the self acknowledges that it is responsible for its moral decisions; moreover, the self as agent is responsible not simply for obedience to some command or law or for the pursuit of an ideal but, more fundamentally, for the content of the decision itself.

In a similar way, Niebuhr's insistence that moral theory is finally accountable to human experience provided a way of overcoming many of the false dichotomies and contradictions which he found in various forms of theological ethics. Analysis of human experience points, he believed, not so much to dichotomies as to polarities in the moral life. It points, for example, to the "polarity" between the "is" and the "ought," between law and freedom, and between institutional and personal relationships. Stated another way, it provides a method for recovering the richness, the complexity, and the multi-dimensionality of moral relationships. It discloses the presence together of value, duty, virtue, and responsibility in morality.

Like H. Richard Niebuhr, Gustafson also begins his ethics with an analysis of moral experience. His approach to ethics, including theological ethics, is similarly phenomenological. Analysis of human experience reveals the basic questions of all ethics. It also discloses the fundamental relationships and processes which are prerequisite for moral decisions and action to take place. Both the method and the form of Christian ethics are the same as those of philosophical ethics; the former differs from the latter only in content. As in the case of Niebuhr, Gustafson does not attempt to derive universal moral standards of value and duty from such rational and empirical analysis. Rather, his purpose is to provide an analytical structure in terms of which the component elements of moral experience and the factors which shape these components can best be understood. For him, also, Christian ethics represents a transformation of the moral life rather than the substitution of an entirely new and different form of morality based on revelation.

While Gustafson and H. Richard Niebuhr both begin their ethics with moral experience, both have focused primarily upon the personal and interpersonal aspects of the moral life. Both show a strong appreciation of the methods and insights of moral philosophy; both also draw upon the social sciences for their insights into the form or structure of human life in history. Gustafson, however, goes beyond Niebuhr in the more careful attention which he gives to the psychological and sociological forces and processes which influence the shaping of character and moral decisions not only of individuals but also of communities. At points he is critical of Niebuhr's anthropology, particularly the latter's concepts of human freedom and human agency. In the end the differences between their respective views of human nature must be resolved by appeal to moral experience. This does not mean that one view will be finally vindicated and the other judged to be in error. Nor does it imply that their differences concerning the scope of human freedom and the proper phrasing of the primary question of theological ethics can be ultimately resolved through the increase of objective, empirical data. It means, rather, that moral experience is the place where moral theory, including both its empirical and rational components as well as its resources in religious faith, is ultimately tried and tested--and re-shaped. Both for Niebuhr and for Gustafson, analysis of moral experience is an ongoing process involving a continuing dialogue--or dialectic--between reason and faith as the agent attempts to understand that experience in both its universal and its particular aspects. We shall return to this issue of the testing of moral theory in terms of experience in the next section of the present chapter. First, however, a brief consideration of the relationship of Gibson Winter's Elements For a Social Ethic to Niebuhr's ethic of responsibility will serve to indicate how Niebuhr's own work might be extended to include a fuller development of a Christian social ethic based upon theistic foundations than he himself provided.

Both H. Richard Niebuhr and Winter are interested in understanding the structure of human existence. Winter's method of analysis is more intentionally phenomenological and more oriented toward the social sciences than was that of Niebuhr. In Elements For a Social Ethic Winter was primarily concerned with "the nature and structure of man as a social being."[8] In The Responsible Self, on the other hand, Niebuhr was primarily concerned with the structure of selfhood although he perceived the self as fundamentally social. Like Niebuhr, Winter was strongly influenced by George Herbert Mead's concept of the social self. However, on the basis of the work of Alfred Schutz and a number of other phenomenologists, Winter believed that Mead's interpretation of human sociality was too behavioristic and that it placed an excessive emphasis upon exteriority (social forms) over interiority (the freedom of the self) in the emergence of mind, the self, and society.[9]

In particular, a return to the world of "lived experience" reveals that the self has a larger role in the constitution of sociality than Mead allowed; hence, Winter modified Mead's concept of the "social self" through an appropriation of the concept of intentionality.[10] The resulting reformulation of Mead's schema represents greater stress on the internal dynamics of the self (its freedom and its intentionality) in comparison with the social forms in which the latter is actualized. The important point for present purposes is that Winter's phenomenological analysis shows how intentionality and social forms are united in human experience.

For Winter, the "We-relation" is the fundamental form of sociality and also of humanness.[11] The task of the social sciences is to describe the empirical forms in which such sociality and humanness have been and are expressed; the task of social ethics, on the other hand, is to evaluate these forms in terms of the possibilities which they hold for future human fulfilment. The social sciences constitute theories of "the conditioned character of practice"; social ethics represents an "evaluative interpretation of the intentional character of practice."[12] The social sciences provide an empirical characterization of events which is essential for responsible social policy, but they are not equipped to deal adequately with the subjective, intentional aspects of sociality. Hence, it becomes the task of social ethics to translate and apply scientific formulations to specific problems of society. In performing this task, ethics gives greater attention to the meaning and expression of intentionality.

For both Winter and H. Richard Niebuhr, ethical reflection is reflection from the perspective of a historical community. Winter calls his approach to social ethics "historical contextualism."[13] Like Niebuhr, he also uses the term "responsible" to describe the ethic which is based upon this approach. Similarities between the two authors include recognition of the following: the co-presence of the past, the present, and the future in moral decisions; the pregivenness of values as part of moral experience; the relational nature of value; the dialogical--or polar-- relationship between the is-ness of experience and the ought-ness of moral claims; and the relativity of all human moral judgments.[14]

Niebuhr is basically a theological ethicist. Winter is primarily interested in social ethics and social policy; hence, he leaves the theological bases of social ethics (e.g., the meaning of human fulfilment) largely undeveloped. Niebuhr analyzes the meaning of responsibility in terms of the "responsible self"; Winter's concern is with "the responsible society."[15] Yet, for Niebuhr the self is both responsible in society and responsible for the communities in which it exists. For him the structure of selfhood is triadic; it always involves the self in relationship to a community and also to some common cause. As social the self is to a large extent conditioned; yet the experience of the self is also the experience of freedom, of transcendence, and of accountability. While Niebuhr does not customarily use the phenomenological language of intentionality in speaking of the self in its freedom, he nevertheless perceives the self as oriented toward the future in intentional action and in anticipation of accountability. Similarly, he also speaks in intentional terms of the three-fold pattern of divine action in creation, governance, and redemption.

Both The Responsible Self and Elements For a Social Ethic are foundational works; as such they provide basic materials for the construction of a social ethic, but in them neither author undertakes this task. Although they reflect different theological perspectives and point to different models of moral agency and responsibility, the two essays are nevertheless complementary. Taken together they make clear the manner in which empirical and theological sources of ethics are conjoined in moral experience. In them Niebuhr and Winter demonstrate the need for both forms of inquiry. Niebuhr does this primarily by employing the method of moral philosophy although the experience which he is seeking to understand has been illuminated and shaped by the empirical sciences as well as by philosophical reflection. Winter, on the other hand, points to the need for both forms of knowledge through an analysis of the empirical and intentional aspects of public policy. Both sources of insight are necessary for an adequate understanding of human selfhood and human sociality and also of the interdependence between the two.

Theological Symbols And The Structure Of Morality

The underlying presupposition of this entire study has been that human experience provides the basis for testing the adequacy of ethical theory. Since faith and reason are united in moral experience, ethics involves an analysis of the relationships between faith and morality. In the present study we have been examining the differences between Christological and theistic forms of ethics, and we have attempted to define these differences in terms of the symbols which selected ethicists have employed in their accounts of reason and revelation, the nature and source of the good, human agency, and social institutions.[16]

In the pages which follow we shall attempt to identify and evaluate certain strengths and weaknesses in the conceptions of the good (moral criteria), human agency, and social institutions based on Christological foundations with those based upon broader, theistic foundations. The primary criteria which we will be using in such evaluation are the adequacy (intelligibility and comprehensiveness) and consistency of the different conceptions, or forms, for the task of social ethics. Within the limits of the present essay, such a comparison and evaluation cannot be exhaustive; nor does it need to be. A major purpose of our study has been to provide a critique of Christocentric ethics by examining the resources of the latter for the special task of social ethics. Our fundamental concern has been the exclusiveness of this approach to theological ethics.

In the discussion which follows, no attempt will be made to argue that Christian ethics should employ only Christological or only theistic symbols of analysis and interpretation. On the contrary, both are needed to account not only for the distinctive but also for the general in the moral activity of Christians. Both are present in Scripture and in Christian tradition. Both have been born out of the attempt on the part of believers to understand their life in relationship to God and the world. Moreover, each of the traditional symbols--e.g., sovereignty of God, image of God, covenant, law, justification by grace, freedom-- has undergone development and reinterpretation in the course of history; in addition, new symbols have emerged to give more adequate expression to faith in new historical contexts. Such re-interpretation of faith in relation to contemporary experience is a continuing process; it is also a dialogical one. It involves both the effort to understand contemporary events in terms of historical faith and also the attempt to comprehend the meaning of faith in the light of new dimensions of human experience--advances in technology, new dimensions of freedom, greater awareness of human interdependence and the limits of the earth's resources.[17]

(1) Moral Criteria

Comparison of Christological and theistic criteria of moral action includes consideration not only of their form and content but also of the manner in which they can be known. Those ethicists who define the good exclusively in Christological terms emphasize the distinctiveness of Christian ethics; those who employ more general theological symbols emphasize the similarities between the latter and other forms of morality. In the first instance, knowledge of the good is limited to those who share the Christian faith; in the second instance, the distinctive in Christian ethics is related in some way to the good which is known to reason. Viewed in terms of the pluralism of contemporary culture, it seems evident that Christians can neither understand their own responsibility in society nor participate in the shaping of the common life on the basis of Christological images and conceptions of the good alone.

As defined by H. Richard Niebuhr, an ethic of responsibility begins with the recognition that this form of moral existence is given to all persons in the very fact of our human interdependence.[18] Responsibility is not experienced fundamentally as an ought or an ideal as if it were a matter of choice; rather, it is experienced fundamentally as a <u>given</u> of our interrelatedness. Interpreted in theocentric terms an ethic of responsibility affirms that God is active in every event in a three-fold pattern of creation-governance-salvation, that all human action is action done in response to the divine action, and that as moral agents all persons are finally accountable to God. The norm of moral action is its "fittingness" as a human response to the divine action, not a duplication of what God is doing. As response to the divine action, this norm directs the <u>intention</u> of the agent away from the self toward the divine will and toward the neighbor-in-relationship to God; it locates <u>responsibility</u> for the use of one's freedom <u>in</u> the agent (accountability); and it <u>universalizes</u> the neighbor (social solidarity). If responsibility to the divine action provides the formal criterion of moral decisions in Niebuhr's ethic, the content of this norm is most fully evidenced in an understanding of the life of Israel as a covenant community, in Jesus Christ as a paradigm of responsibility, and in a transformationist conception of the relationship of Christian ethics to the moral law and natural justice. All of these themes are united in the notion of Christian ethics as response to a three-fold pattern of divine action in creation, governance, and salvation.

Like H. Richard Niebuhr, Barth, Brunner, and Bonhoeffer also use the symbol of responsibility in their interpretations of Christian ethics. For each of the last three writers, however, the structure of responsibility is defined Christologically rather than phenomenologically; it is also interpreted in terms of obedience to the command--or Word--of God as this is disclosed through Jesus Christ. For Barth, the content of the divine command is known only as it is revealed concretely through Christ in each new moment of decision. For Brunner, on the other hand, the command of God is also known indirectly through the "orders of creation"; however, the command of the Creator (justice) stands finally in sharp antinomy with the command of the Redeemer (love).

For Bonhoeffer and Reinhold Niebuhr, also, there is a certain dualism between Christological criteria of human conduct and the requirements of human life in history. In Bonhoeffer's case this dualism is grounded in an eschatological tension between the ultimate and the penultimate; for Reinhold Niebuhr, it is rooted in the radicality of *agape* revealed in the Cross of Christ. Bonhoeffer interprets responsibility in terms of obedience to the command of God which comes to humankind in the mandates; for Reinhold Niebuhr, on the other hand, *agape* is the final measure both of individual and collective life. Viewed from a radically monotheistic perspective, this dualism in the perception of the divine will results in the denial of the unity of God in his relationship to the world and the possibility of integrity, or wholeness, of the self. This does not mean that H. Richard Niebuhr's concept of sin is less radical than that of those who view the relationship of Christ to culture in terms of polarity. It means, rather, that his concept of sin rests upon a less dualistic (Brunner and Bonhoeffer) or perfectionist (Reinhold Niebuhr) understanding of the divine will and a different conception of the self and sin. For H. Richard Niebuhr, theocentric faith is closely correlated with the unity of the self and, in its negative form, with sin understood as idolatry.

Like H. Richard Niebuhr, Gustafson emphasizes the similarities between Christian ethics and ethics based on reason; and, like Niebuhr, he also interprets the relationship between the two in conversionist terms. Both of these writers emphasize the richness and variety of human relationships and a corresponding richness in value and the good. In this respect they differ from Reinhold Niebuhr and Paul Ramsey, both of whom reduce the good to a single moral principle, agape.

Not only is Gustafson critical of Barth's ethics of obedience to the divine command; he also rejects all attempts to define the good in terms of response to the divine action (Lehmann and H. Richard Niebuhr). Such attempts are presumptuous, Gustafson believes, because human beings cannot say "what God is doing"--or commanding--with the certainty or precision which such formulations imply; moreover, they reflect an excessively passive conception of human agency.[19] In contrast, Gustafson defines the good in human conduct as the "imitation of God" and as action which intends the well-being of creation.[20] Both of these symbols are theistic; both affirm a multiplicity of values rooted in creation. Good human conduct is action that is in conformity with what God is "enabling and requiring" human beings to do. Like the divine activity, it intends the preservation and fulfilment of creation out of gratitude to God. Understood in terms of theocentric piety and vision, obedience to God means cooperation with the divine governance in the fulfilment of God's purposes.[21]

Compared with H. Richard Niebuhr, Gustafson's ethic is teleological, rather than responsibilist; it allows greater room for human autonomy; and it provides a larger role for reason in the development of action-guiding principles and values based upon underlying religious beliefs. Yet the differences between Gustafson and Niebuhr are not as sharp as they at times appear.[22] For Niebuhr, the norm of human conduct is the fitting response to what God is doing; for Gustafson, it is human action which intends the "well-being of creation," action in conformity with what God is enabling and requiring human agents to be and do. For Gustafson the content of the good is known more indirectly than it is for Niebuhr, but for both the final norm is the divine will which is being disclosed in and through the processes of history. For this reason the good cannot be defined in static or abstract terms. Both Niebuhr and Gustafson base their ethics upon theistic rather than exclusively Christological foundations; for both, the norm of the good in human action is grounded in the divine activity (or, as Gustafson would prefer, in God's dynamic relationship to the world), and human agents are accountable finally to God for their decisions and their actions.[23] They are in basic agreement concerning the sources, the inclusiveness, and the unity of moral criteria; they are also in agreement concerning the relational nature of the good, obligation, and responsibility. The primary differences between the two are related to their conceptions of God and human agency. Gustafson's interpretation of ethics in terms of teleology and virtue is based to a large degree upon his theological teleology; Niebuhr's ethic of responsibility is rooted theologically in his concept of the sovereignty of God (radical monotheism).

Like H. Richard Niebuhr and Gustafson, Ramsey also bases his ethic upon theistic rather than exclusively Christological foundations. Unlike the former, however, he finds the unity--i.e., the good-defining quality--of Christian ethics in neighbor-love. This is particularly clear in his analysis of virtue, but it is also true of his social ethic. For this reason there is a greater polarity in Ramsey's ethic between love and justice than there is in Niebuhr's ethic of responsibility or Gustafson's ethic of "the imitation of God." Ramsey is also in agreement with Niebuhr and Gustafson in so far as he understands the good finally in relational terms as neighbor-centered love; yet, there is a basic inconsistency in Ramsey at this point, for he tends to equate obedience to *agape*-embodying rules with obedience to Christ. Ramsey attempts to guard against legalism through his appeal to prudence in the application of such rules in medical ethics, for example; however, his rigid conception of rules seems fundamentally inconsistent with a relational conception of the good.

Both Gustafson and Ramsey seek to provide greater moral direction than they find in most forms of contemporary Protestant ethics. Gustafson has attempted to do so primarily in terms of virtue; Ramsey, through the development of rules derived from agape and also through an appeal to natural justice as the latter is transformed by love. Such efforts are consistent with--and even required by--a responsibilist interpretation of Christian ethics. In the latter, however, they would be undertaken in a different ethical framework and on the basis of a different perception of the self. Virtue is a necessary part of Christian ethics, but the latter also includes responsibility for society and culture. Similarly, laws--rules and moral principles-- have an indispensable role in theological ethics; however, the latter must also provide a basis for a critique of all such rules in terms of its most fundamental conception of the good. In his polemic against contextualism and pragmatism in Protestant ethics, Ramsey tends to obscure the relational nature of moral criteria and the role of the good in morality. Theologically, his emphasis upon law rests upon his deontological understanding of the covenant as the fundamental form of God's relationship to the world.

(2) Human Agency

In our discussion of moral criteria we found it necessary to refer to the underlying conception of moral agency included in the corresponding notions of obedience to the command of God, conformity to agape, and response to the divine action. As we turn to a comparison and evaluation of these various concepts of the agent, we will be primarily concerned with the following two issues: (1) the autonomy of the agent in relationship to the ultimate environment of human action and (2) the role of the agent in the determination of moral choices. These issues are interrelated; in a sense they represent two different ways of posing the question of autonomy and freedom in morality. Hence, they will be treated together in the discussion which follows.

As noted above, the most widespread traditional images of moral agency have been those of obedience to law and aspiration after value. In addition to these, the symbol of responsibility has been increasingly appropriated in contemporary theological ethics as well as in philosophical ethics. As H. Richard Niebuhr suggested, the use of this image in ethics grew out of a new conception of the self that had its origins in the social and biological sciences. While it was not entirely new, it represented an emergent understanding of the human agent that differed in significant respects from the older images. Niebuhr called each of these symbols "synecdochic," for each represents an image drawn from a part of moral experience which is used to describe and interpret the whole. The idea of the moral life as response was prefigured in Aristotle and the Stoics, he believed; it was also represented in the biblical _ethos_.

When this symbol first began to be used in ethics, it was generally interpreted in terms of obedience or aspiration as the primary models of human agency. Thus Barth, Brunner, and Bonhoeffer, for example, employed it to restate the traditional concept of obedience. Other ethicists have used the idea to re-interpret morality in essentially teleological terms. Joseph Fletcher, for example, describes the practical, operational style of situation ethics in terms of "moral responsibility."[24] For him, this concept symbolizes the freedom and openness of the agent's response to persons in Christian love. Used in this sense, it is basically a teleological category closely akin to the utilitarian ideal of aspiration after "the greatest good for the greatest number."

Although they do not make "responsibility" a central category in their ethics, Reinhold Niebuhr and Gustafson employ the notion both explicitly and implicitly. For Reinhold Niebuhr, the fundamental problem of a Christian social ethic is two-fold. It includes a clear perception, based upon the gospel, of the realities of our common life; it also includes the preservation of "_a sense of responsibility for_ achieving _the highest measure of order, freedom and justice_ despite the hazards of man's collective life."[25] For Gustafson, Christian ethics is a human response to "what God is enabling and requiring" moral agents to be and do. It is an ethic of "the imitation of God"; it intends the "well-being of creation" even as God does. Although Gustafson is on occasion critical of the use of the image of "response" in Christian ethics because it implies an excessive passivity in the moral agent, the idea is nevertheless implicit in his ethics as a whole, including both the agent's accountability for his/her action and the agent's participation in moral decisions.[26] Like Reinhold Niebuhr, however, Gustafson interprets human response fundamentally in terms of aspirations after goods or values.

Unlike those writers who adopted the idea of responsibility to restate the traditional concepts of obedience and aspiration, H. Richard Niebuhr used it to signify an alternative conception of moral agency and the unity of the moral life before God. For Niebuhr, the re-symbolization of Christian ethics in terms of responsibility rested upon a different perception of the nature and limits of human freedom and a different perception of God's relationship to the world. Both of these ideas were joined together in his notion of human action as response (agency) to the divine action (radical monotheism).

As we have previously noted, an ethic of responsibility has much in common with an ethic of duty and an ethic of ends; yet it represents a fundamentally different structure of morality. As used in contemporary theological ethics, responsibility represents a middle way between legalism and individual autonomy in morality. In Barth, however, obedience to the command of God replaces obedience to rational or revealed law. Interpreted in these terms, responsibility affirms both the unity of the agent and the unity of the divine will; it also affirms both the freedom of the agent and the freedom of God on Christological grounds. However, Barth's conception of moral agency seems in sharp contradiction to the contemporary experience of human freedom and responsibility _for_ the historical forms of culture. Brunner and Bonhoeffer, on the other hand, recognize the vocation to participate freely and creatively in the work of culture as a human task; finally, however, they also understand responsibility in terms of obedience. Humans are ultimately accountable to God for their acts of obedience/disobedience to him in the offices, roles, and relationships which they occupy in society. They have the responsibility to participate as agents--on the basis of human capacities, including reason--in political, economic, and cultural life even when all of the available choices incur guilt. Such responsibility is located, however, within the over-arching framework of obedience within the "orders of creation" (Brunner) or the mandates (Bonhoeffer); moreover, there remains a fundamental dualism between the will of the Creator and the will of the Redeemer, between law and gospel--or, in the language of Bonhoeffer--between the penultimate and the ultimate. Interpreted in deontological terms, responsibility means the freedom to be obedient--and not much more.[27] When it is interpreted in terms of aspiration, on the other hand, responsibility means the search for values and goals which represent the fulfilment of human life and/or creation. Thus, Reinhold Niebuhr, Gustafson, Lehmann, and Fletcher stress the autonomy and creativity in human agency. For Lehmann and Fletcher, however, responsibility remains more unstructured than it is for Reinhold Niebuhr and Gustafson. According to Reinhold Niebuhr, *agape* remains the final norm of human freedom in community, and *agape* leads to the demand for social justice. For Gustafson, human autonomy is limited by what God makes possible and requires through the processes and events of nature and history. Human agents have the responsibility of determining through reason those actions which promote the well-being of creation; moreover, the former are accountable to God for the latter.

In his proposal of a responsiblist interpretation of Christian ethics, H. Richard Niebuhr sought to clarify the meaning of this symbol by focusing upon the structure of moral experience. This structure, he believed, contained four major elements: response, interpretation, accountability, and social solidarity. To define moral activity in terms of this model of self-understanding is to locate responsibility for moral action directly in the agent, and it is also to see the agent primarily as a responder to prior action which provides both the limits and the possibilities for one's present response. It is here that the fundamental difference between H. Richard Niebuhr and the other writers whom we have been considering is joined: Is the moral agent more adequately understood as responder and answerer or as maker and/or as citizen? For Niebuhr the answer to this question was grounded basically in common human experience rather than in particular theological doctrines. The fundamental structure of human life is that of response rather than seeking after goals or obedience to law. It has to do with the question of how men interpret and react/respond to those things which are not in their power.[28]

Response ethics begins, therefore, with an effort to understand the totality of human existence and history in terms of a unified pattern of divine action of creation, ordering, and reconciliation. Responsible action is action which is "fitting"--which corresponds to, is consistent with, and affirms the divine will for the fulfilment of creation. To be human is to exercise <u>creaturely</u> <u>freedom</u> and responsibility in faith. As noted above, an ethic of responsibility does not make the metaphors of aspiration and obedience unnecessary; it does, however, subordinate the latter to the former. Indeed, both man-the-citizen and man-the-maker are responders.[29] Responsibility as the primary and inclusive symbol, however, interprets human action as response of the whole person to many kinds of action in an inclusive moral community. It holds together freedom and limitation, gospel and law, human action and the limitations upon human achievement in a distinctive way.

The adequacy of the model of responsibility will, of course, be determined on the basis of experience. As an <u>alternative</u>, it differs in important respects from Gustafson's ethics of virtue, which seems increasingly akin to teleological ethics,[30] from his theological teleology, which places proportionately greater emphasis upon God as the Creator of new possibilities for the well-being of creation,[31] and from his conception of man as "co-actor" with God.[32] To a certain extent these differences are matters of emphasis; yet, the fundamental structure of Gustafson's ethics seems increasingly to be teleological rather than responsiblist. To make the seeking after goals/values the primary model of ethics is to prompt the query as to whether this model takes sufficient account of the limitations of human life (the restrictions imposed by limited natural resources, by the creaturely limits of technology, by the moral order, by human sinfulness) and of human <u>accountability</u> to God <u>for</u> <u>all</u> <u>that</u> <u>is</u> <u>given</u> <u>concretely</u> in creation.

Niebuhr's ethics of response differs also from Paul Ramsey's basically deontological ethics in so far as the latter focuses primarily upon obedience to principles and rules which are intended to give concrete expression to <u>agape</u>. In contrast to Ramsey's ethics of obligation and duty, Niebuhr's ethics of responsibility recognizes more clearly the relativity of the moral law; it interprets Christian ethics fundamentally in terms of response rather than obedience--even "obedient love";[33] and it understands obligation and duty in more consistently relational--that is to say, dynamic, historical--terms.

The need for a responsiblist model of moral agency and the relationship of the former to models based on obligation and value can be illustrated by reference to the debate in medical ethics concerning research with human subjects. Here responsibility of the scientific community includes taking into account both the rights of research subjects and the possible benefits of such investigations not only to the subjects themselves but also to society, including future generations. The responsibility of the physician/researcher cannot be reduced simply to known obligations--e.g., the avoidance of harm--or to the quest for desirable ends--e.g., the advancement of medical knowledge. The dilemma posed by research with human subjects is <u>how</u> to reconcile the recognized duty to protect the latter with the duty to gain new knowledge for the benefit of humankind. As moral agents, members of the medical community acknowledge themselves to be in fact responsible in this two-fold way; moreover, this responsibility implies the necessity that they participate as agents in the determination of the concrete meaning of this claim which cannot be finally reduced either to known principles of obligation or of value. As moral agents, members of the scientific community are accountable for the manner in which the obligation to protect human subjects is reconciled with the advancement of medical science in particular investigations.[34]

(3) The Covenant Form Of Community

For H. Richard Niebuhr, the conception of the moral life as human response to the divine action was exemplified concretely in the idea of the covenant in the history of Israel. Viewed in terms of the sovereignty of God, the natural communities based on sexuality, politics, and economic dependence were transformed into fundamentally moral communities. Theologically, the conception of human life in terms of covenant was rooted in Israel's perception of God's relationship to the world; but this theological perception was also rooted in Israel's effort to understand her own social and cultural life as a historical community in relationship to God.

The symbol of covenant has been widely used in Christian history to describe the fundamental nature of human existence, but it has been interpreted in quite different and contradictory ways. Within the confines of the present study, for example, Barth, Ramsey, and H. Richard Niebuhr all use it as a primary image of human life in community; yet their interpretations of the concept differ fundamentally at a number of points. These variations are due in part to the variety of models of covenant within Scripture; they are also due to contrasting methods of biblical interpretation and different conceptions of biblical authority. For Barth, especially in the more systematic stages of his work, the concept is basically a Christological, soteriological category. In <u>Church Dogmatics</u> it refers primarily to the purpose for which humankind was created, viz., to be covenant-partners of God. Here Barth does not use the term as a social image to describe human life in society but, rather, as a formal, theological symbol of the end for which humanity was created. Although human beings are created <u>with</u> their fellow-humans, they are not covenant-partners of God by creation. Their true end--the realization of their true humanity--depends solely upon God's sovereign grace. Moreover, Barth understands human existence primarily in personal terms as I-Thou encounters. Human beings are created with their fellow-humanity in order that they may be <u>for</u> the latter; but covenant-partnership with God means obedience to the command of God, not acceptance of human accountability for decisions which shape the common life of human communities. Barth's concept of moral agency does not allow the agent's participation in the decision-making process beyond the decision of obedience, and his exclusively Christological ethics makes empirical social analysis finally irrelevant to theological ethics.

Ramsey follows Barth in making the covenant the central category for defining the meaning and purpose of our creation as human beings. Both interpret this symbol fundamentally in terms of obedience. For Ramsey, however, covenant is a more general anthropological concept. Theologically it is rooted in the biblical idea of covenant between God and man; this means that it is grounded more positively in creation. Not only does created human nature provide the ground-- the external basis--for covenant relationships; the latter are constitutive even of our fallen humanity. All persons exist in covenants, some of which are entered by birth and some by choice. Ramsey defines covenant in terms of fidelity to known individuals and the duty to fulfill recognized obligations that are derived fundamentally from <u>agape</u> but also from natural justice in the service of love. For Ramsey, covenant ethics is sharply opposed to an ethic of ends, including pursuit of a common good. Its focus is upon the preserving work of social justice rather than upon the fulfilment of the possibilities and potentialities of created human nature.

Although H. Richard Niebuhr's concept of covenant resembles that of Ramsey more nearly than it does that of Barth, the former nevertheless implies a fundamentally different concept of community that is rooted in basically different conceptions of moral agency and God's relationship to the world. More particularly, Niebuhr has a larger place for human freedom and a more dynamic understanding of creation than Ramsey. Beginning as he does with the primacy of moral experience, Niebuhr interprets biblical and theological symbols dialogically. This means that the latter are reinterpreted in light of the changing historical experience of those who share the same fundamental biblical story. While the basic structure of images such as covenant remains the same, the particularized content of the latter emerges out of the contemporary experience which they are used to interpret.

The concept of covenant had been distorted by Calvin and Edwards, Niebuhr believed, through the use of mechanistic images to describe the sovereignty of God. In contrast to images drawn from the machine and also from the social contract theories of society, sixteenth and seventeenth century Puritanism provided the basis for a new understanding of covenant grounded in a less deterministic conception of God's sovereignty and a more active, participatory conception of human responsibility in and for society.[35] This interpretation of covenant had many sources, both secular and religious; most significantly, however, it represented an effort on the part of the Puritans to understand their personal and collective life in terms of the biblical idea of covenant. Thus, it was, in a sense, a re-enactment in the seventeenth century of the earlier history of Israel "with variations due to the new experiences of the time."[36] The concept of covenant which emerged from this reinterpretation was deeply dependent upon Scripture, but it was also influenced by the social and cultural experience of the Puritans themselves. Human life was understood fundamentally in relationship to a moral order in which covenant--or promise--constitutes the primary bond, both between God and humanity and within society itself. Such a conception of community presupposed a social rather than an individualistic conception of human nature. It presupposed also that humans are essentially moral beings and that true freedom consists of the ability to commit oneself to a cause rather than the liberty to choose among goods. In the political community covenant meant the binding together in one body of persons who pledged mutual responsibility to and for each other in the governance of society under God. Covenant meant the <u>participation</u> of all citizens in the processes of governance--not simply consent to be ruled by laws that were imposed by others.

In order to distinguish H. Richard Niebuhr's concept of covenant as a symbol of responsibility more clearly from Ramsey's notion of covenant-fidelity, attention should be called to two additional contrasts. First, Niebuhr--much more than Ramsey--recognizes the relational nature of value, duty, and responsibility. Hence, he interprets covenant in terms of response rather than primarily in terms of obedience to rules. Second, whereas Ramsey finds the basic bonds of society in obedience and obligation, Niebuhr locates these in common objects of faith, shared centers of value. For him human communities are primarily faith-communities. This means that the former are based upon and sustained by commitment to a mutual object of loyalty. In this view, commitment to a common center of value is prior to the formation of societies based on contract or upon mutual interest and force.

Interpreted in terms of responsibility, the theological symbol of covenant most adequately expresses the essential nature of human existence as interdependent yet free. To understand collective forms of human life in terms of covenant is to recognize mutual responsibility for the political processes of society, for the ordering of social priorities, and for governance under law. It is also to acknowledge accountability to and for the cause, or purpose, for which the community came into being and by faithfulness to which the latter is sustained and nourished. Fundamentally, covenant represents a conversionist concept of the relationship of Christian faith to culture. It represents the acknowledgement of mutual responsibility and accountability to and for each other under God. Democracy represents a secular form of covenant, but in the West it has been significantly shaped and sustained by its religious roots in Calvinism, particularly in Puritanism.

In this section of our study attention has been focused upon the concept of covenant as a model of Christian social ethics. Our purpose has been to suggest a direction in which an ethic of responsibility might move when it takes up the task of social ethics. Since the idea of covenant has been used in different ways as a dominant symbol in the ethics of Barth and Ramsey, it has been necessary to examine how its meaning is changed when it is interpreted in terms of human response to the creating, ordering, and redeeming action of God. Thus understood, "covenant" signifies human responsibility not simply for obedience but, more fundamentally, for the determination of the content of justice and the common good in response to the conditions and possibilities which are given through the divine action. Such response takes place in a universal community which includes not only humanity but nature and the cosmic environment. Understood in this sense, "covenant" acknowledges the limits of human existence imposed by nature and by human sinfulness; but it also defines the humanity of all in terms of mutual responsibility and accountability of all members of society to and for each other before God. Covenant ethics does not make other approaches to ethics unnecessary. On the contrary, it leads to efforts to define the good and to the pursuit of goods; in so doing, however, it recognizes the limits of human autonomy and the relativity of all human definitions of the good. Covenant leads also to the quest to understand the physical and moral order of the universe in terms of law; but it recognizes the relativity of all human conceptions of law.

The Movement From Theory To Practice

The concept of covenant itself points to the relationship between faith and practice in ethics. As such it exemplifies the two-fold task of ethics: to provide an analysis of moral activity and also to offer moral guidance for concrete choices and decisions. With the possible exception of Lehmann, all of the major writers in our study have given attention to this matter although they differ greatly in the methods of moral reasoning which they employ. For Lehmann, Christian ethics aims not at morality but at maturity. It is not interested in the quality of specific acts, but, rather, in their parabolic significance. In the koinonia the methodology of decision-making is contextualist and intuitive in the sense that the will of God is perceived immediately and directly through the "theonomous" conscience of the believer. For Barth, Christian ethics is a matter finally of obedience to the divine command; nevertheless, he undertakes to provide moral guidance through his analysis of certain spheres, or patterns of relationships, in which all human action takes place and through the development of "directives" which give general guidance toward concrete acts of obedience. As we have seen, however, Barth finally allows no place for empirical reason in the determination of right action and no role for moral agency in the sense of the agent's participation in the latter.

In contrast to Barth, Brunner and Bonhoeffer attempt to provide moral direction in social ethics through a larger role for natural reason in the ordering of society. Brunner does this through the concept of the "orders of creation" and through the sharp antinomy which he draws between the requirements of love and justice. While Christian ethics is a matter finally of obedience to the concrete command of God for Bonhoeffer, the latter attempts to provide moral direction through his concepts of discipleship, conformation, and the mandates.

In different ways Reinhold Niebuhr and Paul Ramsey

both provide moral guidance through principles and/or rules which give more concrete expression to _agape_ as the ultimate norm of human life in both its personal and its collective forms. For Reinhold Niebuhr, love is related dialectically to justice; justice, in turn, is defined in terms of the regulative principles of liberty and equality. While _agape_ remains the final norm of community life, it is related dialectically to the latter through justice, liberty, equality and a historically qualified conception of natural law. Ramsey, on the other hand, moves more directly from the ultimate norm of _agape_ through increasingly specific principles and rules to the subsumption of concrete cases. Niebuhr moves teleologically and pragmatically from a perfectionist conception of love to the social and historical realities of collective life; Ramsey, on the other hand, moves deontologically through a series of love-embodying principles and rules to specific duties which are owed to all members of the community.

Like Ramsey, Gustafson has attempted to provide moral direction in his ethics, but he has done so primarily in terms of virtue, or character. He has also sought to develop action-guiding principles and values based on the religious beliefs of the Christian community, and he has endeavored to state these as fully as possible in terms of moral philosophy. In particular, he has called for a recovery of the pedagogical function of the law and for a continuing effort on the part of the Christian community to identify those qualities which constitute the well-being-of-creation and the common good as symbols of God's purpose for the world.

For H. Richard Niebuhr, also, moral direction is one of the fundamental purposes of ethics. Yet it is precisely concerning this point that one of the major criticisms of his ethics has been made.[37] In an attempt to meet this criticism, we turn in the remainder of this essay to certain directions which the movement from theory to practice might take in a theocentric ethic of responsibility. Such an endeavor is implicit, this writer believes, in Niebuhr's understanding of the socio-historical context of all moral action, in his notion of accountability, and in his idea of an inclusive moral community. More concretely, it is implicit in his understanding of the idea of the covenant both in Israelite history and in Puritanism. According to Niebuhr, Christian ethics is reflection--within a particular historical community--upon the human response to the action and nature of God. This community of faith, moreover, has understood its own moral experience in a variety of ways--partially in terms of law, partially in terms of aspiration and virtue, but more fundamentally, Niebuhr believed, in terms of its response to the creating, ordering, and redeeming action of God.

(1) The Divine Commonwealth

Niebuhr's ethics of responsibility rested theologically upon radically monotheistic faith. Biblically such faith was expressed in the image of the kingdom of God. Other symbols--notably the "City of God" and the "divine commonwealth"--have also been used in Christian history to represent this idea. For Niebuhr, the essential theme expressed by all of these images was the sovereignty of God. Each points to a unified moral order grounded in a single, unified, purposive pattern of divine action as the ultimate environment of all human action.

As a symbol of the divine sovereignty in history, the kingdom of God points to the givenness--the being and the structure--of human existence and to the mode of the divine rule. It does not signify a denial of human freedom although it has often been interpreted in this way. It does not mean a mechanical, fatalistic, or despotic ordering of history. It means, rather, that all human action is ultimately dependent upon a more inclusive pattern of divine action and that all persons are finally accountable to God in their freedom. Individual and collective acts of good and evil are performed by human subjects, but in and through such action God is even now bringing a new creation--a new, universal community--into being. For Niebuhr, such faith is eschatological; it affirms the conviction that the divine rule which is a present though oftentimes hidden reality will in the end become fully manifest. The "divine commonwealth" represented a new symbolization of the kingdom of God in an image which, while maintaining the fundamental conviction of God's sovereignty, reinterpreted the latter in light of a new historical perception of human freedom and human community. Such re-interpretation is a continuing process, made necessary by the changing character of human experience. It is the result of an on-going dialogue between tradition and experience. The birth of new symbols does not make the traditional ones unnecessary; together, they interpret each other. Both the reinterpretation of old images and the creation of new ones are needed to avoid idolatry and to express the living character of faith and history.

A much more recent attempt to give new symbolic expression to the kingdom of God in terms of the "responsible society" is found in the Protestant ecumenical movement. Following its introduction at the Amsterdam Assembly of the World Council of Churches (1948),[38] the concept of the "responsible society" played an important role in ecumenical discussions of the relationship of the church to society for a number of years. The term was initially used to signify the responsibility of the Church for the construction of a new social environment which would protect the personal dimensions of human life against the threats of advancing technological controls. It was also used to describe the social mission of the Church apart from the identification of the latter with any particular economic, social, or political system. The idea of the responsible society was expanded by the Evanston Assembly of the WCC (1954) to give greater recognition to the critical role of institutions in affecting social life and in the achievement of justice. The Evanston Assembly also identified four requirements of justice in relationship to political institutions: the protection of human rights; the guarantee of each person's freedom to express one's own religious, moral, and political convictions; the provision of channels by which the people can change their governments without recourse to violence; and respect for forms of association within society based upon foundations and principles which are independent of the state.³⁹

Although the concept of a responsible society was intended to maintain a dynamic balance between freedom and order, liberty and justice, in reality it reflected the values and priorities of older and more established constitutional societies in contradistinction to those of emergent nations in which order and unity are frequently given priority over individual freedom.⁴⁰ Hence, the idea came under increasing criticism in ecumenical circles. Taking note of this problem, the New Delhi Assembly (1961) called for recognition of the different circumstances faced by new nations which are coming into being and which do not yet have established constitutional processes of social change.

As Bennett suggested in the mid-sixties, the concept of the responsible society needs to be rigorously re-examined in light of the broader experience of the world community. Need for such criticism began to be evident almost from the beginning from the perspective of Christians in totalitarian societies.⁴¹ The underlying difficulties with the earlier interpretations of this concept had to do with the issues with which we have been concerned in this study: the nature of human moral agency, criteria of the good, and the underlying conception of community.

While the concept of the responsible society became an important category in Protestant ethics for at least a decade and a half after Amsterdam, the idea rested upon a variety of theological and ethical presuppositions which were fundamentally inconsistent. For Amsterdam, the concept of a responsible society referred primarily to a goal toward which the churches in all countries should work.⁴² This concept was developed, however, in the context of the theme for the Assembly, "Man's Disorder and God's Design." Clearly the latter included strong elements of obedience and accountability as well as aspiration. In a sense, the more recent emphasis in the social thought of the WCC upon the right of all persons to participate in the political processes of their societies and the increased representation of the churches from the Third and Fourth Worlds in the WCC represents greater recognition of the responsibility which these groups bear for their own social and political life.[43] While this greater freedom is recognized, it is not made absolute, for there is common recognition of the final responsibility of all persons and societies to God. In response to the various forms of liberation theology there has also been greater recognition of the historically conditioned character of all human institutions. In view of the increased pluralism within the WCC as well as within secular society, a conception of community based upon covenant appears more viable in the long run than a conception of community based upon common interests and goals.

It is not surprising, in view of the variety of interpretations of responsibility which we have noted in modern Protestant ethics, that the concept of the responsible society has been similarly understood in different ways in the ecumenical movement. In this respect, it resembles other symbols of Christian faith such as the kingdom of God, covenant, and *agape*. Whether the idea can be recovered as a viable slogan for the social ethics of the WCC is problematic and perhaps unimportant. Beneath this surface issue, however, lies the deeper question concerning the adequacy of whatever symbols may be employed to conceptualize the basic form of Christian social ethics in the contemporary world. Viewed from the perspective of theocentric responsibility, the concept of the responsible society as used in the WCC lacked an adequate understanding of the radicality of the divine judgment upon the social institutions of the West. In addition, it failed to give adequate recognition to the responsibility of particular societies for the development of institutions adapted to their own needs and possibilities. Finally, in the face of the increased pluralism of the contemporary world, the question of the bonding of human community has been raised once again in radical and universal terms. As already suggested, a covenantal conception of community points to the deepest levels of human solidarity in both its interpersonal and communal forms.

(2) Response To The Divine Action

Stated in theological terms, the primary question of an ethic of responsibility is: What is God doing? While this is also the primary question in Lehmann's <u>koinonia</u> ethics, an ethic of responsibility answers it in a distinctive way. According to Lehmann, God is always at work "doing what it takes to make and to keep human life human."[44] Lehmann interprets this reply in exclusively Christological terms. God's action is fundamentally political and messianic. In Lehmann's ethics, however, it is unclear how our human action differs from the divine action. While Gustafson prefers to state the primary question in the following terms: "What is God enabling and requiring me (or us) to be and to do?" he seems to be asking essentially the same question as Niebuhr and Lehmann. His focus, however, is upon the <u>human</u> response to what God is doing. Humans are enabled and required to seek the "well-being of creation" because this is what God wills and seeks.[45]

Stated also in theological terms, the secondary question raised by an ethic of responsibility is: How shall I (we) respond to what God is doing? Other forms of ethics speak of a human response to what God is doing (Lehmann), commanding (Barth, Brunner), or "enabling and requiring" persons to be and do (Gustafson); however, they define such a response primarily in terms of aspiration or obedience. In an ethic of responsibility, on the other hand, emphasis falls upon the ultimate givenness--in terms of being--of both the possibilities and the limits of human action; the latter is, nonetheless, the agent's own action, for it includes the agent's interpretation of "what is going on," his/her participation in the determination of the "fitting" response, and accountability for such action.

In an ethic of responsibility God's relationship to the world is understood in terms of a unified but three-fold pattern of divine action. This pattern corresponds to the fundamental dimensions of human existence. Thus, while it is possible--and necessary--to distinguish between his work of creation, governance, and salvation, all of these forms are interrelated in such a way that none can be properly understood except in relationship to the other two. Such a conception of the unity of the divine action rules out all forms of dualism, including both the separation of human life into two spheres (persons *vs.* community) and perfectionistic conceptions of the good. It is inconsistent with all such dualisms both in God's relationship to the world and in our human response to the divine action.

For H. Richard Niebuhr, this three-fold pattern of divine action and human response is rooted in Scripture and in the experience of Israel and the Christian community.[46] Like obedience to God and aspiration after the good, response to the divine action can be understood in different ways. In each case, interpretation is involved. Fundamentally, however, an ethic of responsibility emphasizes the priority and unity of God's will and the unity of our human response to that action. While it rejects theological and ethical dualism, it does speak in terms of the polarities between moral claims. Such polarities are rooted in the competition of being with being, not in a dualism between being and the good. Moral choices are choices between greater and lesser goods, not between good and evil.

In the first place, radically monotheistic faith means that God is active in every event as Creator. He is present not only as the source of all created being but also as its sustainer and as the creator of new forms and possibilities of being. The appropriate human response to this form of the divine activity is acceptance and affirmation of that which God has created and that which he is even now bringing into being. It is response that includes a human imitation of the divine creativity. While the human capacity to create is limited and dependent, it is nevertheless a means through which God is working to bring about the fulfilment of creation. In terms of virtue, the human response to the Creator is one of gratitude and love to God; it is also a response of love for the neighbor-in-relation-to-God as the Center of all being and value. In an ethic of responsibility that act is most loving or most fitting which most ministers to human need.

Radically monotheistic faith means, in the second place, that God's action is understood also as that of Orderer or Governor. God is not related to the world alternately as Creator and as Orderer; rather, he is related to the latter in a unified pattern of action that includes both creation and governance in every event and every human relationship. Understood in terms of creation, God wills the establishment of a society in which covenant is the ultimate ordering principle. Such a society is symbolized by the kingdom of God. In it human freedom either to obey or to disobey the will of the Creator is presupposed. Since God is sovereign, however, humanity is not free to be disobedient with impunity. As a consequence of the Fall, humankind encounters the Creator also as Judge. Basically, his judgment is upon human pride and idolatry; it is directed against the tendency which is present in all persons and all communities to put themselves in the place of God.

God's relationship to the world as Orderer is an expression of his sovereignty in the face of human sin. As Creator, God wills the establishment of a kingdom based upon the moral order which he has ordained. The upholding of that order is experienced by sinful humanity as judgment, as the divine No against all human efforts to transgress the limits of their creaturely existence and set themselves up in the place of God. This judgment falls both upon individual and upon collective forms of human life. Just as humanity is one in its creation for participation in a community based upon covenant, so it is also one in its Fall and in its confrontation with judgment upon its sin. Human response to the divine governance is, therefore, a response of repentance, of self-denial, and of responsible restraint of the neighbor. As Orderer, God does not will simply the preservation of a creation which has fallen; he wills, rather, a re-ordering--a transformation--of society in conformity with his purposes in creation and salvation. Human response to God's governing activity is not limited to personal forms of repentance and self-denial; it includes responsibility and accountability for the restraint of injustice in both its personal and collective forms. Moreover, since God's action as Governor must always be understood in relationship to his will as Creator, humanity is also responsible for the establishment of positive forms of community based upon covenant, or--stated in more general terms--upon loyalty to a common cause. Commitment to social justice is part of the meaning of covenant. It includes the acceptance of mutual limitation and restraint in the exercise of power and justice; it also means the ordering and structuring of the common life toward the realization of the kingdom of God in and through human history.

Thirdly, radical monotheism means that God is active in every event not only as Creator and Orderer but also as Redeemer. The will of the Creator and that of the Orderer and Redeemer are finally one and inseparable. This means that our human response to God must also be a unified response. It cannot be separated into realms of creation and redemption, the earthly and the spiritual, persons and institutions, law and gospel. Response to God's action as Orderer cannot be properly understood except in relation to his purpose as Savior. This purpose is two-fold. It includes not only the restoration of broken community made possible by the divine work of forgiveness, justification, liberation, and reconciliation; it includes also the creation of new and fuller forms of human life as a whole built upon vicarious love. Response to the redemptive action of God means the acceptance of forgiveness and the granting of forgiveness to others; it means reconciliation [II Cor. 18]; it means the acceptance of the gift of freedom and response to the neighbor in freedom. In relation to the collective forms of life, response to God's liberating action means liberation of the oppressed; it means the transformation of societies based upon fear, suspicion, and narrow loyalties into communities based upon trust and faithfulness to common centers of value within a universal community.

(3) Regulative Principles Of Human Community

The implications of the notions of the divine commonwealth and human response to the divine action are made more concrete through an analysis of certain moral principles and values which are implicit in a covenant conception of community. As we have seen, for H. Richard Niebuhr, the fundamental form of human society is covenant, i.e., the making and keeping of promises. This is also the basic pattern of God's relationship to the world. From the standpoint of monotheistic faith, loyalty in the human community is thus rooted ultimately in faith as trust in the faithfulness of God. This does not mean that the presence of community is dependent upon the presence of monotheistic faith. It means, rather, that the presence of community--even in its negative forms of fear, suspicion, injustice, and violence--points to a universal moral order which monotheistic faith makes intelligible. It means, also, that such faith clarifies and illuminates the nature, or character, of authentic human community.

A responsiblist ethic does not approach the task of social justice from the standpoint of an abstract conception of community as a model for all human communities. Neither does it attempt to derive such a model from idealistic or rationalistic moral principles and values. Rather, it begins with an effort to understand the moral structure of presently existing communities in relational terms. Monotheistic faith does not prescribe a new set of universal values and norms in the place of those which are presently embedded in the fabric of community relationships. On the contrary, it begins with the latter and undertakes to show how these are qualified, radically revised, and transformed when they are viewed in the context of a universal moral order and a correspondingly universal community of being. In short, moral values and principles which define the meaning of covenant have a double rootage in historical social experience and in monotheistic faith.[47] Their concrete meaning in particular forms of community must always be defined relationally and dialogically. Pursuit of this task presupposes the existence of a community of trust and mutual commitment to shared values and/or causes.[48]

In applying the covenant conception of society to particular forms of community, it is possible and necessary to describe the former in terms of more particular values and principles. In a responsiblist ethic the latter are best understood in regulative rather than constitutive terms. Historically, the development of such principles has been rooted in the prophetic tradition and in the effort of Christians to understand their political and social responsibility in terms of monotheistic faith.

While the movement from theory to practice involves a continuing debate about the concrete application of such norms to specific economic and political problems, the former represent guidelines for the determination of social policy. They serve as procedural and directional principles in a responsiblist social ethic. Examples of such norms are the following: freedom, equality, order, justice, and the common good. Many other such values and principles might be identified and utilized in an ethic of responsibility. These are representative, however; and they describe some of the most basic qualities of community life understood in terms of covenant. Significantly, such norms are not derived form a single value, obligation, or virtue. They rest, rather, in the nature of human beings understood both in relationship to each other in a variety of communities and ultimately in relationship to the divine rule in history.

Freedom and equality are grounded in the relationship of all persons to the Creator. As beings made in the image of God, all are endowed with freedom. All are created with the capacity for moral choice, with the capacity to trust or be distrustful, to be loyal or to be disloyal. All are born into relationships of response and responsibility, and all are accountable finally to God for the exercise of their freedom. Moreover, all persons are endowed with equal dignity, for all are dependent upon the Creator for their existence and fulfilment, and all share equally in his love. Since all are created with the desire for freedom and fulfilment, all are entitled to participate in decisions affecting the determination of their well-being.

Order and justice are grounded primarily in the governing action of God. The former are not, however, related to creation primarily in a negative way. On the contrary, both are related directly to creation as the structure or form in which the fulfilment of creaturely human life becomes possible in community. But order and justice also have a negative or preserving function, viz., the restraint of evil which results from human sinfulness. While the preserving work of justice has a certain priority over its positive task of human fulfilment, the former cannot be separated from the latter; nor can it be defined in terms of a different set of moral criteria. In both its negative and its positive forms justice is a condition of order in community. Order rests upon the promise of justice in both its restraining and its creative forms. Since sin is universal, covenant means the acceptance of shared responsibility and mutual accountability for the restraint of evil as well as the pursuit of common goals such as freedom, justice, and peace.

A covenant conception of community also includes an implicit notion of the common good. Theologically the idea of the common good is grounded in the concept of a divine commonwealth. In this respect it serves as a symbol of the ultimate unity and harmony of the divine action in creation, governance, and salvation.[49] As a principle of human community, it expresses the dignity and equality which all persons have in creation. The very possibility for the existence of a community based upon covenant depends upon the presence of a shared faith in a cause which promises fulfilment to all members of the group, not just to the majority. Historically, the idea of the common good has functioned primarily as a distributive concept. As a principle of distributive justice, it provided a criterion for resolving the conflicts of interest among competing groups through reference to the welfare of the whole. In our contemporary setting, however, the idea needs to be reinterpreted to include the equal participation of all not only in the distribution of the common good but also in the determination of what that good might be.[50]

(4) Responsibility In The Formation Of Social Policy

In practice such regulative principles as freedom, equality, order, justice, and the common good are interrelated. Together they serve to interpret each other. To these should be added the principle of universalization, for theocentric ethics extends the horizons of community to include the whole realm of being. This universal community includes not only all of humanity but also the world of nature. Beyond such principles an ethic of responsibility can--and must--move toward their application to concrete social issues in a number of different ways.

On the one hand, it might move toward the construction of a variety of systems of value. Such value systems would be tentative and provisional on account of their historical and cultural relativity; but they would nevertheless constitute important instruments in the development and critiquing of social policy. They would contribute to a more concrete understanding of the manifold values which constitute the common good. They would also play an indispensable role in the setting of community priorities. Gustafson, for example, has made a major contribution to contemporary theological ethics through his emphasis upon the importance of values in the fulfilment of human life and through his application of this method of analysis particularly in the field of medical ethics.

On the other hand, an ethic of responsibility might attempt to provide more specific moral direction in the area of social policy through the development of a concept of moral rights. Indeed, such a concept seems necessary in order to assure the equal protection of the freedom and dignity to which all persons are entitled by reason of their common humanity.[51] These rights would be based upon a Christian understanding of the moral order which underlies and sustains all human community; more particularly, they would be based upon a covenantal understanding of society, the worth of persons as ends, and the inclusiveness of the moral community. Such rights would provide moral direction for both the construction and the critiquing of social policy in all aspects of collective life.

Understood from the perspective of responsibility, policy formation is a process which proceeds dialogically in relationship to concrete social issues and problems. It involves analysis of these problems at both the empirical and ethical levels. Both forms of analysis are interrelated; hence, they must be undertaken together and in relationship to each other. This is necessary for a number of reasons. In the first place, moral concepts such as value, duty, and the fitting are relational terms. Since they refer to empirical relationships, it is obviously important to understand the latter as adequately as possible, whether they pertain primarily to our interpersonal, societal, or ecological relationships. In the second place, empirical analysis is never completely objective or value free. Thirdly, ethical judgments are always conditioned by the limitations and perspectives of the moral analyst. Apart from the participation of people trained in the physical and social sciences, the claim of moralists that they have understood the empirical structures and dynamics of society seems hollow and pretentious. Similarly, persons with ethical insight and training are needed to interpret the moral significance of all such relationships and to point to resources of moral renewal and human fulfilment in both its individual and social forms.

NOTES

Chapter 1

1. See, for example, H. Richard Niebuhr, <u>Christ and Culture</u> (New York: Harper and Row, 1951).

2. See Helmut Thielicke, <u>Theological Ethics, Volume I: Foundations</u>, ed. William H. Lazareth (Philadelphia: Fortress Press, 1966), pp. 359-382.

3. Walter Rauschenbusch gave classic expression to the aims of this movement in <u>Christianizing the Social Order</u> (New York: Macmillan, 1912) and <u>A Theology for the Social Gospel</u> (New York: Macmillan, 1917).

4. Stanley Hauerwas has developed the role of character as a theme in Christian ethics in a very perceptive and suggestive way in <u>Character and the Christian Life: A Study in Theological Ethics</u> (San Antonio: Trinity University Press, 1975). See also his <u>A Community of Character: Toward a Constructive Christian Social Ethic</u> (Notre Dame, Indiana: University of Notre Dame Press, 1981).

5. It would be particularly fruitful to examine the ethics of John Howard Yoder, Stanley Hauerwas, and representative liberation and Roman Catholic theologians in relation to the issues raised in this study. To have included them in the present study, however, would have made the latter excessively long and changed its more specific purpose.

6. For an incisive analysis of the significance of Christ for the moral life of "individual men" in their "personal existence," see James M. Gustafson, <u>Christ and the Moral Life</u> (New York: Harper & Row, 1968). Gustafson deals with many of the writers under consideration in the present study but purposely excludes an analysis of their social ethics in this work (ibid., p. ix).

7. See Gibson Winter, "Introduction," <u>Social Ethics: Issues in Ethics and Society</u>, ed. Gibson Winter, (New York: Harper & Row, 1968), p. 6. As Winter suggests, it would be more precise to use the term "societal" rather than "social" to describe the field of ethics under consideration "since it is the evaluation of societal organization and public policy in the shaping of society with which social ethics is concerned." Since this term seems too awk-

Notes to Pages 6-10

ward for general usage, it is important to specify the meaning of "social" in the present context.

8. Ibid., p. 15.

9. Gibson Winter, Elements for a Social Ethic (New York: Macmillan, 1966), chap. 8. Cf. Maurice Natanson, The Journeying Self: A Study in Philosophy and Social Role (Reading, Massachusetts: Addison-Wesley Publishing Co., 1970).

10. Winter, Social Ethics, p. 17.

11. Winter, Elements for a Social Ethic, p. xiv.

12. Ibid., pp. 85-118.

13. Ibid, p. 99.

14. "Intentionality is man's living toward the structures of his world.... Its subjective dimensions are the constituting intentionalities of embodied consciousness" (ibid., p. 198).

15. For an incisive analysis of the relationship of the empirical sciences to ethics, see James M. Gustafson, Theology and Christian Ethics (Philadelphia: United Church Press, 1974), pp. 215-228.

16. Acceptance of this point is not dependent, of course, upon agreement with the precise balance which Winter strikes between human creativity and social conditioning. Various phenomenologists obviously differ in this regard.

17. For a discussion of the uses of phenomenological analysis in contemporary theological ethics, see E. Clinton Gardner, "Phenomenological Analysis and Normative Ethics in Selected Theological Ethicists," in The American Society of Christian Ethics: Selected Papers (Sixteenth Annual Meeting), ed. Franklin Sherman (Missoula, Montana: Scholars Press, 1975), pp. 29-47.

18. Emil Brunner calls the question of the believer's understanding of the "orders," or the natural forms of community, "the most difficult problem of Christian ethics" (The Divine Imperative, New York: Macmillan Co., 1942, p. 335). Cf. Roger Mehl, "The Basis of Christian Social Ethics," in Christian Social Ethics in a Changing World, ed. John C. Bennett (New York: Association Press, 1966), pp. 44-45. "In other words," Mehl writes, "socialism discovered that the chief problems of social ethics are problems of structures."

Notes to Pages 11-13

19. H. Richard Niebuhr, Radical Monotheism and Western Culture (New York: Harper & Brothers, 1960), pp. 58-60; The Purpose of the Church and Its Ministry (New York: Harper & Brothers, 1956), pp. 44-45.

20. H. Richard Niebuhr, The Responsible Self (New York: Harper & Row, 1963), p. 158. Copyright 1963 Florence M. Niebuhr. All quotations used with permission of the publisher.

21. For an earlier discussion of the issues of faith and revelation in relation to Christology, see H. Richard Niebuhr, The Meaning of Revelation (New York: Macmillan, 1941), esp. pp. 38-42, 138-191.

22. Paul Ramsey, ed., Faith and Ethics: The Theology of H. Richard Niebuhr (New York: Harper & Brothers, 1957), pp. 140-141.

23. Ibid, p. 162.

24. Paul Ramsey, Nine Modern Moralists (Englewood Cliffs, N.J.: Prentice-Hall, 1962), pp. 36-38. This revelational meaning of the term is emphasized by Ramsey when he places Barth's Christological categories in a larger theological context. Thus he speaks of Barth's "Christocentric theological anthropology" but continues to maintain that for Barth "our knowledge into God, into man, and into ethics are...fully Christocentric" (Paul Ramsey, Deeds and Rules in Christian Ethics, New York: Scribner's, 1967, pp. 69-70).

25. Paul Ramsey, "Love and Law," in Reinhold Niebuhr: His Religious, Social, and Political Thought, eds. Charles W. Kegley and Robert W. Bretall, (New York: Macmillan, 1956), pp. 115-117. Speaking of Niebuhr's anthropology and ethics, Ramsey writes: "I would insist that at all points he is at the same time a rational analyst of human nature and a Christocentric theologian"(ibid., p. 115).

26. Gustafson, Christ and the Moral Life, p. 15.

27. It does not lie within the scope of Gustafson's essay to deal directly with the issue of the adequacy of Christomorphic forms of ethical analysis for social ethics.

28. Bennett, Christian Social Ethics in a Changing World, pp. 126-131.

29. Ibid., pp. 289-309.

30. Ibid., pp. 369-381.

Notes to Pages 14-24

31. H. Richard Niebuhr, Responsible Self, p. 157. Cf. also H. Richard Niebuhr, Christ and Culture. Each of the five major types of theological ethics which Niebuhr analyzes in the latter study is defined in terms of the Christ-and-culture problem, i.e., in terms of Christology. Thus Niebuhr writes: "However great the variations among Christians in experiencing and describing the authority Jesus Christ has over them, they have this in common: that Jesus Christ is their authority, and that the one who exercises these various kinds of authority is the same Christ" (ibid., p. 13).

32. Cf. Harvey Cox's criticism of Jürgen Moltmann's theology of hope as "extremely Christological at its base." Cox calls for a theology of hope built on the doctrine of creation or a doctrine of the Spirit because of his "increasing sensitivity to the difficulty which a Christological theology of any sort... has in a world of so many different religions" (Frederick Herzog, ed., The Future of Hope: Theology as Eschatology, New York: Herder and Herder, 1970, pp. 78-79).

33. See, for example, H. Richard Niebuhr, The Kingdom of God in America (Chicago: Willett, Clark and Company, 1937).

34. I am indebted for this insight to James Luther Adams, "The Pragmatic Theory of Meaning," unpublished Presidential Address delivered at the Tenth Annual Meeting of the American Society of Christian Ethics, Washington, D. C., January 24, 1969.

Chapter 2

1. See H. Richard Niebuhr's analysis of faith as trust and loyalty in Radical Monotheism, pp. 16-23.

2. Barth, Church Dogmatics, 4 vols. (Edinburgh: T. & T. Clark, 1936-1969), II/2, pp. 515-516. Volume II/2 copyright 1957 by Karl Barth; all quotations used with permission of the publisher.

3. Ibid., pp. 509-513.

4. Ibid., p. 12.

5. Ibid., p. 511.

6. Ibid., pp. 643, 661-708.

7. Ibid., III/4, pp. 4-5.

8. Dietrich Bonhoeffer, Ethics, ed. Eberhard Bethge (New York:

Notes to Pages 24-30

Macmillan, 1955), p. 56.

9. Ibid., pp. 55-56.

10. Ibid., p. 57.

11. Ibid., p. 25.

12. Ibid., pp. 199-200.

13. Ibid., p. 244.

14. Paul L. Lehmann, Ethics in a Christian Context (New York: Harper & Row, 1963), p. 44. Copyright 1963 Paul L. Lehmann. All quotations used with permission of the publisher.

15. Ibid., p. 45.

16. Ibid.

17. Ibid.

18. Bonhoeffer, Ethics, p. 246.

19. Like Barth and Bonhoeffer, Lehmann also makes obedience the central problem of Christian ethics. For Lehmann, Christian ethics is primarily concerned "with the terms and the territory of obedience" (Lehmann, Ethics in a Christian Context, p. 274).

20. Cf. Gustafson, Christ and the Moral Life, pp. 11-60. While Gustafson is concerned in this study with the significance of Christ for the moral life of individuals in their personal existence, his analysis and critique of Christocentric ethics in that context are quite pertinent to our study of Christian social ethics.

21. On the importance of this work, compare N.H. Søe: "It seems to me no exaggeration to state that the famous ethics of Emil Brunner, Das Gebot und die Ordnungen (1932), more than any other book marks the beginning of modern works on theological ethics." N.H. Søe, "The Personal Ethics of Emil Brunner," in The Theology of Emil Brunner, ed. Charles W. Kegley (New York: Macmillan, 1962), p. 247.

22. Brunner, Divine Imperative, pp. 10-11.

23. Ibid., pp. 128-129.

24. Ibid., p. 209.

25. Ibid. Cf. Emil Brunner, *Dogmatics*, 2 vols. (Philadelphia: Westminster Press, 1950-1952), II, pp. 24-31.

26. Reinhold Niebuhr, *An Interpretation of Christian Ethics* (New York: Harper & Brothers, 1935), pp. 37-61.

27. Ibid., pp. 7-8, 37.

28. Ibid, p. 214.

29. Ibid., pp. 104, 197.

30. Reinhold Niebuhr, *Nature and Destiny of Man*, 2 vols. (New York: Scribner's, 1943), II, pp. 54-55. Copyright 1941, 1943 Charles Scribner's Sons; copyright renewed 1969, 1971 Reinhold Niebuhr. All quotations reprinted with permission of Charles Scribner's Sons.

31. Ibid., p. 73.

32. Ibid., p. 64.

33. Ibid., I, p. 15.

34. Ibid., II, p. 67.

35. Ibid., I, p. 136.

36. Ibid., I, p. 142.

37. Ibid., II, p. 67.

38. Reinhold Niebuhr, *The Self and the Dramas of History* (New York: Scribner's, 1955), p. 232. Cf. *Nature and Destiny of Man*, I, pp. 287-288.

39. For Ramsey's critique of dualism in Brunner's ethic, see Paul Ramsey, *Basic Christian Ethics* (Chicago: University of Chicago Press, 1980), pp. 2-3. All quotations reprinted by permission of The University of Chicago Press. Copyright, 1950, by Charles Scribner's Sons; copyright renewed 1977 by Paul Ramsey. Published 1950. Paperback edition 1980. See also *Nine Modern Moralists*, pp. 181-208 (on Brunner) and pp. 111-147 (on Reinhold Niebuhr).

40. Ramsey, *Nine Modern Moralists*, p. 207.

41. Ibid., p. 208.

Notes to Pages 36-41

42. Ibid., pp. 139-140.

43. Ibid., p. 139.

44. Ramsey, *Basic Christian Ethics*, pp. xiv.

45. Ibid., pp. 343-344.

46. Ramsey, *Nine Modern Moralists*, p. 7.

47. Ibid., p. 5.

48. Ramsey, *Basic Christian Ethics*, p. 23.

49. Ibid., p. 21.

50. Cf. Ramsey, *Nine Modern Moralists*, p. 6.

51. Cf. Paul Ramsey, *The Patient as Person* (New Haven: Yale University Press, 1970), pp. xi-xviii.

52. Paul Ramsey, *War and the Christian Conscience* (Durham, North Carolina: Duke University Press, 1961), p. xx.

53. Ibid., p. xviii.

54. Cf. James M. Gustafson, *The Contributions of Theology to Medical Ethics*, (Milwaukee: Marquette University, Department of Theology, 1975), pp. 43-44. See also Charles E. Curran, "Paul Ramsey and Traditional Roman Catholic Natural Law Theory," in *Love and Society: Essays in the Ethics of Paul Ramsey*, eds. James Johnson and David Smith (Missoula, Montana: Scholars Press, 1974), pp. 47-65; see, esp., p. 56.

55. Ramsey, *Basic Christian Ethics*, pp. 20-22.

56. Paul Ramsey, *Christian Ethics and the Sit-In* (New York: Association Press, 1961), p. 22; *The Patient as Person*, p. xii.

57. Paul Ramsey, "Some Rejoinders," *The Journal of Religious Ethics* 4:2 (Fall, 1976), p. 190.

58. Lehmann, *Ethics in a Christian Context*, p. 274.

59. Ibid., pp. 268-284, esp. p. 275; cf. Barth, *Church Dogmatics*, II/2, pp. 509-551.

60. H. Richard Niebuhr, *The Responsible Self*, pp. 42-46.

Notes to Pages 41-46

61. Ibid., p. 44.

62. Ibid., p. 45.

63. Cf. Libertus A. Hoedemaker, The Theology of H. Richard Niebuhr (Philadelphia: Pilgrim Press, 1970), p. 63: It is Niebuhr's understanding of Christian faith which "allows for the freedom to start freely in human moral existence, not because this is a common ground we share with all men to begin with, but because we can treat it as such, inspired by our particular standpoint."

64. H. Richard Niebuhr, Radical Monotheism, pp. 33, 42.

65. Ibid., p. 32.

66. H. Richard Niebuhr, Christ and Culture, pp. 190-256.

67. H. Richard Niebuhr, Radical Monotheism, pp. 38-48.

68. H. Richard Niebuhr, Responsible Self, pp. 161-178.

69. Cf. Hoedemaker, Theology of H. Richard Niebuhr, p. 64.

70. Ramsey, Faith and Ethics, p. 148.

71. H. Richard Niebuhr, Radical Monotheism, p. 111.

72. Gustafson, Christ and the Moral Life, pp. 1-3.

73. James M. Gustafson, Can Ethics Be Christian? (Chicago: Universtity of Chicago Press, 1975), pp. 13-24. See, also, James M. Gustafson, Ethics from a Theocentric Perspective, I: Theology and Ethics (Chicago: University of Chicago Press, 1981), pp. 115-154, esp. pp. 115-129. This important volume appeared after the present essay had been completed except for final revisions. At key points in the present study, however, an effort has been made to show how Ethics from a Theocentric Perspective, I, is related to Gustafson's earlier works. Basically, the former represents a more systematic elaboration and development of the latter.

74. James M. Gustafson, Christian Ethics and the Community (Philadelphia: United Church Press, 1971), pp. 101-126.

75. Gustafson, Ethics from a Theocentric Perspective, I, p. 115.

76. For the clearest and fullest statement of this aspect of Gustafson's ethics, see ibid., esp. pp. 87-113.

77. Gustafson, Can Ethics Be Christian?, pp. 156-157.

78. Ibid.; cf. Ethics from a Theocentric Perspective, I, p. 327.

79. Gustafson, Can Ethics Be Christian?, pp. 148-149.

80. Ibid., pp. 114-116.

81. Ibid., pp. 102-103, 112-116.

Chapter 3

1. Brunner, Divine Imperative, pp. 111, 291.

2. Barth, Church Dogmatics, II/2, pp. 559-561.

3. Ibid., III/4, p.4.

4. Ibid., II/2, p. 661.

5. Ibid., III/4, p. 25.

6. Ibid.

7. Ibid., II/2, p. 586.

8. Ibid., p. 561.

9. Ibid., p. 609.

10. Ibid., p. 606.

11. Ibid., p. 605.

12. Ibid., p. 566.

13. Ibid., p. 586.

14. Ibid., III/4, pp. 24-31.

15. Ibid., p. 31.

16. Ibid., II/2, pp. 683-700.

17. Ibid., p. 699.

18. Cf. ibid., IV/2, pp. 751-824.

Notes to Pages 55-62

19. Ibid., II/2, pp. 641-661.

20. Ibid., p. 578.

21. Ibid., p. 569.

22. Ibid., IV/2, pp. 727-840.

23. Brunner, Divine Imperative, pp. 111-113.

24. Ibid., pp. 122-131.

25. Ibid., pp. 210-336.

26. Emil Brunner, Justice and the Social Order (London: Lutterworth Press, 1945).

27. Brunner, The Divine Imperative, p. 314.

28. For Barth love is also an act, but as such its practice is limited to the Christian community where such practice can be mutual. Friendliness is the duty which Christians owe to nonbelievers. In any event, love is not limited in its application to relationships between two individuals, and community is conceived in more inclusive terms. Moreover, love is not made the totality of the divine command even in the order of redemption. See Barth, Church Dogmatics, IV/2, pp. 803-809.

29. Bonhoeffer, Ethics, p. 57.

30. Ibid., pp. 17-25.

31. Ibid., pp. 192-230.

32. Dietrich Bonhoeffer, The Cost of Discipleship, rev. and unabridged edition (New York: Macmillan, 1959); cf. Barth, Church Dogmatics, IV/2, pp. 533-534. See also Gustafson, Christ and the Moral Life, pp. 168-171.

33. Bonhoeffer, Ethics, pp. 252-267; cf. Barth, Church Dogmatics, III/4, pp. 29-30. For a fuller discussion of the spheres and mandates, see below, Chapter 6.

34. Ramsey, Basic Christian Ethics, p. 115.

35. Reinhold Niebuhr, Nature and Destiny of Man, II, pp. 246-247.

36. Ibid., p. 246.

Notes to Pages 62-66

37. Ibid., I, p. 285.

38. Gordon Harland, The Thought of Reinhold Niebuhr (New York: Oxford University Press, 1960), pp. 40-41.

39. Cf. Reinhold Niebuhr, An Interpretation of Christian Ethics, p. 147: "The ideal possibility for men involved in any social situation may always be defined in terms of freedom and equality. The highest good consists in freedom to develop the essential potentialities of their nature without hindrance....the next highest good is equality; for there is no final principle of arbitration between conflicting human interests except that which equates the worth of competing individuals."

40. Reinhold Niebuhr, Self and the Dramas of History, p. 151.

41. See Ramsey, Nine Modern Moralists, pp. 122-124, 140-142.

42. Reinhold Niebuhr, Faith and History (New York: Scribner's, 1949), p. 183.

43. Reinhold Niebuhr, Nature and Destiny of Man, I, pp. 280-300. See also Harry R. Davis and Robert C. Good, Reinhold Niebuhr on Politics (New York: Scribner's, 1960, pp. 163-179.

44. Ramsey describes Reinhold Niebuhr as a "radical revisionist" among natural law theorists. Ramsey's implied criticism of Niebuhr for his failure to derive a more structured ethic from his essentialist understanding of human nature reflects Ramsey's more rationalistic, deductive approach to natural law whereas Niebuhr's radical revision of the latter is based on a more dynamic, existential conception of human nature and a more historical understanding of the rational norms of human history. See Ramsey, Nine Modern Moralists, pp. 111-147.

45. Reinhold Niebuhr, Nature and Destiny of Man, I, pp. 154-155.

46. Reinhold Niebuhr, Faith and History, p. 183.

47. Ramsey, Basic Christian Ethics, pp. xi, 388.

48. Ibid., pp. 21-24, 45.

49. Ibid., p. 148.

50. See ibid., p. 116: "When right relation to neighbor has been established, then and then only....as a secondary though quite essential concern, does it enter into a Christian's head for his neighbor's sake to ascend whatever scale of values he may find

Notes to Pages 66-70

reasonably creditable"(italics added).

51. See Ramsey, Deeds and Rules, pp. 108-109.

52. Paul Ramsey, Fabricated Man (New Haven: Yale University Press, 1970), p. 122.

53. See Paul Ramsey, The Just War: Force and Political Responsibility (New York: Scribner's, 1968), p. 431. Cf. Paul Ramsey, "The Case of the Curious Exception," in Norm and Context in Christian Ethics, eds. Gene H. Outka and Paul Ramsey (New York: Scribner's, 1968), pp. 132-133. See also Paul F. Camenisch, "Paul Ramsey's Task: Some Methodological Clarifications and Questions," in Johnson and Smith, Love and Society, pp. 76-77.

54. Compare the distinction which Ramsey makes between the "ethics of consent" and "ethics in the consent situation" (Patient as Person, pp. 3-12).

55. Outka and Ramsey, Norm and Context in Christian Ethics, p. 73.

56. Ibid., p. 74.

57. See ibid., p. 75: "Our model of the component stages in moral reasoning can, therefore, be stated as follows: ultimate norm (agape, utility, self-realization, etc.); general principles; defined-action principles, or generic terms of approval and generic offense-terms; definite-action rules, or moral-species-terms; then the subsumption of cases."

58. Ramsey, Basic Christian Ethics, p. 219.

59. Ibid.

60. Ibid., p. 210.

61. Ibid., p. 219.

62. I Cor. 13:4-7.

63. Ramsey, Basic Christian Ethics, pp. 327-337.

64. Ibid., pp. 338-343.

65. Ibid., pp. 351-366.

66. Ramsey, Nine Modern Moralists, pp. 6-8.

Notes to Pages 71-76

67. Ramsey, Basic Christian Ethics, p. 388.

68. Ramsey, Deeds and Rules; see esp. pp. 1-5.

69. Ramsey, Patient as Person, pp. xii-xiv.

Chapter 4

1. Lehmann, Ethics in a Christian Context, p. 45.

2. Ibid., p. 46.

3. Ibid., p. 159.

4. Ibid., p. 101.

5. Elsewhere Lehmann defines the will of God as "forgiveness and justice and reconciliation" [Paul Lehmann, "The Foundation and Pattern of Christian Behavior," in Christian Faith and Social Action, ed. John A. Hutchinson (New York: Scribner's, 1953), pp. 112-113.] If developed, these themes could provide a more comprehensive structure for Christian ethics than those which he employs in Ethics in a Christian Context.

6. Lehmann, Ethics in a Christian Context, p. 144.

7. Ibid., pp. 61, 63.

8. Ibid., p. 72.

9. Ibid., p. 54.

10. Ibid., p. 55.

11. Ibid.

12. Ibid., p. 122.

13. Ibid. While Lehmann praises Luther's Sermon on Good Works as "perhaps the most important ethical treatise of the sixteenth century," he goes much farther than Luther in separating the form of an act from its symbolic, or parabolic, meaning (p. 40). Lehmann criticizes the Reformers' concept of the "threefold office of the law" as being too preceptual (p. 78).

14. Cf. Gustafson, Can Ethics Be Christian?, pp. 148-149, 158-159. Gustafson describes the methodologies of Barth, H. Richard Niebuhr, and Lehmann as "intuitive." This element is much

Notes to Pages 76-81

stronger--at least in principle--in Lehmann than it is in Niebuhr and Barth.

15. Lehmann, Ethics in a Christian Context, pp. 358-359. Lehmann calls this a "theonomous" conscience.

16. Ibid., p. 130.

17. H. Richard Niebuhr, Radical Monotheism, pp. 100-113.

18. Ibid., p. 107.

19. Ibid., p. 100.

20. Ibid., p. 103.

21. Ibid., p. 108.

22. H. Richard Niebuhr, Responsible Self, p. 61.

23. Ibid., pp. 65-68; see also pp. 161-178.

24. See Albert R. Jonsen, Responsibility in Modern Religious Ethics (Cleveland: Corpus Publications, 1968), p. 147.

25. H. Richard Niebuhr, Responsible Self, p. 65.

26. Ibid., pp. 162-173.

27. On the virtues of Christ, see H. Richard Niebuhr, Christ and Culture, pp. 11-29; on Christian ethics as response to the divine action, see James W. Fowler, To See the Kingdom (New York: Abingdon, 1974), pp. 151-200; on the role of Scripture, see Waldo Beach and H. Richard Niebuhr, eds., Christian Ethics: Sources of the Living Tradition (New York: Ronald Press, 1955), pp. 10-45, and Niebuhr, The Responsible Self, pp. 149-178; on the relations of the moral law to Christian ethics, see Ramsey, Faith and Ethics, pp. 140-172. See, also, E. Clinton Gardner, "Responsibility and Moral Direction in the Ethics of H. Richard Niebuhr," Encounter 40 (Spring, 1979): 143-168.

28. H. Richard Niebuhr, Christ and Culture, pp. 11-29.

29. H. Richard Niebuhr, Radical Monotheism, p. 41.

30. Ibid.

31. H. Richard Niebuhr, Christ and Culture, p. 19; Radical Monotheism, p. 42.

Notes to Pages 81-83

32. Fowler speaks of a "tacit covenantal structure" of human community in Niebuhr (Fowler, To See the Kingdom, p. 206).

33. See Ramsey, Faith and Ethics, pp. 140-172. Ramsey speaks of the promise which Niebuhr's ethics contains "of a dynamic ethics of redemption which does not simply build upon yet does not jettison the ethics of creation" (p. 168).

34. H. Richard Niebuhr, "Evangelical and Protestant Ethics," in The Heritage of the Reformation, ed. E. J. F. Arndt (New York: Richard R. Smith, 1950), p. 226; cf. H. Richard Niebuhr, Meaning of Revelation, p. 167.

35. Arndt, Heritage of the Reformation, p. 226.

36. Gustafson, Can Ethics Be Christian?, pp. 156-157.

37. Gustafson, Ethics from a Theocentric Perspective, I, pp. 235-251. Gustafson's concept of God as Redeemer differs radically from the classical Christian tradition. In a theocentric theology life after death is not necessary, Gustafson believes, since God does not exist to satisfy human desires (p. 184). Gustafson does speak of redemption in two ways, however, viz., redemption from fatedness and from sin (pp. 248-251). In his Christology he draws primarily upon the narratives of the synoptic gospels; however, the traditional biblical eschatological symbols are not sustainable in a theocentric conception of the divine governance (p. 268).

38. Ibid., p. 273.

39. Ibid., p. 264.

40. Ibid., pp. 201-204.

41. Ibid., p. 106.

42. Gustafson, Christ and the Moral Life, p. 258.

43. Gustafson, Ethics from a Theocentric Perspective, I, pp. 270-271. Particularly in this volume, Gustafson is reluctant to ascribe intentionality to God since this term connotes "intelligence" and "will," both of which may imply an anthropomorphic view of God. Hence, he prefers to speak of God's purposes. In a more general sense, however, Gustafson's conception of God's relation to the world may be appropriately described in terms of "intention" and "will" (ibid., p. 113; cf. Contributions of Theology, pp. 18-19).

233

Notes to Pages 84-90

44. See James M. Gustafson, "Moral Discernment in the Christian Life," in Outka and Ramsey, Norm and Context in Christian Ethics, pp. 17-36. See also Gustafson, Ethics from a Theocentric Perspective, I, pp. 333-338.

45. Gustafson, Christian Ethics and the Community, pp. 83-100.

46. See Gustafson, Christ and the Moral Life, pp. 264-271.

47. Gustafson, Can Ethics Be Christian?, pp. 163-168.

48. Lehmann, Ethics in a Christian Context, pp. 358-359.

49. Gustafson, Christ and the Moral Life, pp. 265-271.

50. Gustafson, Ethics from a Theocentric Perspective, I, p. 276.

51. Gustafson, Can Ethics Be Christian?, pp. 114-116.

52. Gustafson, Contributions of Theology, pp. 18, 44.

53. Ibid., pp. 31-38, 76-78; cf. Ethics from a Theocentric Perspective, I, p. 106.

54. Gustafson, Can Ethics Be Christian?, p.78.

55. Gustafson, Christ and the Moral Life, p. 248.

56. Gustafson, Christian Ethics and the Community, p. 202.

57. Ibid., pp. 153-163.

58. Cf. Gustafson, Ethics from a Theocentric Perspective, I, pp. 339-340. The moral requisites for the sustenance and fulfilment of life will be treated more fully in Volume II of this work, Ethics and Theology (forthcoming).

Chapter 5

1. H. Richard Niebuhr, Responsible Self, pp. 47-68.

2. Ibid., p. 155.

3. Ibid., p. 157.

4. Cf. Ramsey, Basic Christian Ethics, pp. 89, 388.

5. Barth, Church Dogmatics, III/2, p. 208.

Notes to Pages 91-95

6. Ibid., p. 243.

7. Ibid., pp. 274-275.

8. Ibid., p. 321.

9. Ibid., pp. 249-285.

10. Ibid., p. 273. "[I]f humanity does not consist first and last in this freedom, it does not exist at all."

11. Ibid., p. 324.

12. Barth, ibid., III/1, pp. 96-97.

13. Ibid., p. 231.

14. Ibid., III/2, p. 136.

15. See Charles C. West, Communism and the Theologians (Philadelphia: Westminster Press, 1958), pp. 285-325; cf. Robert E. Willis, The Ethics of Karl Barth (Leiden: Brill, 1971), p. 438.

16. Barth, Church Dogmatics, III/4, pp. 3-46. Barth pursues this task in the remainder of ibid., III/4 and IV/2.

17. Ibid., III/4, pp. 30-31.

18. Ibid., II/2, p. 641.

19. Ibid., pp. 642-643.

20. Ibid., p. 662.

21. Ibid., pp. 644-645.

22. Emil Brunner, Man in Revolt (Philadelphia: Westminster, 1947), pp. 526, 532-533.

23. Ibid., p. 170; cf. Divine Imperative, p. 62.

24. Brunner, Man in Revolt, p. 170. See also Emil Brunner, Nature and Grace (London: Geoffrey, 1946), p. 31.

25. Brunner, Man in Revolt, p. 480.

26. Ibid., p. 50.

27. Ibid., pp. 135, 201-203.

Notes to Pages 96-100

28. Ibid., pp. 273-274.

29. Ibid., p. 11.

30. Brunner, Divine Imperative, p. 208.

31. Ibid.

32. Brunner, Man in Revolt, p. 146.

33. Ibid., pp. 525-526.

34. Brunner, Divine Imperative, pp. 148-151.

35. Ibid., pp. 209-210.

36. Bonhoeffer, Ethics, p. 8.

37. Ibid., pp. 63-64.

38. Ibid., pp. 18, 22.

39. Ibid., p. 192.

40. Ibid., pp. 203, 209-210.

41. Ibid., pp. 194-267. The deontological character of Bonhoeffer's ethics is even more pronounced in his earlier work, Cost of Discipleship.

42. Bonhoeffer, Ethics, p. 241.

43. Ibid., p. 425.

44. Ibid., p. 211.

45. Ibid., p. 216. Cf. Letters and Papers from Prison, ed. Eberhard Bethge (New York: Macmillan, 1962), p. 20: Free responsibility "depends upon a God who demands bold action as the free response of faith, and who promises forgiveness and consolation to the man who becomes a sinner in the process."

46. Bonhoeffer, Ethics, p. 216.

47. See Michael R. Weed, "Conscience in Protestant Ethics: An Examination of Protestant Views of the Nature and Function of Conscience Focusing on the Thought of Select Contemporary Theologians" (Ph.D. dissertation, Emory University, 1978).

Notes to Pages 101-107

48. Ramsey, Basic Christian Ethics, p. 263. Ramsey's concept of the "imago Dei" lacks clarity at a number of points. It is unclear, for example, whether this image is present in all men or whether it exists only where persons "like a mirror" obediently reflect God's will in all of their life and actions. It is also unclear how the "acquired image" is related to salvation and in what sense rationality is "an imago Dei" in man (pp. 255-264).

49. Ramsey, Patient as Person, p. xii; Christian Ethics and the Sit-In (New York: Association Press, 1961), pp. 22, 26.

50. Ramsey, Christian Ethics and the Sit-In, pp. 31-32.

51. Ramsey, Patient as Person, p. xii.

52. There are a number of unresolved issues related to the concept of the covenant in Ramsey's ethics. How, for example, are covenant claims based upon birth related to those based upon choice or need? See Johnson and Smith, Love and Society, pp. 74-75.

53. Ramsey, Patient as Person, p. 9.

54. Paul Ramsey, Fabricated Man, pp. 30-39, 87-88. To separate radically what God has joined together in parenthood--viz., the unitive and the procreative purposes of sex and marriage--means "a refusal of the image of God's creation in our own" (p. 39). The covenant of parenthood lies at "the heart of the humanum in sex, marriage, and generation"(p. 88).

55. Lehmann, Ethics in a Christian Context, pp. 90-95.

56. Ibid., p. 104.

57. Ibid., p. 119. Cf. Karl Barth, Christ and Adam (New York: Harper & Brothers, 1957), pp. 26-35.

58. Lehmann, Ethics in a Christian Context, pp. 120-121, 148-154.

59. Ibid., p. 154.

60. Ibid., pp. 156-159.

61. Ibid., p. 122.

62. Ibid., p. 123.

63. Ibid., p. 141.

64. Ibid., p. 152.

65. Ibid., pp. 348-352. As Gustafson points out, however, Lehmann does not make clear how the human ethical act is related to the divine activity. On the one hand, the former may be interpreted as a response to the divine intention through human intentions that are consistent with the latter; on the other hand, it may be a duplication of the pattern of divine action. If Lehmann intends the former, he does not give adequate attention to the role of moral reasoning in ethical reflection; if he intends the latter, he obscures the difference between God's action and human activity (Gustafson, Christ and the Moral Life, p. 258).

66. Lehmann, Ethics in a Christian Context, pp. 358-359.

67. Ibid., p. 366.

68. Reinhold Niebuhr, Nature and Destiny of Man, II, p. 55.

69. Cf. ibid., p. 204.

70. Ibid., I, p. 150.

71. Ibid., p. 152.

72. Ibid., pp. 178-186.

73. Ibid., pp. 186-203.

74. Cf. ibid., pp. 231-240.

75. Ibid., pp. 208-219.

76. Ibid., pp. 219-227. See also Kegley and Bretall, Reinhold Niebuhr, p. 437, where Niebuhr acknowledges the inadequacy of this formula.

77. Reinhold Niebuhr, Nature and Destiny of Man, I, p. 222.

78. Ibid., p. 270.

79. Reinhold Niebuhr, The Children of Light and the Children of Darkness (New York: Scribner's, 1960), p. xiii.

80. Reinhold Niebuhr, Nature and Destiny of Man, I, p. 143.

81. Ibid., II, pp. 48-52, 287-321.

82. Gustafson, Christ and the Moral Life, p. 139.

83. Niebuhr uses this phrase in "Theology and Political Thought in the Western World," The Ecumenical Review 9 (April, 1957), pp. 253-262. See also Harland, Thought of Reinhold Niebuhr, pp. 189-192.

84. Hutchison, Christian Faith and Social Action, p. 241.

85. Gustafson, Can Ethics Be Christian?, p. 159.

86. Ibid., pp. 114-116.

87. Gustafson, Ethics from a Theocentric Perspective, I, p. 242.

88. Gustafson, Can Ethics Be Christian?, p. 14. See also Christ and the Moral Life, pp. 240-271.

89. Gustafson, Contributions of Theology, pp. 31-38; Ethics from a Theocentric Perspective, I, pp. 106, 307.

90. See James M. Gustafson, Protestant and Roman Catholic Ethics (Chicago: University of Chicago Press, 1978), pp. 108-119. For Gustafson's concept of sin, see Ethics from a Theocentric Perspective, I, pp. 293-317.

91. H. Richard Niebuhr, Responsible Self, pp. 47-68.

92. Ibid., p. 53. In response to the question: "What is possible for human agents?" the deontologist replies, "That we should rule ourselves as being ruled, and not much more" (ibid., p. 52).

93. Ibid., pp. 56, 159-160.

94. Ibid., p. 59.

95. Ibid., pp. 60-61.

96. Ibid., p. 126.

97. Ibid., p. 173. See also H. Richard Niebuhr, "The Idea of the Covenant and American Democracy," Church History XXIII (1954):133.

98. Ibid., p. 101.

99. Cf. Richard E. Crouter, "H. Richard Niebuhr and Stoicism," The Journal of Religious Ethics II (1974):142. "Perhaps this (human freedom) dimension of Niebuhr's thought is the truly understressed and problematic aspect of his systematic position, even though his major works...take care to present his understanding of the way in which man is free while standing in a

Notes to Pages 123-132

relationship of wider and ultimate dependence."

100. H. Richard Niebuhr, Responsible Self, p. 170.

Chapter 6

1. Barth, Church Dogmatics, III/4, p. 24.

2. Ibid., III/2.

3. Ibid., III/4.

4. Ibid., III/2, pp. 75-77. In this connection see Barth's discussion of the "Phenomena of the Human" (ibid., pp. 71-132).

5. Ibid., III/4, p. 44.

6. West, Communism and the Theologians, p. 205.

7. Barth, Church Dogmatics, III/2, pp. 208, 243-274.

8. West, Communism and the Theologians, pp. 244-245.

9. Karl Barth, Community, State, and Church: Three Essays, with an Introduction by Will Herberg (Garden City, New York: Doubleday, 1960), pp. 149-189.

10. Ibid., p. 188.

11. See Edward LeRoy Long, Jr., A Survey of Christian Ethics (New York: Oxford University Press, 1967), pp. 200-203; West, Communism and the Theologians, pp. 200-204; Barth, Community, State, and Church, pp. 31-38; and John H. Yoder, Karl Barth and the Problem of War (Nashville: Abingdon Press, 1970), pp. 119-131.

12. Barth, Community, State, and Church, p. 183.

13. Lehmann, Ethics in a Christian Context, p. 115.

14. Ibid., p. 120.

15. See James T. Laney, "A Critique of Radical Contextualist Ethics" (Ph. D. dissertation, Yale University, 1966), p. 157.

16. Lehmann, Ethics in a Christian Context, p. 144.

17. Ibid., p. 153.

18. Ibid., p. 144.

19. Ibid., pp. 141, 143.

20. Ibid., p. 55.

21. Ibid.

22. Ibid., p. 90 (italics added).

23. Paul Lehmann, The Transfiguration of Politics (New York: Harper & Row, 1975).

24. Ibid., pp. 261-262.

25. Ibid., p. 262.

26. There is a striking similarity between Lehmann's conclusion at this point and Barth's appeal to necessity as a possible justification of war in exceptional cases (Barth, Church Dogmatics, III/4, pp. 461-462). It should be noted, however, that Barth's appeal to necessity comes under the category of "the exceptional case" which presupposes a general rejection of resort to arms.

27. Brunner, Divine Imperative, pp. 122, 291.

28. Ibid., pp. 330-339.

29. Ibid., pp. 337-338.

30. Ibid., pp. 128-129.

31. Ibid., p. 222.

32. Emil Brunner, Justice and the Social Order, pp. 20, 86.

33. Ibid., p. 116.

34. Ibid., p. 117.

35. Bonhoeffer, Ethics, p. 73.

36. Ibid., p. 252. Bonhoeffer elswhere identifies these, alternatively, as labor, marriage, government, and church (ibid., p. 73).

37. Ibid., p. 76.

38. Ibid., p. 257.

39. Ibid., pp. 84-100.

40. Ibid., p. 92.

41. Ibid., p. 103.

42. Laney, "A Critique of Radical Contextualist Ethics," pp. 134-147. Cf. James T. Laney, "An Examination of Bonhoeffer's Ethical Contextualism," in A Bonhoeffer Legacy, ed. A. J. Klassen (Grand Rapids, Michigan: Erdmans, 1981), pp. 306-310.

43. Reinhold Niebuhr, Nature and Destiny of Man, II, p. 211.

44. Ibid., p. 188.

45. Ibid., pp. 96-97.

46. Reinhold Niebuhr, Self and the Dramas of History, p. 165.

47. Ibid., p. 34.

48. Ibid., p. 163.

49. Ibid., pp. 35-36.

50. Reinhold Niebuhr, Christian Realism and Political Problems (New York: Scribner's, 1953), p. 196.

51. Reinhold Niebuhr, Nature and Destiny of Man, I, p. 208.

52. Reinhold Niebuhr, Christian Realism, pp. 120-121.

53. Ibid., p. 134. For Niebuhr's criticism of Augustine's conception of charitas and amor dei, see ibid., pp. 139-140. Niebuhr agrees essentially with Nygren that, under the influence of Plotinus, Augustine misinterpreted the New Testament concept of agape. In reducing love of the neighbor to a form of love for God, Augustine lost sight of the New Testament meaning of agape as the meeting of the neighbor's need. Secondly, by making God the only worthy object of love (amor dei), Augustine obscured the notion of sacrificial love as the ultimate meaning of agape.

54. Gordon Harland, The Thought of Reinhold Niebuhr (New York: Oxford University Press, 1960), p. 180.

55. Ibid., pp. 193-195.

56. Reinhold Niebuhr, Nature and Destiny of Man, II, p. 244.

57. Ibid., p. 204.

58. Reinhold Niebuhr, "The Christian Faith and the Economic Life of Liberal Society," in Goals of Economic Life, ed. Dudley Ward (New York: Harper Brothers, 1953), p. 451.

59. See Long, Survey of Christian Ethics, pp. 216-226.

60. Reinhold Niebuhr, Nature and Destiny of Man, II, pp. 257-258.

61. Ibid., p. 248.

62. Reinhold Niebuhr, Faith and History, pp. 188-189.

63. Cf. Arthur Schlesinger, Jr., "Reinhold Niebuhr's Role in American Political Thought and Life," in Reinhold Niebuhr, Kegley and Bretall, eds., pp. 126-150.

64. Harland, Thought of Reinhold Niebuhr, pp. 186-192.

65. Reinhold Niebuhr, "Theology and Political Thought in the Western World," p. 256.

66. Quoted in Kegley and Bretall, Reinhold Niebuhr, p. 161.

67. H. Richard Niebuhr, Responsible Self, p. 78.

68. Ibid., p. 73.

69. Ibid., pp. 71-79.

70. H. Richard Niebuhr, Radical Monotheism, pp. 24-37.

71. Ibid., pp. 49-89. See also Kingdom of God in America and "The Idea of Covenant and American Democracy."

72. H. Richard Niebuhr, "The Triad of Faith," The Andover Newton Theological Bulletin XLV (October, 1954), pp. 3-12.

73. Ibid., p. 12.

74. Ibid., p. 9. See also Responsible Self, pp. 79-89.

75. H. Richard Niebuhr, Radical Monotheism, p. 41.

76. Ibid.

77. Ramsey, Patient as Person, p. xii. Cf. Fabricated Man, p. 38: "Men and women are created in covenant, to covenant, and for covenant."

78. Ramsey, Basic Christian Ethics, pp. 331-337.

79. Ibid., pp. 336-337.

80. Ibid., p. 337.

81. Ramsey, Nine Modern Moralists, pp. 5-7.

82. Ramsey, War and the Christian Conscience, pp. xxii-xxiii.

83. Ramsey, Basic Christian Ethics, pp. 373-388.

84. Ibid., p. 388.

85. Ramsey, War and the Christian Conscience, pp. xxi, 112.

86. Ibid., p. xxi.

87. Ibid., p. 112.

88. Ramsey, Patient as Person, pp. xi-xii.

89. Ibid., p. xiv.

90. Ibid., p. xii.

91. Cf. Charles E. Curran, "Paul Ramsey and Traditional Roman Catholic Natural Law theory," in Love and Justice, Johnson and Smith, eds. pp. 52-56.

92. Cf. Gustafson, Protestant and Roman Catholic Ethics, pp. 150-151.

93. Ramsey, Patient as Person, p. xii; Christian Ethics and the Sit-In, p. 22.

94. Ramsey, Christian Ethics and the Sit-In, p. 28.

95. Ramsey, Nine Modern Moralists, pp. 5-7.

96. Ibid., p. 5.

97. Cf. Gustafson, Can Ethics Be Christian?, pp. 82-116. See also Ethics from a Theocentric Perspective, I, pp. 235-251.

Notes to Pages 168-179

98. For a discussion of the church, see James M. Gustafson, *Treasure in Earthen Vessels: The Church as a Human Community* (New York: Harper & Brothers, 1961), esp. pp. 99-112. For an analysis of the relationship of Christian ethics to secular community, see *Christian Ethics and the Community*.

99. James M. Gustafson, *The Church as Moral Decision-Maker* (Philadelphia: Pilgrim Press, 1970), pp. 63-80.

100. Ibid., p. 66.

101. Ibid., pp. 71-76.

102. This section was written before the publication of *Ethics from a Theocentric Perspective, II: Ethics and Theology*.

103. Gustafson, *Church as Moral Decision-Maker*, pp. 172-175, 202.

104. Cf. Gustafson, *Protestant and Roman Catholic Ethics*, p. 140: "The writings of Thomas Aquinas, in my judgment, present the most comprehensive and coherent (that is, systematic) account of theological ethics in the history of Christianity."

105. Gustafson, *Can Ethics Be Christian?*, p. 158.

106. Gustafson, *Protestant and Roman Catholic Ethics*, pp. 114-119.

107. Ibid. Cf. *Contributions of Theology*, pp. 47-52. Significantly, however, Gustafson finds Rahner's ethic excessively individualistic and anthropocentric.

108. Gustafson, *Can Ethics Be Christian?*, p. 173.

109. Ibid.; *Contributions of Theology*, pp. 93-95.

110. Gustafson, *Theology and Christian Ethics*, p. 145; *Can Ethics Be Christian?*, pp. 114-116.

111. Gustafson, *Theology and Christian Ethics*, p. 285.

112. Gustafson, *Ethics from a Theocentric Perspective*, I, pp. 316, 338-342. This task will be undertaken in the forthcoming Volume II of this work.

Chapter 7

1. H. Richard Niebuhr, *Responsible Self*, p. 42.

Notes to Pages 179-186

2. Cf. James M. Gustafson and James T. Laney, eds., On Being Responsible (New York: Harper & Row, 1968), p. 15.

3. Maurice Mandelbaum, Phenomenology of Moral Experience (Baltimore, Maryland: Johns Hopkins Press, 1969), p. 35.

4. H. Richard Niebuhr, Responsible Self, p. 63. Stated in theological terms, this primary question becomes, "What is God doing?" (ibid., pp. 122-126, 169).

5. This is not surprising since phenomenology did not develop as a self-conscious movement in this country until much later than it did in Europe and since it followed a largely independent course here. In this country the early development of this movement was rooted to a large extent in the radical empiricism of William James. See James M. Edie, ed., New Essays in Phenomenology (Chicago: Quadrangle Books, 1969).

6. H. Richard Niebuhr, "Triad of Faith," pp. 3-4.

7. Cf. Jonathan Edwards, The Nature of True Virtue (Ann Arbor, Michigan: University of Michigan Press, 1960). See also Roland A. Delattre, Beauty and Sensibility in the Thought of Jonathan Edwards (New Haven: Yale University Press, 1968).

8. Winter, Elements for a Social Ethic, p. xiv.

9. Ibid., pp. 88-99.

10. Ibid., pp. 91, 103.

11. Ibid., p. 117.

12. Ibid., p. 262.

13. Ibid., p. 224.

14. See ibid., p. 230. Winter specifically cites Niebuhr's essay "The Center of Value," as being especially helpful for understanding the norms of sociality.

15. Ibid., pp. 254-285.

16. For an analysis of the role of symbolic forms in ethics, see H. Richard Niebuhr, Responsible Self, pp. 151-160. "Symbol and reality participate in each other." Symbols give "intelligibility and form" to human experience. They shape the manner in which we apprehend and interpret the latter.

17. For an analysis of the authority of religious symbols and criteria for the selection of such symbols, see Gustafson, <u>Can Ethics Be Christian?</u>, pp. 117-144.

18. Knud E. Logstrup, <u>The Ethical Demand</u> (Philadelphia: Fortress Press, 1971), p. 113: "[I]t is not within our power to determine whether we wish to live in responsible relationships or not; we find ourselves in them simply because we exist."

19. Gustafson, <u>Can Ethics Be Christian?</u>, pp. 148-150, 156-157.

20. Ibid., pp. 115-116.

21. Gustafson, <u>Ethics from a Theocentric Perspective</u>, I, p. 317.

22. Ibid., p. 242: "The religious community <u>responds</u> to the signs of ordering of nature and society as marks of the divine sustenance and governance. It perceives its moral and social task to be to relate to that sustenance and governance in a <u>fitting</u> way, to relate to all things in a manner <u>appropriate</u> to their relations to it (italics added)."

23. Ibid., p. 242, 317.

24. Joseph Fletcher, <u>Moral Responsibility: Situation Ethics at Work</u> (Philadelphia: Westminster Press, 1967), esp. pp. 231-241.

25. Reinhold Niebuhr, "Christian Faith and Social Action," in John A. Hutchison, ed., <u>Christian Faith and Social Action</u>, p. 236 (italics added).

26. See Gustafson, <u>Ethics from a Theocentric Perspective</u>, I, pp. 273-274. Gustafson is primarily critical of the application of the response model of human agency to humanity's relations to God.

27. Cf. H. Richard Niebuhr, <u>Responsible Self</u>, p. 52.

28. Ibid., p. 170.

29. Ibid., p. 136.

30. Gustafson, <u>Christ and the Moral Life</u>, pp. 2-3.

31. Gustafson, <u>Can Ethics Be Christian?</u>, pp. 25-81.

32. Gustafson, <u>Contributions of Theology</u>, p. 52; cf. <u>Ethics from a Theocentric Perspective</u>, I, pp. 242, 317.

33. Ramsey, Basic Christian Ethics, p. xi.

34. See, e.g., Jay Katz, ed., Experimentation with Human Beings (New York: Russell Sage Foundation, 1972); Charles Fried, Medical Experimentation: Personal Integrity and Social Policy (New York: American Elsevier, 1974). See also Gustafson, Theology and Christian Ethics, pp. 245-271.

35. H. Richard Niebuhr, "The Idea of Covenant and American Democracy," esp. pp. 130-135.

36. Ibid., p. 130 (italics added).

37. See Gardner, "Responsibility and Moral Direction in the Ethics of H. Richard Niebuhr," pp. 143-168.

38. J. H. Oldham, "A Responsible Society," in The World Council of Churches, Man's Disorder and God's Design: The Amsterdam Series, Vol. III: The Church and the Disorder of Society (New York: Harper & Row, n.d.), pp. 120-154.

39. James Hastings Nichols, Evanston: An Interpretation (New York: Harper & Row, 1954), pp. 127-130.

40. Bennett, Christian Social Ethics in a Changing World, pp. 378-381.

41. Edward Duff, S.J., The Social Thought of the World Council of Churches (New York: Association Press, 1956), p. 193, esp. n. 2.

42. Ibid., p. 192.

43. The Third Assembly of the WCC (New Delhi, 1961) was the first to meet outside of the West. The Fourth Assembly met at Uppsala (1968); and the Fifth in Nairobi (1975). See Ernest W. Lefever, Amsterdam to Nairobi (Washington, D.C.: Ethics and Public Policy Center, 1979), pp. 12-46.

44. Lehmann, Ethics in a Christian Context, p. 101.

45. Gustafson, Can Ethics Be Christian?, pp. 114-116, 156-157.

46. For a fuller treatment of these themes in Niebuhr's lectures, see Fowler, To See the Kingdom, pp. 151-200. See also E. Clinton Gardner, Biblical Faith and Social Ethics (New York: Harper & Row, 1960), Chapters 5 and 7, for an interpretation of Christian ethics as response to the divine activity.

47. Cf. H. Richard Niebuhr, Radical Monotheism, p. 69.

Notes to Pages 214-217

48. For H. Richard Niebuhr, community never rests exclusively either upon interest or upon interest and power; loyalty of its members to each other and to a common cause is always also present in some form (ibid., pp. 65-68).

49. For Niebuhr's use of this concept in relation to God's governing action, see Fowler, To See the Kingdom, pp. 193-196.

50. Compare the Reports of Sections VIII and X of the "Conference on Faith, Science, and the Future," sponsored by the World Council of Churches (Cambridge, Massachusetts, July 12-24, 1979). These reports were entitled, respectively, "Economics of a Just, Participatory and Sustainable Society" and "Toward a New Christian Social Ethic and New Social Policies for the Churches" (World Council of Churches, Geneva, Switzerland, 1979). In this conference as a whole, justice, participation, and sustainability served as regulative criteria of social policy. As such they proved to be useful principles in the analysis and development of public policies affecting societies at different stages of technological development.

51. See Joseph L. Allen, "A Theological Approach to Moral Rights," The Journal of Religious Ethics II (Spring, 1974):119-141.

INDEX

Adams, James Luther, 222
Allen, Joseph L., 249
Aquinas, Thomas, 70, 119, 245
Aristotle, 119, 137
Augustine, 10, 125, 145-146, 161-162, 242

Barth, Karl, 3, 11-15; Christological anthropology, 90-93, 127-129; community, 126-131; covenant, 23, 55, 91-92, 198-199; directives, 54-55, 93, 203; divine command, 23-24; good (the), 50-60, 94; moral agency, 90-97, 194; moral evil, 92; responsibility, 55, 93-94, 188-189; social ethics, 129-131; special ethics, 127-129; spheres, 53-54, 93, 203; starting point, 22-27, 177;
Bennett, John C., 4, 13-14, 28, 106, 207
Bentham, Jeremy, 159
Bergson, Henri, 180
Bonhoeffer, Dietrich, 3-4, 11, 13-15; community, 134-135, 138-141; conscience, 99; deputyship, 59; ethics as formation, 24-25, 59; good (the), 25, 50; law-gospel, 98-100; moral agency, 90, 97-100; penultimate, 139-141, 195; responsibility, 59, 93, 97-100, 188-189, 194-195; starting point, 24-27, 177
Brunner, Emil, 3-4; community, 134-138; dualism, 30, 58, 97, 137-138; good (the), 50, 56-59; moral agency, 90, 93-97; orders of creation, 57, 96, 136-138, 203; philosophical ethics, 29; responsibility, 93, 95-96, 188-189, 194-195; sin, 96; starting point, 28-30, 34-36, 177
Buber, Martin, 152
Bultmann, Rudolf, 120

Calvin, John, 200
Camenisch, Paul F., 230
Character, see Virtue
Christian ethics, 21-22; contextualism, 26-27; and philosophical ethics, 25, 29, 37, 40-42, 46; see also Starting Point
Christocentrism, 5, 10-17; critique of H. Richard Niebuhr, 11, 13-15; in social ethics, 10; meanings of, 11-17; Ramsey, 37-38
Community, structures of, 125-174; dualism of creation and redemption, 134-151; structures of redemption, 126-134; transformation of community, 151-174
Cooley, George Horton, 152
Covenant, Barth, 23, 55, 91-92, 198-199; H. R. Niebuhr, 80, 155-156, 198, 213; Ramsey, 39, 70-72, 101-104, 116, 156-166, 198-201
Cox, Harvey, 222
Crouter, Richard E., 239
Curran, Charles E., 225, 244

Delattre, Roland, A., 246
Duff, Edward, 248

Edwards, Jonathan, 180-181, 200
Ethics, purpose of, 9, 203
Existentialist theology, 2-3

Fletcher, Joseph, 193, 195
Fowler, James W., 232, 233

Gardner, E. Clinton, 220, 232, 248
Gogarten Friedrich, 29
Good (The), 49-87; common good, 118, 173-174, 204; conformity to moral principle, 60-72; in Catholic ethics, 49; obedience to command of God, 50-60; response to divine action, 73-87
Gustafson, James M., character, 5, 45, 48, 84, 87; common good, 118, 173-174, 204; community, 151-152, 167-174; good (the), 47-48, 82-87, 116, 118, 173-174, 189-190; moral agency, 82, 104-105, 116-119; moral direction, 84-86, 174, 191, 204; moral experience, 40-41, 45-47; moral theology, 118-119, 171-172; Scripture, 84-85; social ethics, 170-171; starting point, 40-41, 45-48, 178-179, 182-183, 209; teleology, 86, 116-119, 167-170, 174, 190-191, 193-194; theocentric piety, 83; transformationist ethics, 46, 48, 118, 167, 172-173, 189; virtues, 5, 48, 86-87, 170-173, 191, 204

Haering, Bernard, 118
Harland, Gordon, 229, 238, 243
Hartmann, Nicolai, 77
Hauerwas, Stanley, 219
Hobbes, Thomas, 161
Hoedemaker, Libertus A., 226

Institutions, see Community

James, William, 180, 246
Jonsen, Albert R., 232
Justice, 176, 214-216; see Brunner, dualism; R. Niebuhr, love and justice; Ramsey, love and justice

Kant, Immanuel, 77, 119-120
Kingdom of God, 17, 205-206, 208

Laney, James T., 240, 242, 246
Lazareth, William H., 13
Lefever, Ernest W., 248
Lehmann, Paul, 4, 14-15; community, 126, 131-134; God's messianic action, 74-75, 105-106, 132-134; good (the), 73-76; <u>koinonia</u> ethics, 26, 73-76, 131-132, 203; maturity, 74-76; moral agency, 104-109, 195; moral principles, 132-134; new humanity, 105-109; social policy, 132-134; starting point, 25-26, 105, 177, 209; teleological ethics, 75-76, 104-109; theonomous conscience, 108, 203; violence, 134
Løgstrup, Knud E., 247
Long, Edward LeRoy, 240
Love, as moral norm, 31-34, 60-72; and justice, see R. Niebuhr and Ramsey; relation to other virtues, 64-65, 68-70, 87
Luther, Martin, 10, 97, 231

Mandelbaum, Maurice, 179-180
Mead, George Herbert, 7, 151, 180, 183-184
Mehl, Roger, 220
Moltmann, Jürgen, 222
Moral agency, images of, 89-125, 192-198; deontological, 90-104; responsiblist, 119-125, 192; teleological, 104-119

Natural law, 13, 37; see Gustafson, moral theology; Reinhold Niebuhr; Ramsey
Neo-orthodox theology, 2-3
Nichols, James Hastings, 248
Niebuhr, H. Richard, community, 151-156; covenant, 80, 155-156, 198, 213; critique of Christocentrism, 11, 14-15;

fitting (the), 76-82, 121, 123; good (the), 73, 76, 121-124; moral agency, 89, 119-125; moral direction, 204-217; moral experience, 40-45; moral law, 81-82; radical monotheism, 4-5, 11, 42-44, 151, 153, 189, 191, 194, 205, 209-213; relational value theory, 77-78, 156; responsibility, 78-80, 97-100, 119-124, 152, 188-202; self, 152-155; starting point, 40-45, 178-186, 209; transformationist ethics, 43, 81-82, 153, 189; virtues of Jesus Christ, 79-80

Niebuhr, Reinhold, 3, 4, 12, 14, 189; agape, 31-34, 60-65, 147, 189; anthropology, 109-115, 143; community, 134-135, 141-151; love and justice, 61-65, 114-116, 141, 146-150, 203-204; moral agency, 104-105, 109-116, 195; natural law, 64, 146, 149; pragmatism, 115-116, 149-151; realism, 31, 113, 145-148, 151; sin, 111-114, 144-145; Social Gospel, 31, 60-61; starting point, 30-36, 177; teleological ethics, 60, 114-116, 193-194

Nygren, Anders, 242

Oldham, J. H., 248

Phenomenology, of moral experience, 5-8, 41, 78-79, 84, 133-134, 167; of social world, 5-8, 15-16, 175-176; see also Gustafson, H. R. Niebuhr, Schutz, Winter

Plato, 77

Puritanism, 200, 202, 205

Radical monotheism, 4-5, 11, 42-44, 151, 153, 189, 191, 194, 205, 209-213

Rahner, Karl, 118

Ramsey, Paul, Christocentrism, 11-12, 14-15, 36-38, 101; community, 151-152, 156-157; covenant, 39, 70-72, 101-104, 116, 156-166, 198-201; deontology, 5, 66-68, 197; just war, 66-67, 162-163; love and justice, 66, 69-70, 102, 157-166; medical ethics, 66, 68, 71, 103, 162-164; moral agency, 90, 100-104; natural law (justice), 5, 35, 37-40, 68, 70, 161, 164-166; obedient agape, 36, 39, 65-72, 189, 191; rules, 67-68, 71, 191-192, 203-204; social ethics, 157-160, 164-166, 170; starting point, 34-40, 178; transformationist ethics, 35, 37, 39, 161-166; virtues, 68-70

Rauschenbusch, Walter, 60, 219

Revelation, 15-16, 19; see also Christocentrism, Starting Point

Rousseau, J. J., 159-161

Royce, Josiah, 154, 160

Schlesinger, Arthur, Jr., 243

Schutz, Alfred, 7-8, 183

Self, intentionality, 7-9; see also Moral Agency

Social ethics, 6-10, 17-19, 176-186

Social Gospel, 4, 10, 17, 31, 60

Social sciences, 6-9, 17-19, 128-129, 176-186

Söe, N. H., 13, 223

Starting point for Christian ethics, 21-48, 177-186; Barth, 22-27; Bonhoeffer, 24-27; Brunner, 28-30; 34-36; Christology, 22-27; Christology and creation, 28-40; Gustafson, 40-41, 45-48; Lehmann, 25-27; moral experience, 40-48; Niebuhr, H. R., 40-45; Niebuhr, Reinhold, 30-36; Ramsey, 34-40

Symbols, Theological, 14, 17, 186-202; community, 198-202; human agency, 192-198; moral criteria, 187-192; see also Moral Agency

Theocentric ethics, 5, 12, 14, 17, 43, 46, 80, 83, 173, 208; compared with Christocentric ethics, 175-217; see also Radical Monotheism
Thielicke, Helmut, 3-4
Troeltsch, Ernst, 4, 180

Value, 15, 77-78, 82-87, 156, 216
Virtue, 5, 48, 68-70, 79-80, 86-87, 170-173, 191, 204; see also Love, Justice

Weber, Max, 180
Weed, Michael R., 236
West, Charles C., 235, 240
Winter, Gibson, 6-10, 175-176, 183-186
World Council of Churches, 12-13, 206-209, 249

Yoder, John Howard, 219, 240